To Pauline
lots of l
Donald xxx
29th June 2012

..... and love to William
x xxxx

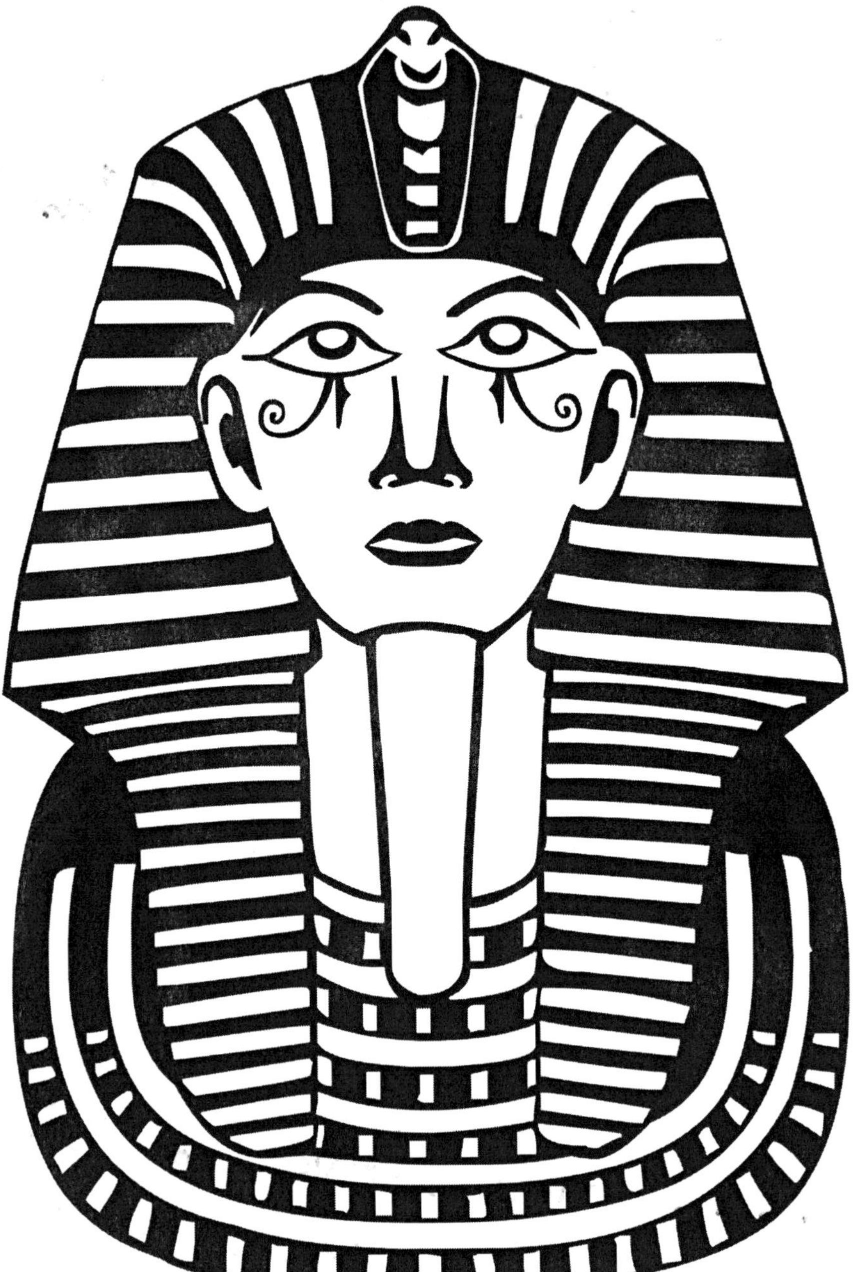

HIEROGLYPHS AND ARITHMETIC OF THE ANCIENT EGYPTIAN SCRIBES

Version 1

by

Donald Frazer

Chief Pyramid Builder,
Sesh and Polymath.

Copyright © 2012 by Donald Frazer.

Library of Congress Control Number: 2011962540
ISBN: Hardcover 978-1-4691-3645-5
Softcover 978-1-4691-3644-8
Ebook 978-1-4691-3646-2

Donald Frazer has asserted his right to be identified as the author of this work including all hieroglyphic fonts seen herein.

All rights reserved. This book contains material protected under international laws and treaties. Any unauthorized reprint or use of this material is prohibited. No part of this book may be reproduced or transmitted in any form or by any means, electronic or mechanical, including photocopying, recording, or by any information storage and retrieval system, without permission in writing from the copyright owner.

Copyright © Egyptian Pabulum 2011 UK Copyright Service 333433
Egyptian Fonts (1-9)

EgyptianPabulum@Sky.com

This book was printed in the United States of America.

To order additional copies of this book, contact:
Xlibris Corporation
0-800-644-6988
www.xlibrispublishing.co.uk
Orders@xlibrispublishing.co.uk

CONTENTS

0.0.0 Preface..15
    0.1.0 Book Structure 15
        0.1.1 Part One Overview..15
        0.1.2 Part Two Overview..15
        0.1.3 Part Three Overview...15
        0.1.4 Part Four Overview 16
    0.2.0 Hieroglyphs and Jargon...16
    0.3.0 Map of Ancient Egypt...18
    0.4.0 Dynastic Periods and Kingdoms of Ancient Egypt...........19

1.0.0 Chapter One—Writing in the Time of the Pharaohs...............21
    1.1.0 The Basics About Hieroglyphs..23
        1.1.1 The Word Hieroglyph...23
        1.1.2 The Rosetta Stone 24
    1.2.0 Papyri and Scribes in Ancient Egypt...............................26
        1.2.1 Papyrus..26
        1.2.2 The Scribe 26
        1.2.3 Scribal Egocentricity..28
        1.2.4 Scribal Immortality..28
    1.3.0 Ideograms..32
        1.3.1 Idea-Pictures 32
        1.3.2 The Vertical Stroke..32
        1.3.3 Common Ideograms..33
        1.3.4 The Artistic Beginnings of Written Words............34
    1.4.0 Phonograms..35
        1.4.1 Sound-Writing..35
        1.4.2 Twenty-four Phonemes..35
        1.4.3 Rebus Principle 36
        1.4.4 Vowels 37
        1.4.5 Uniliterals...39
        1.4.6 Biliterals 40
        1.4.7 Triliterals 41

1.5.0 Determinatives 42
    1.5.1 A Dual Purpose 42
    1.5.2 Some Generic Determinatives 43
    1.5.3 Cartouche Determinatives..45
1.6.0 Direction of Reading Hieroglyphic Writing......................46
    1.6.1 Read towards Figures 46
1.7.0 Plurals and Duals 47
    1.7.1 Repetition Replaces 'S'...47
1.7.2 Specific Quantities...49
1.8.0 Gender...50
    1.8.1 Nouns Are Something Substantive 50
1.9.0 Prepositions..52
    1.9.1 Similarities with English..52
1.10.0 Number Basics 54
    1.10.1 Base Ten 54
1.11.0 Transliteration and Translation..55
    1.11.1 Translation..55
    1.11.2 Transliteration 55
    1.11.3 The Ancient Egyptian Alphabet 56
1.12.0 English Phonetics for Common Egyptian Hieroglyphs ..59
    1.12.1 Overview of the List of Phonograms 59
    1.12.2 Using the Hieroglyphic Sign List....................60
        1.12.2.1 Column 1—Hieroglyphs 60
        1.12.2.2 Column 2—Key 60
        1.12.2.3 Column 3—Brief Description..............61
        1.12.2.4 Column 4—Sound 62
        1.12.2.5 Column 5—Examples of Usage...........63
    1.12.3 Commonly Used Ancient Egyptian Phonograms64
1.13.0 Main Egyptian Hieroglyphs for Whole Numbers 96
1.13.1 Rope, Fingers, and Polliwogs...96

> §Notes of Interest
>
> Pictures of these creatures baffled Egyptologists for a very long time. They had no idea what they were looking at; when they discovered that the Nile was teaming with them, they realized that they were looking at tadpoles!

```
2.0.0 Chapter Two—Ancient Egyptian Arithmetic
    and Units of Measure ................................................................. 99
    2.1.0 Counting With Hieroglyphic Numbers ........................... 101
        2.1.1 The Development of Number Systems ............... 101
        2.1.2 Hieroglyphs For Numbers From 0 to 9 ............... 102
        2.1.3 Hieroglyphs for Numbers in Multiples of 10 ...... 102
        2.1.4 Hieroglyphs for Numbers in Multiples of 100 .... 103
        2.1.5 Hieroglyphs for Numbers in
              Multiples of 1000 ................................................. 103
        2.1.6 Hieroglyphs for Numbers Greater Than 1000 ..... 104
        2.1.7 Keyboard Locations of
              Hieroglyphic Numbers ......................................... 104
        2.1.8 Ad Hoc Numbers ................................................. 105
    2.2.0 Big Number Examples .................................................. 106
        2.2.1 Repetition Method ............................................... 106
        2.2.2 Multiplication Method ........................................ 107
    2.3.0 Cardinal Numbers ......................................................... 109
        2.3.1 Masculine or Feminine ........................................ 109
        2.3.2 Common Cardinal Numbers ................................ 110
        2.3.3 Gender Exceptions .............................................. 112
    2.4.0 Ordinal Numbers ........................................................... 112
        2.4.1 Order in the Ranks .............................................. 112
        2.4.2 Common Ordinal Numbers ................................. 113
    2.5.0 Fractions ....................................................................... 114
        2.5.1 The Mouth Hieroglyph ........................................ 114
```

        2.5.2 R-Notation Fractions 114
        2.5.3 R-Fraction Exceptions 115
        2.5.4 Bulky Fractions 116
        2.5.5 The Paradox of an Ordinal Fraction 117
        2.5.6 Common Arithmetic Hieroglyphs 119
    2.5.7 Simple Arithmetic Examples 122
    2.6.0 The Eyes of Horus 122
        2.6.1 Belief Development with Time 122
        2.6.2 The Wadjet Eye 123
        2.6.3 The Murder of Osiris 124
        2.6.4 The Corn-Measure 125
        2.6.5 Hekat Fractions and Ro 126
        2.6.6 Eye-Part Combinations 126
    2.7.0 The Ro-measure 127
        2.7.1 A Mouthful of Grain 127
        2.7.2 Ro Expressed as Fractions of a Hekat 127
    2.8.0 The Sacred Ratio 128
        2.8.1 Natural Form 128
        2.8.2 Divine Proportion 128
        2.8.3 Phi (φ) 129
        2.8.4 Golden Pyramids 130
    2.9.0 Measuring Length 131
        2.9.1 The Cubit 131
        2.9.2 Ancient Egyptian Units of Length 132
        2.9.3 Multiples of Units 134
    2.10.0 Measuring Area 135
        2.10.1 Ancient Egyptian Units of Area 135
        2.10.2 References to Centaroura and Decaroura 137
        2.10.3 Examples of Adding Areas 138
    2.11.0 Measuring Volume 139
        2.11.1 Ancient Egyptian Units of Volume 139
        2.11.2 Jobs for the Boys 141
    2.12.0 Measuring Weight 143
        2.12.1 The Deben 143
        2.12.2 Ancient Egyptian Units of Weight 143
    2.13.0 Measuring Time 144
        2.13.1 Pharaohs Used Several Calendars 144
        2.13.2 The 365-Day Calendar 145
        2.13.3 Ancient Egyptian Units of Time 146
        2.13.4 The 24-Hour Day 147

- 2.13.5 Calendars...148
- 2.13.6 General Date and Time Vocabulary 150
- 2.13.7 Examples of Date Structure 151
- 2.13.8 Ordinal Units of Time 152
- 2.13.9 Translating Modern Dates................................153
- 2.13.10 The Stela by Ity 154
- 2.13.11 Hours and Minutes......................................155
- 2.13.12 Examples of the Time of Day........................156
- 2.13.13 Using Time to Measure Distance 157
- 2.14.0 Measuring Strength of Bread and Beer.......................157
  - 2.14.1 Pefsu (Pesu)...157
  - 2.14.2 The Pefsu Formula 158
- 2.15.0 Measuring Slope 158
  - 2.15.1 Modern Inclination by Degrees 158
  - 2.15.2 The Seked...158
  - 2.15.3 Angle of Slope for Different Sekeds 161
  - 2.15.4 Common Sekeds for Pyramids.......................162
  - 2.15.5 The Cubit as a Prime Number 163
  - 2.15.6 The Rhind Papyrus Problem 56 164
    - 2.15.6.1 The Scribe's Solution 164
    - 2.15.6.2 Converting Cubits to Palms 165
- 2.16.0 Addition and Subtraction 167
  - 2.16.1 The Importance of Text Direction 167
  - 2.16.2 Tables Used as Ready Reckoners...................168
  - 2.16.3 Hieroglyphic Vocabulary for Arithmetic..........170
  - 2.16.4 Examples of Simple Arithmetic 172
- 2.17.0 Multiplication...173
  - 2.17.1 The Method of Doubling................................173
  - 2.17.2 Multiplying by Ten 176
- 2.18.0 Division...177
  - 2.18.1 Multiplication in Reverse..............................177
  - 2.18.2 An Example—957 Divided by 11 179
- 2.19.0 More about Aliquot Fractions 180
  - 2.19.1 Reasoning that Remains a Secret....................180
  - 2.19.2 Dividing a Loaf Problem...............................180
  - 2.19.3 Work and Bread for All 181
  - 2.19.4 Breaking down Fractions 182
- 2.20.0 Calculating Areas of Geometric Shapes 183
  - 2.20.1 Area of a Square or Rectangle 183
  - 2.20.2 Area of a Triangle..184

2.20.3 Area of a Circle 185
  2.20.3.1 The Rhind Papyrus Problem 50 185
2.20.4 Area of a hemisphere 187
2.21.0 Calculating Volumes 188
  2.21.1 Jars used for Volume 188
  2.21.2 Volume of a Block..188
  2.21.3 Volume of a Cylinder 189
  2.21.4 Volume of a Pyramid..194
  2.21.5 Volume of a Frustum..194
    2.21.5.1 How was the Frustum
             Formula Derived?..196
    2.21.5.2 The Moscow Papyrus
             Frustum Problem...196
    2.21.5.3 Modern Derivation of
             Frustum Formula...197
2.22.0 Algebraic Mathematics 200
  2.22.1 Algebra Origins...200
  2.22.2 Degree of an Equation 201
  2.22.3 First-Degree Equations 201
  2.22.4 Second-Degree Equations................................201
  2.22.5 Third-Degree Equations and Higher 202
  2.22.6 Exceptions to the Degree Rule.........................202
  2.22.7 A Practical Example of Degree Rule 202
  2.22.8 Types of Ancient Egyptian
         Mathematical Problems..204
  2.22.9 Aha Problems 207
  2.22.10 The Hundred Loaf Problem 207
  2.22.11 False Position 210
  2.22.12 False Position Method of Computation...........210
  2.22.13 A Simple False Position Example 212
  2.22.14 The Hundred Loaf Problem Continued...........214
  2.22.15 Rhind Mathematical Papyrus Problem 24 216
  2.22.16 Rhind Mathematical Papyrus Problem 25 218
  2.22.17 Rhind Mathematical Papyrus Problem 26 220
  2.22.18 Rhind Mathematical Papyrus Problem 27 221
  2.22.19 Rhind Mathematical Papyrus Problem 28 223
  2.22.20 Rhind Mathematical Papyrus Problem 29 224
  2.22.21 Solving Equations by
         the Method of Division 227
  2.22.22 Division by Fractional Expressions 227

    2.22.23 Rhind Mathematical Papyrus Problem 30 229
    2.22.24 Rhind Mathematical Papyrus Problem 31 232
    2.22.25 Rhind Mathematical Papyrus Problem 32 235
    2.22.26 Rhind Mathematical Papyrus Problem 33 236
    2.22.27 Rhind Mathematical Papyrus Problem 34 240
    2.22.28 Complexity in a Solution 242
2.23.0 Ship's Part Problems 243
    2.23.1 Indecipherable Ship's Problems 243
    2.23.2 Problem 3 from the Moscow Papyrus...............243
    2.24.1 A Measure of Flour...245
    2.24.2 Problem 8 from the Moscow Papyrus...............248
    2.24.3 Problem 69 from the Rhind
           Mathematical Papyrus...250
    2.24.4 Problem 69 Proof using Eye-fractions 251
2.25.0 Baku Problems 255
    2.25.1 Problem 11 from the Moscow Papyrus.............255
    2.25.2 Problem 23 from the Moscow Papyrus.............257

3.0.0 Chapter Three—Reference Material 259
    3.1.0 Selected Bibliography 261
    3.2.0 Glossary 264
    3.3.0 Keyboard Maps 284
        3.3.1 Physical Keyboard Views.....................................284
    3.3.2 Character to Hieroglyph Index Mappings 334
        3.3.2.1 Font Filename Egypt1.ttf 334
        3.3.2.2 Font Filename Egypt2.ttf 335
        3.3.2.3 Font Filename Egypt3.ttf 336
        3.3.2.4 Font Filename Egypt4.ttf 337
        3.3.2.5 Font Filename Egypt5.ttf 338
        3.3.2.6 Font Filename Egypt6.ttf 339
        3.3.2.7 Font Filename Egypt7.ttf 340
        3.3.2.8 Font Filename Egypt8.ttf 341
        3.3.2.9 Font Filename Egypt9.ttf 342
    3.4.0 Fonts Copyright and Licence Information 343
        3.4.1 Electronic License Agreement 343
            3.4.1.1 License Grant...343
            3.4.1.2 Copyright 344
            3.4.1.3 Disclaimer and Limited Warranty........344
    3.5.0 Font Installation Instructions 345
        3.5.1 Installation Guide...345

3.5.2 Font Installation for Generic Windows® Users ..345
3.5.3 Font Deletion for Generic Windows® Users 345
3.5.4 Windows® XP Users 346
3.5.5 Windows® 95/98/2000/ NT4® Users.................346
3.5.6 Windows® 7 Users 347
3.5.7 Re-installation of Standard Fonts........................347
3.5.8 Font Installation for Generic Macintosh® Users 351
3.6.0 Common Problems Encountered with Font Usage 352
    3.6.1 Kerning Problems 352
    3.6.2 AutoCorrect Problems...353
3.7.0 Hieroglyphic Character Manipulation.......................354
    3.7.1 Formatting Fonts 354
    3.7.2 Desk-Top Publishing...355
    3.7.3 Word Processing..355
        3.7.3.1 Generic Overview of Microsoft® Works... 355
        3.7.3.2 Generic Overview of Microsoft® Word 356
    3.7.4 Spreadsheets and Tables......................................356
3.8.0 Trademark and Registration Notices............................357
3.9.0 Index 361

4.0.0 Chapter Four—Special Edition CD-Rom 367

§ Notes of Interest

There are records of wheels being used as far back as the Old Kingdom. The ancient Egyptians had very little use for the wheel because it was not very practical in agricultural or desert areas. Not until the New Kingdom, when the chariot was introduced to the army, did the usage of wheeled transport increase. Donkeys, oxen, and boats remained the commonest means of transport.

To Gordon; a tenet of a scribe, 'A king that refuses the truth for falsehood is like a poisoned well that never tastes new rain; he is a sinner to himself and his followers.'

Warning, warning, warning!

A few words of caution for those who intend to type hieroglyphs, but never read any instruction manual before starting a job. (Don't look at me; I have the only flat-pack chest of drawers with the handles on the inside.) Before it is too late, disable everything in your word-processing package that has anything to do with AutoCorrect. Otherwise you will inherit the curse of the pharaohs.

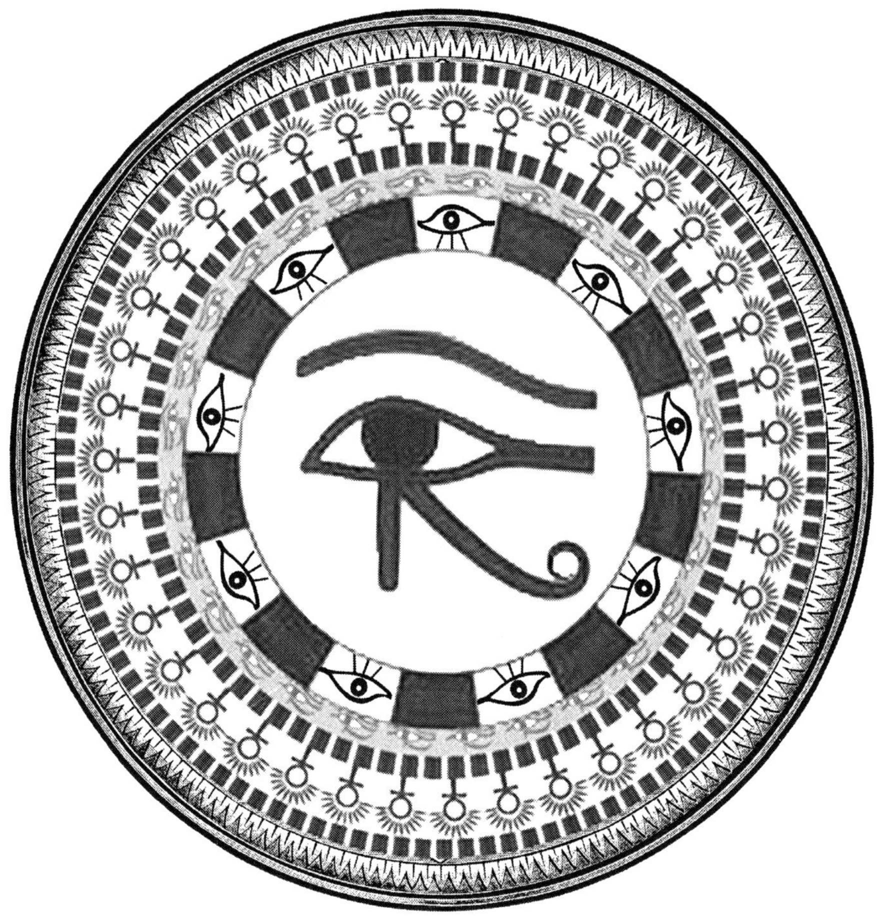

0.0.0 PREFACE

0.1.0 BOOK STRUCTURE

0.1.1 PART ONE OVERVIEW

Part one is an introduction to the ancient Egyptian language and includes a table describing the phonetic sounds of different hieroglyphs and how they relate to the English language. It explains how to write your own simple messages in ancient Egyptian hieroglyphs without getting too involved in pure grammar or syntax.

0.1.2 PART TWO OVERVIEW

This part of the book is an introduction to ancient Egyptian mathematics. It tries to explain the different ways in which Egyptian scribes thought about numbers and fractions, sometimes quite alien to our modern approach to mathematics. Part two will leave you in no doubt that the ancient Egyptians were very capable of performing complex calculations, even though they had no concept of numerical zero. Part two also describes the different units of measure used for length, area, volume, slope, and time and explains how the units were used.

0.1.3 PART THREE OVERVIEW

Part three explains how to install your fonts and provides keyboard maps, which can be used as an alternative way of finding the hieroglyphs you want. If the specific keyboard location for a hieroglyph or other symbol cannot be found in the general body of the text, you will certainly find the location in the keyboard maps at the end of this book. Part three also gives you tips on how to be more artistic with your hieroglyphs, such as rotating and stretching them. At the end of part three, there is also a glossary and index. There are probably many words in this book that you may not be familiar with. As a help, these words are usually explained in the text more than once; a glossary also provides a very quick source of answers to some questions.

0.1.4 PART FOUR OVERVIEW

Part four of the special edition version of this book consists of a PC or Apple computer® readable CD-Rom, which contains all the hieroglyphs used in the text. The hieroglyphs on the CD-Rom are in the format of nine keyboard fonts. This means that after installing the CD, you can use hieroglyphs with any package on your PC or Mac as long as the package uses normal fonts. The hieroglyphs can also be manipulated and printed in the same way as all the regular fonts that you use on your PC, laptop, or Apple computer®. For all other versions of this book, which are not special editions, the fonts are available as a download that are included in the overall price of the book.

0.2.0 HIEROGLYPHS AND JARGON

In some ways, the understanding of ancient Egyptian hieroglyphs is easier than many modern languages; it is certainly a lot more fun. One of the difficulties we sometimes encounter when trying to understand the system of hieroglyphs is the confusing linguistic terminology.

The confusing terminology associated with the study of Egyptian hieroglyphs is not that different to the problems associated with the jargon relating to computing, or whatever the subject is called these days! Terminology with academics must be fashionable; for things to be fashionable they must be changed, not always for the better.

For example, later on you will come across the term 'ideogram'; some authors prefer to use the words and phrases 'sense-signs', 'idea-writing', 'sound-meaning', 'picture glyph', or 'pictogram'. While some of these words and phrases may be helpful, they can also be misleading.

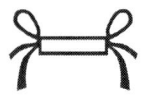

When describing dates, some modern books talk about BCE (Before the Common Era) and CE (Common Era) instead of the classical terms of BC and AD. Except for the suffix change from BC and AD to BCE and CE respectively, all the dates look identical. Allegedly, the justification for this is the politically correct but indefensible idea that reference to Christ is offensive; it is probably more to do with fashion. As you will discover later, the ancient Egyptians based all their dates and calendars on subjects of worship, such as kings, gods, and deities. Wherever possible, we have tried to stick to traditional terminology and that includes a common sense portrayal of dates.

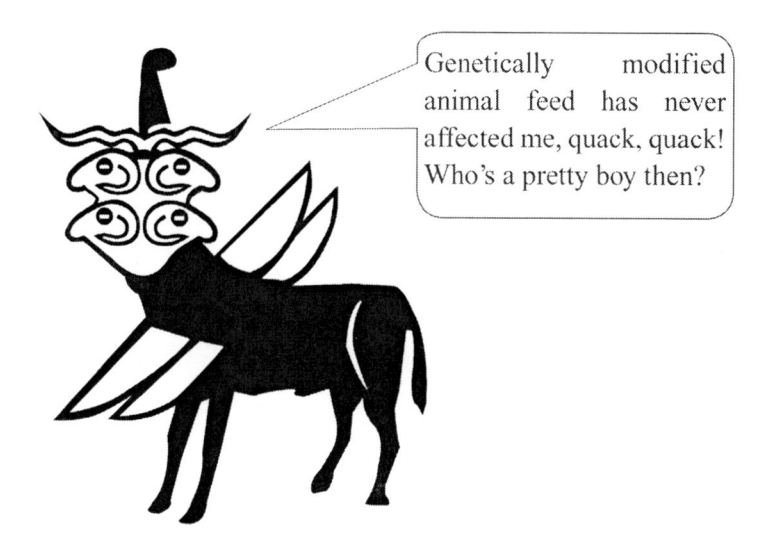

Genetically modified animal feed has never affected me, quack, quack! Who's a pretty boy then?

The beast above is the Egyptian male god Qebui, Lord of the North Wind. He is depicted as a man with four ram heads, or, as a winged four-headed ram. Nearly all of the strange fictitious hybrid creatures discovered in ancient Egyptian art and writings were born out of serendipity. Each element that makes up such a creature bears some rich symbolic significance. This is one of the reasons why a single god can be represented by a variety of different hybrid animals. It very much depends on which aspects or powers of the god need to be invoked or pacified at that moment in time.

0.3.0 Map of Ancient Egypt

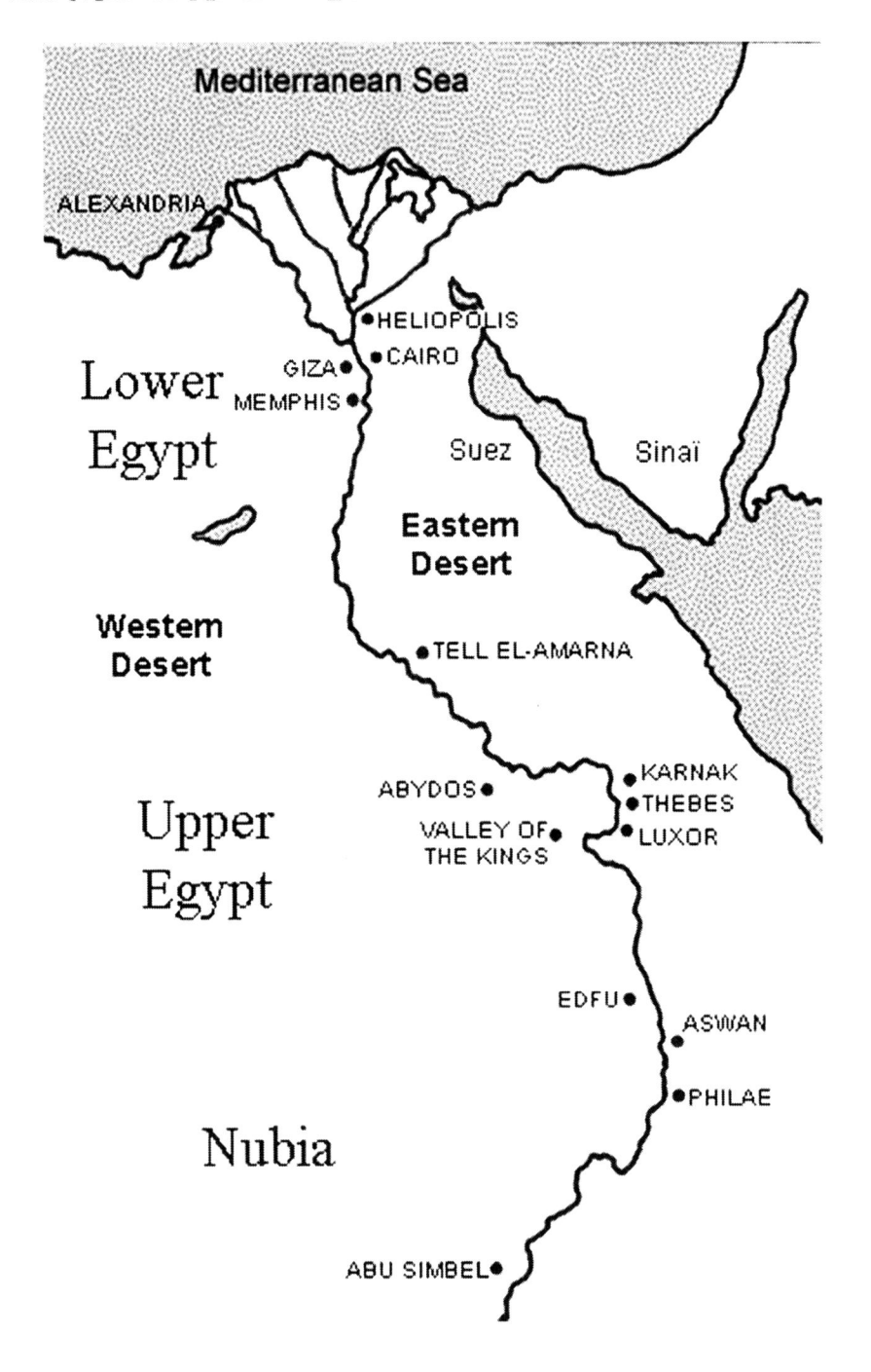

0.4.0 DYNASTIC PERIODS AND KINGDOMS OF ANCIENT EGYPT

Egyptologists divide ancient Egyptian civilization into four main dynastic periods: the old, middle, new, and the late kingdoms. These main Dynastic Periods are separated from each another by the first, second, and third intermediate periods. During these intermediate periods, political divisions and weak rulers fragmented the central government and disrupted the administrative authority of the country.

Time Period	Dynasties	Powerful Rulers
Early Dynastic Period 3100-2600 BC	1-3	Menes, Djoser
Old Kingdom 2600-2160 BC	4-8	Cheops, Chephren, Mycerinus, Pepy I, II
First Intermediate Period 2160-2040 BC	9-11	
Middle Kingdom 2040-1700 BC	11-13	Amenemmes I, II, III
Second Intermediate Period 1700-1570 BC	14-17	
New Kingdom 1570-1070 BC	18-20	Amosis I, Amenophis I, II, III, Tuthmosis I, II, III, IV, Hatshepsut, Akhenaten, Tutankhamun, Ramesses II, III
Third Intermediate Period 1070-600 BC	21-25	Economic troubles and civil wars weaken Egypt. There are up to 4 pharaohs ruling different parts of Egypt at the same time.

Late Kingdom 600-332 BC	26-30	Constant threats from Assyrians, Babylonians, and Persians. During the reign of Nectanebo II, Egypt was conquered by Persians; this marked the end of native Egyptian rule.
Greco-Roman Period 332 BC-395 AD	30 BC Egypt was a Roman province	Alexander the Great, Ptolemy, Cleopatra, Octavius

1.0.0 Chapter One

Writing in the Time of the Pharaohs

1.1.0 THE BASICS ABOUT HIEROGLYPHS

1.1.1 THE WORD HIEROGLYPH

The word 'hieroglyphs' goes back to a Greek origin composed of two parts, 'hieros', which means sacred, and 'gluphe', which means inscription or engraving. These two words combined mean 'sacred inscription'. Hieroglyphic writings started to appear before 3200 BC and remained in active use until the eleventh century AD. This life span of more than 4,000 years makes Egyptian hieroglyphs the longest continually attested language in the world.

The modern English language is based on a twenty-six-letter alphabet, although this was not always the case. The number and nature of the letters in the English alphabet have varied considerably over the centuries. For example, in the latter quarter of the tenth century, there were only twenty-three letters in the English alphabet. Ancient Egyptian writing uses about two thousand hieroglyphic characters. It is hard to define the exact number of hieroglyphs because you end up getting involved in complex classifications. Some hieroglyphs consist of combinations of one or more hieroglyphs, while others have elements removed. As an example, because the ancient Egyptians were a very superstitious people, they would often depict a snake cut in half. The question is, do we class the complete snake as one hieroglyph and the separate pieces as another hieroglyph or even two more hieroglyphs?

Most hieroglyphs are pictures of real items, common objects that existed in ancient Egypt; others for reasons of economy are abbreviations of existing hieroglyphs. Hieroglyphs can represent a sound or an idea associated with the object.

1.1.2 THE ROSETTA STONE

Thanks to the discovery of a piece of carved stone, we are able to decipher hieroglyphs. In 1799, a soldier digging a fort in Rosetta, Egypt found a large black stone with three different types of writing on it. The writing was a message about Ptolemy V, who was an ancient Egyptian ruler. Because the message was written during the time when the Greeks ruled Egypt, one of the three languages was Greek. The other two were demotic and hieroglyphic.

It was soon realized that the three languages on 'The Rosetta Stone' said the same thing and that hieroglyphs were a decipherable script. Even though people could read Greek, they could not understand how to match up the Greek words with hieroglyphic words. For years, no one was able to understand how the hieroglyphic message corresponded to the Greek writings. Then in 1819 an English doctor, Thomas Young had a breakthrough translating the name Ptolemy. He realized that the hieroglyphs that spelt 'Ptolemy' were enclosed in a cartouche, so he was able to match it up to the Greek spelling.

This opened the door for a young French Egyptologist named Jean Champollion who in 1822 managed to translate the names of more than seventy of the Egyptian kings. This discovery enabled him to equate the unfamiliar hieroglyphs with familiar Greek words and to translate the majority of the entire message.

§ 1.1.2 Notes of Interest

The Nile has a length of 6,690 kilometres as per 'Chambers Book of Facts'; it is the longest river in the world. It runs from Eastern Africa to the Mediterranean. The Southern section of the Nile between Aswan and Khartoum is separated by six cataracts, or rapids, caused by outcrops of rocks in the riverbed.

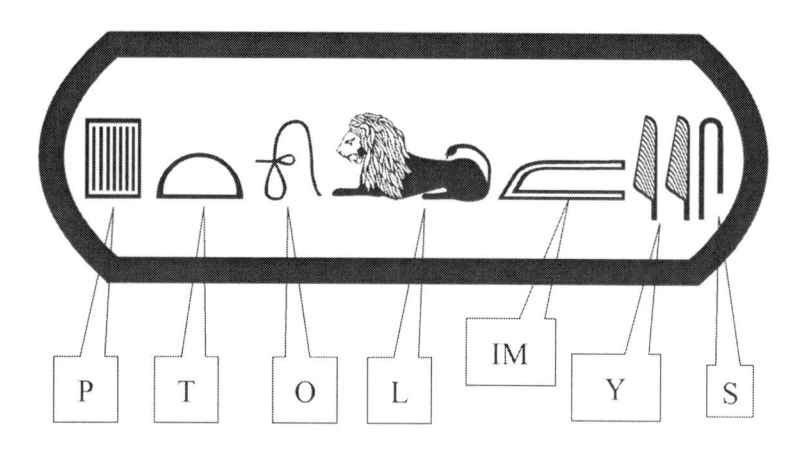

Hieroglyphs and Arithmetic of the Ancient Egyptian Scribes

| P | T | O | L | IM | Y | S |

The spelling above for 'Ptolemy' may look a bit odd, but it must be remembered that everything is spelt phonetically. There were often numerous ways of spelling the same words, all of which could be correct.

Of the two thousand different hieroglyphs about five hundred of these were commonly used. Many of them could have two or even three different functions depending upon how they were used.

The way in which a hieroglyph was integrated with the other hieroglyphs dictated what type it was, which meant it could be an ideogram, phonogram, or a determinative. All these possible different uses of a hieroglyph will be explained later. Each of these types meant that the same hieroglyph could deliver a different message depending upon its context in a sentence. Even if a hieroglyph was multi-purpose, it could only represent one of these types at a time.

To avoid writing confusing, erroneous, or meaningless messages, the ancient Egyptians would have had to pay particular attention when using hieroglyphs that could be used for a number of different purposes. Any poor positioning or incorrect combinations of hieroglyphs with others could completely change the meaning of a sentence; errors carved in granite could not be painted over or rubbed out!

1.2.0 Papyri and Scribes in Ancient Egypt

1.2.1 Papyrus

The word paper comes from papyrus, the reed that came from the banks of the Nile. The papyrus plant has disappeared from Egypt, but has survived in Nubia. The papyrus plant is a species of reed more specifically a sedge plant (Latin; Cyperus papyrus).

To the ancient Egyptians, the papyrus plant was of great economic importance. Sedges are grass-like plants which generally grow in wet ground, have triangular stems and inconspicuous flowers. By cutting the stems of this plant into strips and pressing them flat, the pith of the stems acted as a binding agent. This allowed the ancient Egyptians to make a type of paper we call papyrus, the name being derived from that of the plant; the plural for which is papyri. The word papyrus can be used in a fairly general way, it is also a manuscript written on papyrus.

The sedge was the symbol for Lower Egypt, while the bee stood for Upper Egypt. Boats, baskets, and sandals were woven from the plant. It gained its major cultural impact when it was being used in the manufacture of papyrus. Papyrus was the main writing material in ancient Egypt for thousands of years, and was exported all over the Roman Empire.

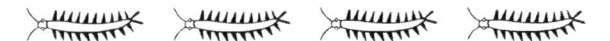

1.2.2 The Scribe

Another name for a scribe was a Sesh. Scribes belonged socially to what we would refer to as middle class elite. They were employed by the state as bureaucrats and administrators to the pharaohs, its army, and temples.

Sons of scribes were brought up in the same scribal tradition, sent to school, and upon entering the civil service, inherited their father's positions. The profession of scribe was very much a protected job and wherever possible, kept within a very small circle of people. Scribes were also considered part of the royal court and did not have to pay taxes or join the military.

It is believed that only four people in a thousand could read and write in ancient Egypt. Egyptian scribes were the majority of this small group. They were professional writers; administrative and economic activities were documented by them, they would copy out official records, documents, letters, poems, and stories. They were also the accountants of their day and could perform complex mathematical calculations.

Monumental buildings such as the pyramids were erected under their supervision, and they kept check of stocks such as how much was harvested, calculate the amount of food needed to feed tomb builders, and monitor and order supplies for the temples and the army.

If it were not for the ancient scribes documenting business and everyday life during the time of the pharaohs, we would have very little understanding today of ancient Egypt and its people.

§ 1.2.2 Notes of Interest

The 'Book of the Dead' was the most popular and longest lasting collection of funerary texts created by the ancient Egyptians for the protection and guidance of the deceased. It came into use before circa 1550 BC and remained in widespread use for more than a millennium and a half.

1.2.3 Scribal Egocentricity

In a prayer addressed by a scribe to the god Thoth, the patron of his profession, there is little room for doubt that the role played by scribes in the development of the various professions in ancient Egypt was well recognized. The prayer is as follows:

> *Come to me, O Thoth, August ibis[1], O god beloved of Khmun, secretary of the Ennead[2], come to me, to advise me; give me skill in thy craft which is better than all other crafts, for men have found that he who is skilled therein becomes a nobleman-dignitary.*
>
> *I have seen many for whom thou did act and now they are members of the Thirty[3], strong and wealthy because of what thou hast done.*

It was a favourite theme of many scribes of ancient Egypt to say that the skilled trade of a scribe surpasses all other trades; what a surprise! This was not only a belief articulated by the scribes, but it is borne out by an examination of the biographies found in tombs about the careers of political, administrative, and learned professionals of the time.

[1] August was the time the ibis migrated.
[2] The Ennead was a group of nine gods.
[3] The Thirty were the traditional Grand Jury of Egypt.

1.2.4 Scribal Immortality

As mentioned earlier, ancient Egyptian scribes were unusually conscious of the significance and desirability of their profession. The following papyrus from the end of the nineteenth dynasty stresses that the scribe's writing was a more efficacious route to immortality than his building of tombs. Scribe's may have been deeply involved in documenting the religious beliefs and laws relating to the afterlife through ancient gods, tombs, complex procedures, and pyramids, but from this document some scribes seem to have had a slightly different perspective to the matter.

The document is a song discovered in a tomb, that suggests a scribe's papyri are read and remembered long after his tomb and those of others have crumbled and are forgotten. It says that their names are still proclaimed on account of the documents which they have produced, so the memory of him who made them will last to the limits of eternity. You might think for reasons of blasphemy the scribe that wrote this song would be executed. Although the risk was probably miniscule, considering few people could read and write and even less people were allowed to see anything in a tomb.

There does seem to be a rather sceptical tone of its author towards the efficacy of building tombs to ensure a place in the afterlife for eternity. This song was found in the tomb of King Intef, The Justified.

He is happy, this good prince!
Death is a kindly fate.
A generation passes, another stays,
Since the time of the ancestors.

The gods who were before, rest in their tombs,
Blessed nobles too, are buried in their tombs.
Yet those who built tombs, their places are gone.
What has become of them?
I have heard the words of Imhotep and Hardedef,
Whose sayings are recited whole.
What of their places?
Their walls have crumbled; their places are gone, as though they had never been!
None comes from there;
To tell of their state, to tell of their needs, to calm our hearts,
Until we go where they have gone!
Hence rejoice in your heart!
Forgetfulness profits you,
Follow your heart as long as you live!
Put myrrh on your head, dress in fine linen,
Anoint yourself with oils fit for a god.
Heap up your joys; let your heart not sink?
Follow your heart and your happiness,

Do your things on earth as your heart commands!
When there comes to you that day of mourning,
The weary-hearted hears not their mourning.
Wailing saves no man from the pit!
Make holiday, do not weary of it!
Lo, none is allowed to take his goods with him,
Lo, none who departs comes back again!

In another document, it explains the advantages of being a scribe, in that it will save you from taxation and will protect you from all labours. It then goes on to compare the scribal profession to menial occupations, to the great benefit of the scribe's. It mentions that not only are the physical conditions of his work better than those of other occupations, since he is ordinarily in charge of those engaged in hard work, but the scribe may rise to the position of magistrate.

§ 1.2.4 Notes of Interest

The term 'Pyramid Texts', derive their name from the fact that they appear on the internal walls and walls of adjoining rooms of the burial chambers of pyramids. Texts mainly written on the inner surfaces of wooden coffins, the outside of coffins, and sometimes also on tomb walls or papyri are known as 'Coffin Texts'. All these texts reflect the importance that was attached to securing the happy existence of the dead in the afterlife.

The predominant content of these texts were compositions such as ritual spells, the rest were hymns, prayers, litanies and magical spells for warding off dangerous animals.

At the beginning of the New Kingdom, an innovation in funerary customs took place, which was the use of anthropoid coffins to replace rectangular sarcophagi for new burials. These coffins were so called, because they took on the recognisable shape of a body. In an anthropoid coffin, the position of the head and shoulders of the mummy inside can be easily visualised. Funerary texts also developed over time and started to include a lot of art work making them very lengthy.

These new style anthropoid coffins lacked sufficient space on their surfaces to inscribe the new collection of funerary spells. This development no doubt influenced the emergence and wide acceptance of papyrus rolls as the usual medium for texts. Papyri of any length, with a variable number of spells, could be rolled up and placed inside the coffin, to be at hand by the deceased if needed.

1.3.0 IDEOGRAMS

1.3.1 IDEA-PICTURES

The hieroglyphs that represent real objects, actions, or some closely related notion are called ideograms or sometimes pictograms. The word 'ideogram' is derived from the Greek wording *'idea'* and *'gramma'*, which mean 'form' and 'writing' respectively.

1.3.2 THE VERTICAL STROKE

When a hieroglyph could represent a sound but was required to function as an ideogram, a vertical stroke was often positioned beneath the hieroglyph which ensured its use as an ideogram. For example, a picture of a mouth on its own represents the sound of the letter 'R', whereas with a single stroke beneath it, it means 'mouth'.

Using the sun as an example of an ideogram, it could simply mean 'the sun' or it could depict the closely related notion of 'daytime'.

The stroke not only highlights the usage of a hieroglyph as an ideogram, but also indicates that there is only one of these items. Also, ideograms may consist of two or more hieroglyphs. This means that a sentence may not be immediately readable until it is realized that a combination of hieroglyphs is actually one ideogram. The following table should help shine some light on the matter.

1.3.3 Common Ideograms

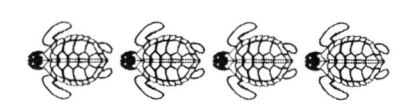

Ideogram	Meaning	Ideogram	Meaning
	King		Fall
	Herds-man		Build
	Give Birth		Sun God Re
	Thoth		Chnum
	Anubis		Seth
	Man		Face
	I or me		Weep
	Eye		Nose
	Soul or spirit		Arm
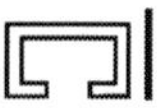	House		Year

Ideogram	Meaning	Ideogram	Meaning
	Neck		Ear
	Heart		Nestling
	Wedjat Eye		Old
	Mouth		Herds- man
	Sun		Sun God Re
	Legs		Chnum
	Hear		Hathor
	Turtle		Head

1.3.4 THE ARTISTIC BEGINNINGS OF WRITTEN WORDS

It is quite possibly that most ancient languages started as a series of pictures that were used to decorate items in the environment of the artists. The items decorated may have included the walls of dwellings, caves, and everyday objects. Even painted or tattooed symbols that adorned the skin of people may have been the beginnings of modern language.

  2.22.23 Rhind Mathematical Papyrus Problem 30 229
  2.22.24 Rhind Mathematical Papyrus Problem 31 232
  2.22.25 Rhind Mathematical Papyrus Problem 32 235
  2.22.26 Rhind Mathematical Papyrus Problem 33 236
  2.22.27 Rhind Mathematical Papyrus Problem 34 240
  2.22.28 Complexity in a Solution 242
 2.23.0 Ship's Part Problems 243
  2.23.1 Indecipherable Ship's Problems 243
  2.23.2 Problem 3 from the Moscow Papyrus..............243
  2.24.1 A Measure of Flour 245
  2.24.2 Problem 8 from the Moscow Papyrus..............248
  2.24.3 Problem 69 from the Rhind
   Mathematical Papyrus...250
  2.24.4 Problem 69 Proof using Eye-fractions 251
 2.25.0 Baku Problems 255
  2.25.1 Problem 11 from the Moscow Papyrus............255
  2.25.2 Problem 23 from the Moscow Papyrus............257

3.0.0 Chapter Three—Reference Material 259
 3.1.0 Selected Bibliography 261
 3.2.0 Glossary 264
 3.3.0 Keyboard Maps 284
  3.3.1 Physical Keyboard Views...................................284
 3.3.2 Character to Hieroglyph Index Mappings.......................334
  3.3.2.1 Font Filename Egypt1.ttf 334
  3.3.2.2 Font Filename Egypt2.ttf 335
  3.3.2.3 Font Filename Egypt3.ttf 336
  3.3.2.4 Font Filename Egypt4.ttf 337
  3.3.2.5 Font Filename Egypt5.ttf 338
  3.3.2.6 Font Filename Egypt6.ttf 339
  3.3.2.7 Font Filename Egypt7.ttf 340
  3.3.2.8 Font Filename Egypt8.ttf 341
  3.3.2.9 Font Filename Egypt9.ttf 342
 3.4.0 Fonts Copyright and Licence Information 343
  3.4.1 Electronic License Agreement 343
   3.4.1.1 License Grant...343
   3.4.1.2 Copyright 344
   3.4.1.3 Disclaimer and Limited Warranty........344
 3.5.0 Font Installation Instructions 345
  3.5.1 Installation Guide..345

3.5.2 Font Installation for Generic Windows® Users ..345
3.5.3 Font Deletion for Generic Windows® Users 345
3.5.4 Windows® XP Users 346
3.5.5 Windows® 95/98/2000/ NT4® Users.................346
3.5.6 Windows® 7 Users 347
3.5.7 Re-installation of Standard Fonts.......................347
3.5.8 Font Installation for Generic Macintosh® Users 351
3.6.0 Common Problems Encountered with Font Usage 352
3.6.1 Kerning Problems 352
3.6.2 AutoCorrect Problems...353
3.7.0 Hieroglyphic Character Manipulation...........................354
3.7.1 Formatting Fonts 354
3.7.2 Desk-Top Publishing...355
3.7.3 Word Processing..355
  3.7.3.1 Generic Overview of Microsoft® Works... 355
  3.7.3.2 Generic Overview of Microsoft® Word 356
3.7.4 Spreadsheets and Tables......................................356
3.8.0 Trademark and Registration Notices..............................357
3.9.0 Index 361

4.0.0 Chapter Four—Special Edition CD-Rom 367

---

§ Notes of Interest

There are records of wheels being used as far back as the Old Kingdom. The ancient Egyptians had very little use for the wheel because it was not very practical in agricultural or desert areas. Not until the New Kingdom, when the chariot was introduced to the army, did the usage of wheeled transport increase. Donkeys, oxen, and boats remained the commonest means of transport.

To Gordon; a tenet of a scribe, 'A king that refuses the truth for falsehood is like a poisoned well that never tastes new rain; he is a sinner to himself and his followers.'

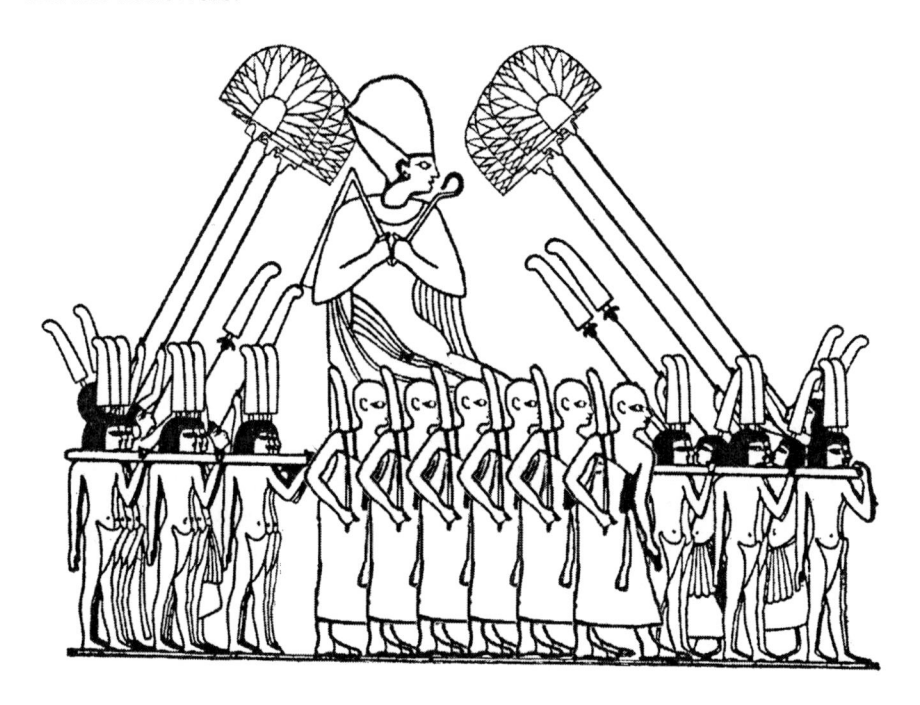

Warning, warning, warning!

A few words of caution for those who intend to type hieroglyphs, but never read any instruction manual before starting a job. (Don't look at me; I have the only flat-pack chest of drawers with the handles on the inside.) Before it is too late, disable everything in your word-processing package that has anything to do with AutoCorrect. Otherwise you will inherit the curse of the pharaohs.

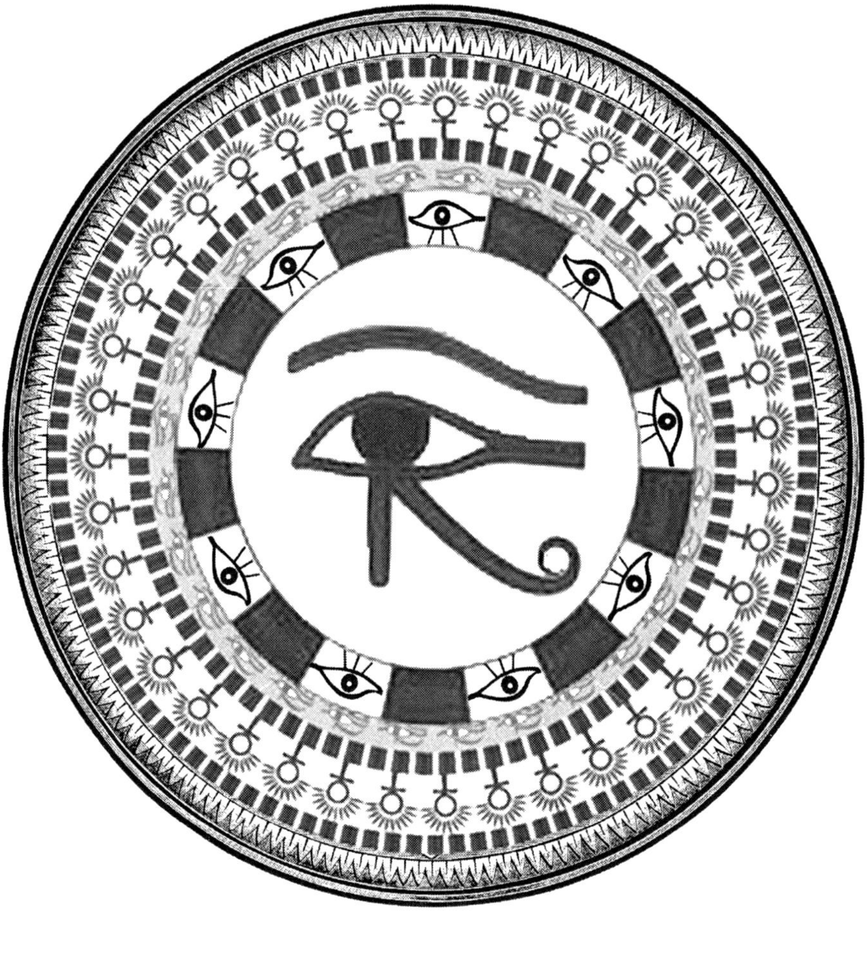

Pictorial art was a precursor to hieroglyphic writing, a very early and important function of which was to provide a visible record of facts and events.

1.4.0 PHONOGRAMS

1.4.1 SOUND-WRITING

The hieroglyphs that represent particular sounds which are used to construct words in the same way as our Western alphabetic characters, are called phonograms. The word 'phonogram' is derived from the Greek wording *'phone'* and *'gramma'*, which mean 'sound' and 'writing' respectively.

1.4.2 TWENTY-FOUR PHONEMES

The ancient Egyptians used twenty-four different phonemes, sounds, to distinguish one word from another in their native tongue. Each phoneme was represented by one or more special hieroglyphs called phonograms. These phonograms allowed them to spell out everything that they required. The phonograms that represent the twenty-four phonemes are referred to as the 'alphabet'.

It was entirely the scribe's choice which hieroglyph to use when a number of hieroglyphs were available that represented the same sound. Sometimes the size or shape of the space available for writing or carving determined the choice.
The neatness and the aesthetic appearance played a major role as well.

Modern languages throughout the world use a wide range of different sounds. Consequently, if you are required to write a sentence phonetically in one language to sound the same as that in an alternative language, it may not be possible to make the two sentences sound exactly alike. The language you are writing in may not possess the necessary phonograms. Even though, ancient Egyptian is a phonetic language and does not rely too much on spelling accuracy, we still have problems performing a character for character textual translation into Standard English.

The English alphabet lacks certain sounds that can exactly match some sounds found in the ancient Egyptian hieroglyphic alphabet. The reverse is also true. Some sounds used in the English alphabet cannot be expressed by phonograms in the ancient Egyptian alphabet either. In such cases where we may be looking for equivalent sounds, we must always settle for an approximation.

The advanced Egyptologist is more concerned with the meanings of sentences and words rather than how they sound. They get around this problem by adopting a system called transliteration, which we will discuss in more detail later.

1.4.3 Rebus Principle

The idea that symbols could be used to represent the sounds of a language rather than represent real objects, is known as the rebus principle and is one of the most significant ancient discoveries leading to the development of writing. Not only did this principle apply to the development of the ancient Egyptian written language, but it was also the precursor to the development of the alphabets used in modern languages as well.

A rebus is a message spelt out in pictures that represents sounds rather than the things they are pictures of. For example the picture of an eye, a bee, and a leaf can be put together to form the English rebus meaning 'I be-lieve', which has nothing to do with eyes, bees, or leaves. Consider the following two examples of rebuses:

The pictograms 👁 and 🦌 represent 'I-deer' and form the rebus 'idea'.

The pictograms 👁, 〰 and 🐑 represent 'eye-sea-ewe' and form the rebus 'I see you'.

This principle is adopted in many parts of the ancient Egyptian system of spelling with hieroglyphs.

The term 'rebus' can refer to the use of one or more pictograms representing one or more phonograms. In the beginning, ancient Egyptian writing relied heavily on pictographic signs representing concrete objects. Words which cannot be represented easily by means of a picture, such as proper names, ideas, and function words, were difficult to write. The rebus principle provided the means to overcome this limitation. Fully developed hieroglyphs read in rebus fashion were in use at Abydos in ancient Egypt as early as 3400 BC.

A famous ancient Egyptian rebus statue of Ramses II consists of three hieroglyphic elements. A large falcon representing Horus the sun god—RA, who is standing behind a sitting child—MES, and the child is holding a sedge plant stalk in his left hand—SU. Remember, we are not looking at these hieroglyphs from the perspective phonograms. These three items compose the rebus RA-MES-SU or as we prefer Ramesses.

Two main types of sound writing evolved from the development and extension of the rebus principle; syllabic and alphabetic writing. The English language is purely alphabetic, although from the example of the rebuses above, it can be seen how easy it is to construct a syllabic rebus from English words.
Ancient Egyptian hieroglyphs can demonstrate both types of writing.

It is even possible to compose a rebus that is both of an alphabetic and a syllabic nature, for example:

$$H + \text{(ear)} = \text{Hear}$$

When you contemplate how language gradually develops, you may be right in thinking that there is no coincidence in the fact that the word 'ear' is part of the word 'hear'.

1.4.4 VOWELS

Although vowels were used in the spoken language, they were not generally written. Where a vowel might be used is where a word began with a vowel or where it might be confusing if vowels were left out, such as with the names of people or places. For example in English, words can be abbreviated by leaving out vowels.

$$\text{Rd} = \text{Road}, \text{Drv} = \text{Drive}$$

When these abbreviations are read aloud, they are spoken with the vowels included. Some hieroglyphs are close to vowel sounds in the English language; these are considered as weak consonants. Due to the lack of English sounding vowels in Egyptian hieroglyphs, any symbols that are used to represent a vowel sound cannot be anything else except an approximation to the required sounds. Ancient Egyptian is no different to any other language with respect to dialect; this always plays a major role in pronunciation. Therefore vowels will have a variety of different soundings but still mean the same. The American pronunciation of the letter 'o' is a good example.

Hieroglyphs can represent a single sound, or, for reasons of economy or convenience two or more sounds.
A hieroglyph that represents one sound is called a uniliteral hieroglyph. Those that represent two sounds combined are called biliterals and those that represent three sounds are called triliterals.

Some authors prefer to use the terms 1-consonant, 2-consonant, and 3-consonant for the terms uniliteral, biliteral, and triliteral respectively. Some biliterals and triliterals are totally unpronounceable to English speakers.

Many symbols had the same meanings or sounds. The symbols used depended on the historic period they were written in, and as previously mentioned, the space available for the writing and the artistic preference of the scribe.

It must also be borne in mind that because hieroglyphs were used over such a vast time span, the sounds of different phonograms changed in that time. In order to be absolutely accurate, you must be aware of the historical time period you are working in when translating or writing hieroglyphs.

For example, it is thought that the hieroglyph that represents a door bolt may possibly have sounded like 'TH', later it became more like 'Z' then even more recent 'S'. This is why it is generally accepted as a phonogram for a 'Z' or 'S'.

Another point to be wary of is the pronunciations of phonograms in different articles you may read. The different dialects between authors can cause large variations in the pronunciation of the same phonograms. Much of the modern literature available today has come from American and French sources. As we are all aware, if you are not accustomed to some American dialects, the pronunciation of some words can sound peculiar to us. No doubt Americans have similar problems with some Scottish, Welsh, and London dialects.

In many translations into English of European literature and vice versa, the editors have obviously had difficulties in finding the correct pronunciations of some sounds. Sometimes it seems as though the translators have concentrated on the body-text of the material, but not realized that the sounds of some words were more important than their literal translation.

The internet can be guilty of this, many texts are translated on mass into English for the benefit of all, or they can be translated at the touch of a button by 'clever' software. These programs are chiefly concerned with literal translation, syntax, and grammar; they have no comprehension of which alphabetic letters produce the same or similar sounds in an alternative language.

1.4.5 UNILITERALS

If you wish to use any of the hieroglyphs on your PC but have problems locating them on your keyboard see sections; 1.12.2, 1.12.3, 3.3.1 and 3.3.2.

Uniliteral Hieroglyph	Pronounced	Uniliteral Hieroglyph	Pronounced
𓄿	A	𓂧	D
𓃀	B	𓆑	F
𓎡	C	𓉔	H

1.4.6 Biliterals

Biliterals are hieroglyphs where one alphabetic character replaces two alphabet characters. The sound of the biliteral hieroglyph is the same as the sound of the two alphabetic characters it replaces. Biliterals help eliminate large numbers of simpler characters.

Sometimes a uniliteral appears next to a biliteral in a word and acts as a sort of sound compliment. The reason for this is not entirely clear, but in such circumstances the uniliteral is not read. For example if we consider the following hieroglyphic word:⌑⌑ = PR R, we read PR not PRR.

There are two rules for uniliteral accompanying biliterals;

1. If a uniliteral has the same sound as the second hieroglyph in the biliteral sound, then the uniliteral sound is not read as a separate sound.
2. If a uniliteral sound differs from the second biliteral sound, then the uniliteral is read as a separate sound.

One reason for adding these silent characters seems to be that lines of text can be lengthened without altering the message. Keeping things symmetrical was very important to the ancient Egyptians.

> § 1.4.6 Notes of Interest
>
> The number of ancient Egyptian words which can be classed as interjections is very small. These include 'lo', 'hail', 'hail to thee', 'hey', 'behold', 'would that' and of course 'yes' and 'no'.
>
> Yes   No

Biliteral Hieroglyph	Pronounced	Biliteral Hieroglyph	Pronounced
	PR		MW
	SW		TP
	SN		GB
	WN		MS

1.4.7 TRILITERALS

Triliterals are hieroglyphs where one alphabetic character replaces three alphabet characters. The sound of the triliteral hieroglyph is the same as the sound of the three alphabetic characters it replaces. Triliterals like biliterals help eliminate large numbers of simpler characters.

Triliteral Hieroglyph	Pronounced	Triliteral Hieroglyph	Pronounced
	SPR		DWA
	DMD		DBA
	STP		SMA
	NFR		WAS

1.5.0 Determinatives

1.5.1 A Dual Purpose

A determinative is a hieroglyph added to the end of a word which has been spelt out in phonograms. The determinative helps clarify any doubts about the meaning of the word by eliminating confusion. The determinative has two purposes. First, it shows that the hieroglyphs preceding it are to be read as phonograms rather than ideograms; and second, it clarifies the meaning of the word. The writings that precede the determinative are put in context. When a hieroglyph is used as a determinative, it does not represent a sound.

Consider the following simplistic example which could have several meanings using modern day symbolism:

Hieroglyphs and Arithmetic of the Ancient Egyptian Scribes   43

The above could mean 'eye heart ewe', 'I see a heart of a sheep', 'I Heart U', 'I Love You' or 'I love sheep'. We can eliminate the confusion by adding a popular valentine symbol as a determinative:

This additional symbol is associated with Cupid, the god of love. Use of this symbol as a determinative implies that the statement relates to matters of love, and effectively says 'I Love You'.

The last symbol above is the Egyptian hieroglyph that is the determinative for eating, drinking, and speaking. So it would mean either 'I love to eat lamb' or 'I talk about love to sheep'. To avoid further confusion, maybe a determinative for mint sauce should be added, if there were such a thing!

1.5.2 SOME GENERIC DETERMINATIVES

Determinative	Meaning	Determinative	Meaning
	Man, person.		Nose, smell, joy, contempt.
	Woman.		Nose, smell, joy, contempt.

![]	Child, young.	![]	Eye, see, actions of eye.
![]	Old man, old, lean upon.	![]	Arm, bend arm, cease.
![]	Official, man in authority.	![]	Walk, run.
![]	Exalted person, the dead.	![]	Walk backwards.
![]	Exalted person, the dead.	![]	Irrigated land.
![]	Exalted person, the dead.	![]	Land.
![]	God, king.	![]	House, building.
![]	King.	![]	Sacred bark.
![]	King.	![]	Knife, cut.
![]	Goddess, queen.	![]	Hoe, cultivate, hack.
![]	Goddess, queen.	![]	Life, live.
![]	High, rejoice, support.	![]	Bird, insect.

	Praise, supplicate.		Small, bad weak.
	Force, effort.		Fish.
	Eat, drink, speak.		Snake, worm
	Lift, carry		Cattle
	Weary, weak		Cattle
	Enemy, foreigner		Wood, tree
	Enemy, death		Corn
	Lie down, death, bury		Sun, light, time
	Lie down, death, bury		Star
	Mummy, likeness, shape.		Book, writing, abstract
	Head, nod, throttle.		Grain.

1.5.3 Cartouche Determinatives

Basically, a cartouche is used to hold the name of a king or other royal personage; for this reason it acts as a determinative. The titulary of a king can consist of five great names and, in addition, a lot of flattery. For example, the full titulary of Sesostris the First is as follows:

1. Horus *Life of births*;
2. Two Ladies *Life of births*;
3. Horus of Gold *Life of births*;
4. King of Upper and Lower Egypt *Kheperkera*;
5. Son of Re *Sesostris; granted life, stability, and wealth, like Re:eternally*.

There is a high probability that if you had met Sesostris when he was alive, you would be required to kneel before him. If you need to access any cartouches displayed in the table below with your PC or I, Section 1.12.2 explains how to do this.

⊖	E1 ?	Original cartouche form; called a 'Shen Ring' and represents a double rope encircling the entire region ruled over by the sun. Hence in calculations it means all that is; infinity. Reads from top to bottom
⬭	E1 @	Later vertical cartouche form; reads from top to bottom.
⬯	E1 <	Later horizontal cartouche form; means circuit; reads from left to right.
⬯	E1 >	Later horizontal cartouche form; means circuit; reads from right to left.

1.6.0 Direction of Reading Hieroglyphic Writing

1.6.1 Read towards Figures

English is always read from left to right. Hieroglyphic writing was written in columns or rows. The reading direction for hieroglyphs is determined by the direction that human and animal figures face; you always read towards figures.

Hieroglyphs could be written for reading from left to right—

Usually they were written to be read from right to left—

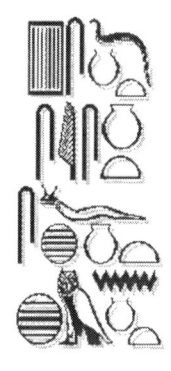

Columns were read from top to bottom. The Egyptians liked symmetry. If hiero-glyphs were inscribed in one column, they would often inscribe the same text in an opposite column, except the writing would be reversed. In the left column, you start at the top, read left to right, then down one line and continue. In the right-hand column, you start at the top but read right to left then down a line and continue.

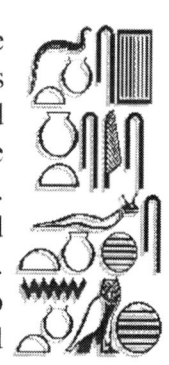

1.7.0 PLURALS AND DUALS

1.7.1 REPETITION REPLACES 'S'

In the English language, when we wish to denote a quantity of something greater than one, we simply add an 's' to the end of a word. 'House' becomes 'houses' and 'tree' becomes 'trees'.

In ancient Egypt, a common way of showing the plurality of something, making the noun a plural, was to repeat the hieroglyphs thus:

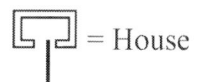

= House

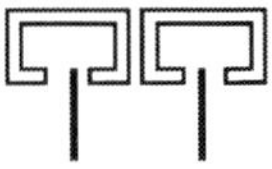

⌐⌐ ⌐⌐ = Two houses (Duality)

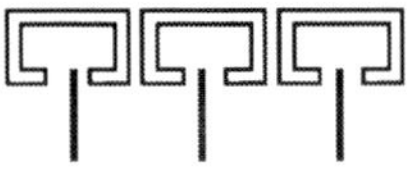

⌐⌐ ⌐⌐ ⌐⌐ = Houses, any number more than two

In later styles of writing a 'determinative of plurality' consisting of three strokes or dots in various patterns came into general use:

Determinatives of Plurality					
|||	ooo / ooo	ooo	ooo	ı'ı	ı'ı	ı ı ı

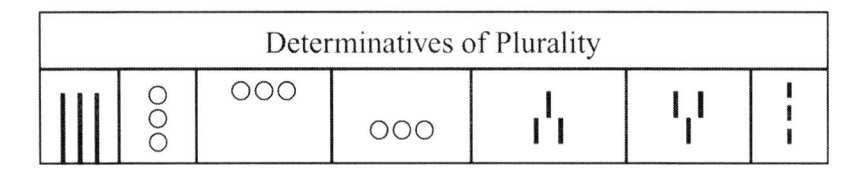

For example:

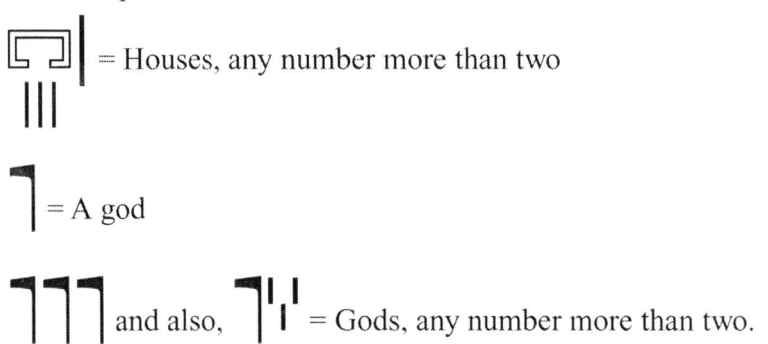

⌐⌐ / ||| = Houses, any number more than two

↑ = A god

↑↑↑ and also, ↑ı'ı = Gods, any number more than two.

Drawing three bars or dots saved the scribe having to draw the same hieroglyphs thrice to represent plurality, not duality. To show duality the scribe had no option, he had to duplicate the appropriate hieroglyphs no matter how complex.

Where words are more complicated and consist of a number of hieroglyphs, repeating the determinative serves the same purpose:

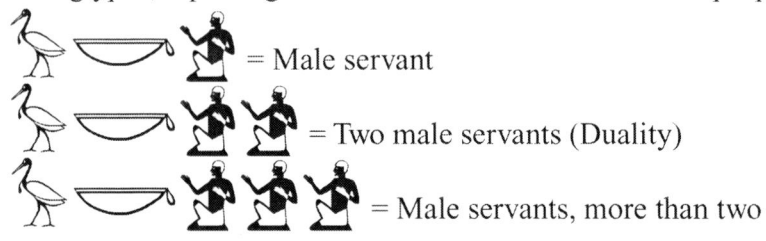

= Male servant

= Two male servants (Duality)

= Male servants, more than two

A valid alternative to the line of hieroglyphs above would be:

🪶⌒𓀀 ||| = Male servants, more than two

Sometimes the hieroglyph of a quail chick was added to the end of a word to indicate that it was plural. If the quail chick were added it was placed before any determinatives for the word.

If a quail chick hieroglyph had been used to signify plurality, the rules for the use of determinatives of plurality, and repetition of the word's determinative as explained above still apply. Consider the following singular form of the word for 'bird' or 'fowl':

= **Singular for bird**

The following are all valid alternatives for the plural of the above singular hieroglyphic word for 'bird':

The quail chick could just as easily be absent from all of the examples!

When determinatives of plurality were not used, it must have taken the scribe a tedious amount of time to repeat some hieroglyphs.

1.7.2 SPECIFIC QUANTITIES

If the ancient Egyptian scribe were required to write about a specific number of items, he usually left the word in the singular form and put the required quantity on the end of the word.

For example, if the scribe were required to write 'ten loaves', he would write in hieroglyphs 'loaf ten'. Let us look at an example of 1527 trees; because we must use the word 'tree' in the singular form, we do not use (🐦) or any determinative of plurality.

〰️ 🏠 🌱 🌀🌀 @ ∩∩ |||| =Tree 1527

Numbers will be explained later, just accept this example for the moment.

1.8.0 GENDER

1.8.1 NOUNS ARE SOMETHING SUBSTANTIVE

First, it is useful to be reminded that nouns are words typically used to refer to people, objects, living things, ideas, something substantive and the like.

In ancient Egyptian, all nouns are treated as either masculine or feminine, and in a similar way to the French language, words are given a gender often for no obvious reason. In the ancient Egyptian language there is no 'it', as there is in the English language.

The gender of nouns used in ancient Egyptian texts is very easily identified; feminine nouns almost always end in (⌒), whereas masculine nouns rarely end in anything to indicate gender. Also there are no special words for 'the' or 'a' in classical ancient Egyptian. This means the word 'man' can mean either 'a man' or 'the man'; usually one or the other of the formats will suggest itself after translation from ancient Egyptian into English.

As mentioned earlier, when a word is plural a (🐦) is sometimes added.

In the case of a feminine word, the (🦅) would be placed before the (⌒) so that the word still ends with (⌒) and can clearly be identified as feminine. Let us consider the hieroglyphs for the word 'tree', which in ancient Egyptian is a feminine word:

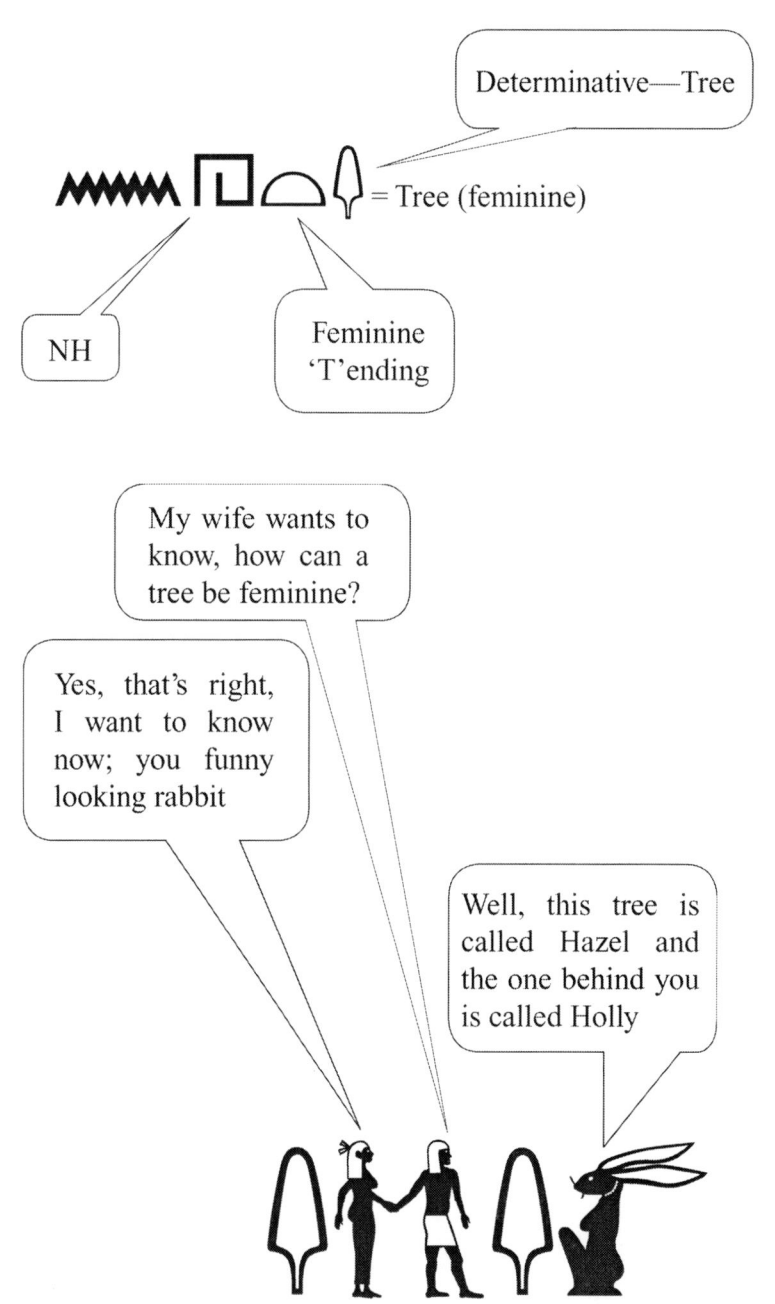

〰〰 ⌷ ⌒ 🌳 = Tree (feminine)

Determinative—Tree

NH

Feminine 'T' ending

My wife wants to know, how can a tree be feminine?

Yes, that's right, I want to know now; you funny looking rabbit

Well, this tree is called Hazel and the one behind you is called Holly

The hieroglyphs for 'tree' in the singular shown earlier can be made plural; 'trees', by using a triple determinative as shown below.

= Trees (feminine)

Remember, the use of a double determinative would have meant we were dealing with two trees, duality. If the scribe was getting short of wall space or papyrus, he may have decided to take a less long-winded approach and wrote the word trees as follows:—

= Trees (feminine)

1.9.0 PREPOSITIONS

1.9.1 SIMILARITIES WITH ENGLISH

One feature of ancient Egyptian that is similar to English is in the use of prepositions. Prepositions are words that are 'pre-posed', or put before others, to indicate locations (in), directions (towards), times (during), accompaniment (with) and how things are done (by). A preposition is a word marking a relationship between a noun and other words.

Hieroglyphic Preposition	Meaning
	in, with, from, as
	by
	to(*wards people*), for
	with
	to(*wards place*), at

For example:

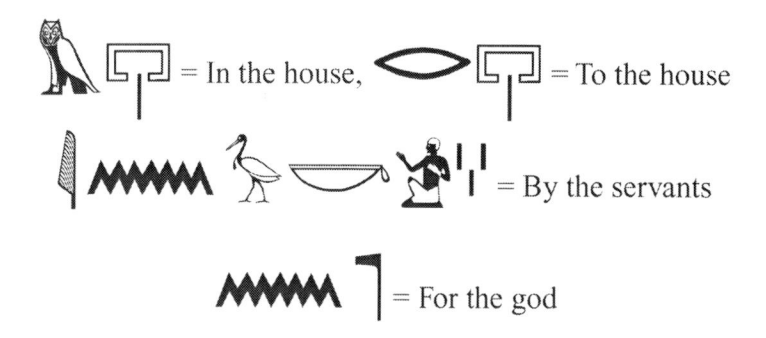

[owl][house] = In the house, [mouth][house] = To the house

[reed][water] [ibis][bowl][seated servant][strokes] = By the servants

[water] [god flag] = For the god

§ 1.9.1 Notes of Interest

While you can't substitute one word for another, each term can appear in so many different forms that there was no need for a scribe to consult a dictionary for its spelling. Let us take an example. To write 'the living' based upon the ankh hieroglyph (☥), all of the following are valid spellings, and this list is by no means complete either!

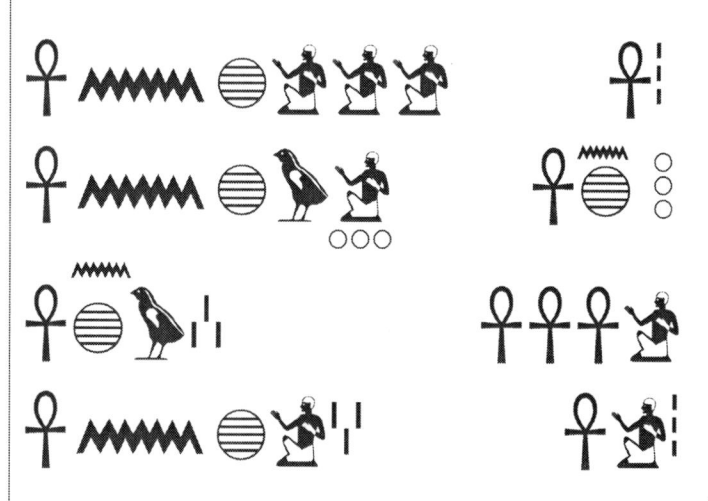

1.10.0 NUMBER BASICS

1.10.1 BASE TEN

A more detailed explanation of the way in which the ancient Egyptians counted and processed numbers will follow later in the section on mathematics. For the moment, we will accept the fact that the ancient Egyptian numbering system was based on units of 10.

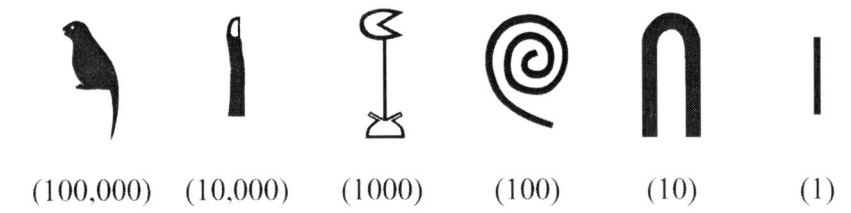

(100,000) (10,000) (1000) (100) (10) (1)

To write a number, the hieroglyph which represented the appropriate magnitude of base ten was simply repeated as many times as was necessary. The same rule applied to the units, units were repeated as necessary up to the required value; if ten were reached then these individual units would all be replaced by a single hieroglyph that represented ten.

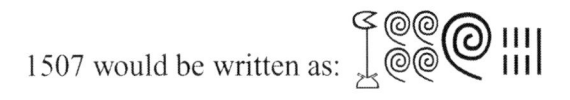

1507 would be written as:

The ancient Egyptian numbering system differed from ours in that our system is positional. Positional means that each column represents a different order of magnitude; in our case based on powers of ten. For example the units, tens, hundreds and thousands etc, all have their own position in a number made up of a string of digits. If a column in a particular sequence of numbers has no value for that position, a zero is inserted. The ancient Egyptians always maintained a rule where their numbers were positioned in order of magnitude, but they had no use for a zero.

Where we would happen to use one or more zeros in a string of numbers, they simply closed any gaps where you would expect a zero to be.

1.11.0 Transliteration and Translation

1.11.1 Translation

Transliteration must not be confused with translation. Translation means to convert written or spoken words from one language into another and retain the original meaning as close as possible. For example, the following words and sentences written in ancient Egyptian hieroglyphs are translated into English words and sentences.

A wretch of a washer man

1.11.2 Transliteration

Transliteration is a process of converting the characters of a written text into another set of characters. Egyptologists have developed a number of different alphabets for the purpose of transliterating ancient Egyptian hieroglyphs. Recording words and sentences written in hieroglyphs can be very tedious, time consuming, and sometimes prone to errors.

By writing a special character that represents a particular hieroglyph can make life a lot easier for the Egyptologist. These special characters are usually taken from the English alphabet, but they can be of their own design depending on which transliteration alphabet is being used.

For example, the same ancient Egyptian hieroglyphic sentence above is now transliterated as follows.

$$\d{h}wrw \quad n \quad r\underline{h}ty$$

Egyptologists use the system of transliteration to compile dictionaries of ancient Egyptian hieroglyphs and words. Transliteration allows hieroglyphs and the words constructed from them to be more easily catalogued and cross referenced.

There are a number of different character sets available for transliteration; some authors have even invented their own. The sound that a particular hieroglyph represents may be very consistent but how it is interpreted with different transliterative fonts can appear spurious. For example the letter 'H' can be pronounced in numerous ways depending upon your nationality. The system below demonstrates the traditional style which has always been based on English-sounding characters.

§ 1.11.2 Notes of Interest

Working conditions were quite good for craftsmen working on some tombs in the Valley of the Kings. They worked eight-hour days and received one in every ten days off. However, they were able to take other days off as they needed for special reasons. These reasons included, hangover, wrapping a dead person, burying a dead person, making libations for the dead, being ill, being bitten by a scorpion, having an argument with the wife, and female family members menstruating.

1.11.3 THE ANCIENT EGYPTIAN ALPHABET

Hieroglyph	Description	Transliteration	Sound
	The Egyptian Alphabet		
	Vulture	3	Glottal stop—'A'

Hieroglyphs and Arithmetic of the Ancient Egyptian Scribes

𓇋	Flowering reed	i	Soft 'I' or 'e' sometimes consonantal 'Y' or 'ee' sound.
𓇌	Two Reed Flowers or two oblique strokes	y	consonantal 'Y'
𓂝	Forearm	$\mathord{\text{ʕ}}$	Unknown to English, varied throughout history. Guttural sound, like 'Ah'
𓅱	Quail Chick	w	W
𓃀	Foot	b	B
𓊪	Stool	p	P
𓆑	Horned Viper	f	F
𓅓	Owl	m	M
𓈖	Water	n	N
𓂋	Mouth	r	R
𓉔	Reed Shelter	h	H

⦵	Wick of twisted flax	*ḥ*	Unknown to English. Emphatic 'h'. Like 'ha' on camera lens before polishing.
⊖	Ball of string	*ḫ*	Like 'ch' in Scottish Loch.
	Animal's Belly with teats	*ẖ*	Like 'ch' in German 'ich'
	Bolt or folded cloth	*s*	S
	Pool	*š*	SH
	Hill slope	*ḳ*	Like 'Q' in queen or 'K' sound in Quran.
	Basket with handle	*k*	K
	Jar stand	*g*	G
	Loaf of bread	*t*	T
	Tethering Rope	*ṯ*	No close English equivalent. Like 'ch' or 'tj' in tune.
	Hand	*d*	D
	Snake	*ḏ*	DJ or J as in June or to some dialects dune.

§ 1.11.3 Notes of Interest

The priesthood, especially in the upper echelons was a very powerful occupation. Priests were able to gain honours, wealth, and titles. People believed that the priests were in the presence of the gods everyday. Therefore, many people made gifts to the priests to gain favour with the gods or ask for something on their behalf.

The kings were considered to be an incarnation of the god Horus on earth and for this reason, they were believed to be gods in their own right. This divine status meant that they were able to converse with the gods and supposedly keep them happy on behalf of their people. Having said this, the kings were not immune to donating gifts, bestowing land, titles and other rewards to the priests. For this reason, high priests became very wealthy and powerful. It appears that the kings did not have as much faith in their own godly status as everyone else was led to believe.

1.12.0 English Phonetics for Common Egyptian Hieroglyphs

1.12.1 Overview of the List of Phonograms

The following list is by no means complete. Many hieroglyphs have been excluded from the list either because the sounds that they represent are unpronounceable or there is no English language equivalent for them. It is common to find more than one ancient Egyptian hieroglyph that is a phonogram for the same English alphabetical sound. Some of the hieroglyphs are a phonogram for a combination of English alphabetic letters. If you are attempting to write a sentence phonetically using different hieroglyphs, take care in your choice of hieroglyphs where English letters may represent a number of different sounds. For example words containing the letter 'Y' or 'I' require special attention. The letter 'Y' in the words 'many' and 'by' are different phonetically. The same is true for the letter 'I' in the words 'bit' and 'bite'. Consequently the phonographic hieroglyph for the letters 'Y' and 'I' in the words 'byte' and 'bite' respectively, could be exactly the same; they are identical phonetically.

1.12.2 USING THE HIEROGLYPHIC SIGN LIST

Excluding the heading, the following table of ancient Egyptian hieroglyphs is in five columns. Each column serves the following function:

1.12.2.1 COLUMN 1—HIEROGLYPHS

This column contains a list of individual hieroglyphs. Even though a symbol in this column may be a combination of hieroglyphs, it is still treated as a single hieroglyph. Each hieroglyph in this column is a phonogram and represents the sound equivalent of one or more letters found in the English alphabet.

Many of the hieroglyphs found in the keyboard fonts contain a lot of detail which is not noticed if too small a point size is used. To realize the full benefit of the detail, as large a point size (character size) should be used as possible. Many of the hieroglyphs in this text are in a point size of 48 or even greater.

1.12.2.2 COLUMN 2—KEY

If you need to type particular hieroglyphs from a computer keyboard, then this column tells you which buttons to press. Of course, before you can type any of these hieroglyphs, the appropriate hieroglyphic fonts

Hieroglyphs and Arithmetic of the Ancient Egyptian Scribes 61

must first be installed onto your computer. For example, if you were required to find the hieroglyph A which represents a netting needle filled with twine, you would notice that the code in the key column would say 'E5 A'. The first two characters tell you the name of the font to use, in this case 'E5', which means that you must switch to the Egyptian5 font. Of course, in the same way you use any keyboard font, you need not switch if you are already using the font you require. The third character tells you which key to press, in this case capital 'A'. Take care, there is a difference between upper and lower case keyboard buttons, they will give you different hieroglyphs.

To make life as easy as possible, many of the letters on the keyboard actually give you the hieroglyphic phonogram by alphabetic letter that you require. Of the nine Egyptian fonts from Egypt1 to Egypt9, the lower font number is more likely to give you the phonogram that you require.

Having said this, always check the tables or keyboard mapping if you have any doubts. When both the upper and lowercase keyboard characters seem to offer the phonograms you require, usually the uppercase character will provide the more exact phonogram.

While working with the Egypt1 font, typing 'CAT' in uppercase, would give you the hieroglyphs as seen on the right; which are the correct phonograms for the word 'cat'.

On the other hand, if you had switched to the Egypt8 font instead, you would have this set of hieroglyphs on the right. This says two Hekats and a Deben.

1.12.2.3 Column 3—Brief Description

For modern day ancient Egyptian enthusiasts such as ourselves, many of the hieroglyphs can look quite alien. A modern day person may only be able to take a guess at what some of these hieroglyphs are pictures of.

This can be particularly true when some hieroglyphs are viewed in isolation. In such cases, only when they are seen as an integral part of a group of hieroglyphs as in a mural, can they be more easily identified. Even then it might still be extremely difficult to identify what particular hieroglyphs are supposed to be pictures of. There is a general consensus of opinion amongst most modern-day Egyptologist, as to what the majority of all the hieroglyphs are supposed to be pictures of. The identification of only a few hieroglyphs remains in serious doubt.

Column three gives a partial description as to what Egyptologists believe each of these hieroglyphs represent.

1.12.2.4 COLUMN 4—SOUND

The letters and combinations of letters in this column provide an indication of what the hieroglyph in column one would replace if you were converting words phonetically from English into ancient Egyptian. The English letters help show how you would pronounce the hieroglyphic phonogram in English. If the English letters offer a variety of sounds depending on their context, then you must check with column five to ensure that you are using the correct hieroglyph.

Letters in this column separated by a slash (/), mean that the hieroglyph in column one can represent either of these sounds depending upon the context in which the hieroglyph is used.

Letters in lowercase represent sounds that accompany the sounds of the capital letter(s), but are very weak and are sometimes silent. In fact, any string of capital letters is often unpronounceable if an attempt is made to pronounce the lowercase letters with any strength.

Staying within the confines of the English Language, the hieroglyphs that represent phonograms that are unpronounceable have been excluded from this table. No doubt if this column were translated to function for some other modern languages, we may find that additional phonograms could be included while others might need to be excluded.

Many of these pronunciations are approximations or a compromise of a number of slightly different sounds. This is because the ancient Egyptians gradually changed the pronunciation of many hieroglyphs over the millennia. Also, the populous from different districts had their own characteristic manner in which to pronounce words. We have the same problem today; people from different parts of the same country or even the same city can have alternative pronunciations for the same words.

To be more accurate with the pronunciation of the phonograms, you need to know which period in ancient Egyptian time you are dealing with. You also need to know the particular area of Egypt that the phonograms were being used in to determine the ancient Egyptian dialect. Do not forget, if you are writing your own messages in hieroglyphs, you may spell the same words different to someone else. If you both speak with a different dialect, it is possible that your spellings for the same word are different and yet still correct. For example, someone with a North-eastern dialect may say 'I like to wark to walk'; after translation, for the benefit of Southerners, it reads, 'I like to walk to work'. Another example; 'Are you shore you like the sea shore?' Translated from TV presenter English, it now reads, 'Are you sure you like the sea shore'?

1.12.2.5 COLUMN 5—EXAMPLES OF USAGE

This column provides a sample of words or part words with one or more alphabetic letters enclosed within brackets. The parenthesized letters are an attempt at showing what the corresponding hieroglyphic phonogram in column one should sound like. Saying the sound you are looking for out loud often helps to improve your choice of phonogram. This is particularly true when searching for hieroglyphs to replace multi-sounding letters such as 'Y'. A different hieroglyph would be required to replace the letter 'Y' in each of the following words, 'many', 'yellow', 'ploy' and 'byte'.

Hyphens indicate where other partial or complete words may be attached to the parenthesized letters.

Warning, do not be heard in public repeatedly muttering out loud words and sounds in an effort to test the pronunciation of phonograms. This often results in you receiving a lot of strange looks. Some people may think that you are seriously disturbed; they may even approach you and talk to you in quiet reassuring tones!

1.12.3 COMMONLY USED ANCIENT EGYPTIAN PHONOGRAMS

West Wind	Ancient Egyptian Phonograms	East Wind

Hieroglyph	Key	Brief Description	Sound	Examples of Usage
	E1 A	Vulture	A	Cockney h(a)t; Short 'A', c(a)t, b(a)t, s(a)t, f(a)t (approximation)
	E1 a	Forearm with palm facing up.	A	Rough throaty breath-in 'A', close to (e); (eh), h(ai)r, b(ea)r, t(ai)r, w(ai)r, c(a)re (long soft A, approximation)
	E2 A	Vertical and also horizontal wooden column.	Aa	Hard-long A; k(a)rt, b(a)ltic, b(a)lsam, (aa)rdvark, c(a)rp, sal(aa)m, advoc(aa)t, b(a)rn, baz(aa)r, k(a)rt
	E2 a			
	E3 A	Leg and arm means horn	AB	(Ab)out, (ab)ack, (ab)sent, (ab)solute, debat(ab)le, adapt(ab)ility, (ab)ility, (ab)ly, admir(ab)le, (ab)le-
	E3 a	Chisel, means be ill or friend	AB/ mr	

Glyph	Code	Description	Translit	Pronunciation
(mast)	E4 A	Mast of boat and same with forearm, means stand	AHa	Very abrupt, throaty (aha); b(ah)aist, m(aha) raja, casb(ah), autob(ah)n, tom(aha)wk, m(aha)tma, cheet(ah),—(ahe)dr-
(mast with forearm)	E4 a			
(netting needle)	E5 A	Netting needle filled with twine, spool; reel	AJ	(J) sounds like (DJ); (aj)ar, m(aj)or, m(aj)esty, p(aj)amas, tr(aj)ectory, (adj)acent, (adj)ourn, a(dj)ust
(crested ibis)	E5 a	Crested ibis, means be glorious; spirit; spirit-like-nature	AK	K like ch in scottish Loch; la(ck), ta(ck), J(ack)
(cormorant)	E1 ;	Cormorant bird, means revenue	AK	K like Arabic Q in Quran; (acc)ount, (ak)imbo, pla(que) anor(ak), p(ack), qu(ack)
(well +)	E1 +	Well full of water	AM	-gr(am)-, (am)pere, ad(am)ant, dyn(am)ics, (am)algamate, (am)ass, (am)phi-, bamboo,—(am)ble
(well -)	E1 -			

☥	E1 =	Sandal strap; symbol of life	ANKh	A(nch)or, t(ank), (ank)le, b(ank), c(ank)er, s(ank), pl(ank), h(ank)y-p(ank)y, hum(ank)ind
🦆	E1 &	Head of duck, means bird	APD	L(apd)og, sn(apd)ragon, tr(apd)oor, sl(apd)ash
🎒	E5 \	Bag for clothing, means prepare; dread	APR	(Apr)il, (apr)on, (apr)icot, c(apr)ice, mal(apr)op, p(apr)ika, s(apr)ophyte, t(apr)oom, t(apr)oot, wr(apr)ound
∞	E1 \	Band of string or linen, a garland, or tie for papyrus roll	ARK	(Ark), aardv(ark), b(arque), h(ark)en, m(arqu)ee, m(ark)er, b(ark), m(ark)et, d(ark), (arc)light, (arck)ed, alt(arc)loth
🦎	E1 /	Lizard, means many	ASHA	(Asha)med, p(asha), un(asha)med, w(asha)ble, w(ashe)r, (ashe)n, b(ashe)s, fl(ashe)d, backw(ashe)s

Hieroglyphs and Arithmetic of the Ancient Egyptian Scribes

🐗	E2 V	Hippopotamus head. Means attack, striking power, moment.	AT	(At)mosphere, (at)om, (at)oned, (at)rocity, (At)lantic,—i(at)ry,—st(at), acclim(at)ize, ch(at)ty, am(at)eur, (at)oll, (at)tach
🦁	E1 ,	Lion head with paw, means front or Prince	AT/ hat	(Hat) with almost silent H.—i(at)rics,—i(at)ry,—st(at), acclim(at)ize, ch(at)ty, am(at)eur, (at)oll, (at)tach, ch(at)eau
	E1 .	Spine with issue of marrow at both ends, means stretch out	AW	(Aw)ait, (aw)ake, (aw)ay
	E1 B	Foot	B	(B)et, (b)uy, (b)ag,—a(b)ility,—a(b)ly, (a)t,—a(b)leibility, (b)ig, (b)ottom
🦩	E3 B	Jabiru bird, means soul, represents a wandering spirit; ba.	BA	(Ba)t, a(ba)ck, canni(ba)l, (ba)rrier, (ba)g, sam(ba), arm(ba)nd, ala(ba)ster, (ba)r(ba)rian, (ba)rrage (ba)lloon
	E2 B	Pot possibly used as lamp, means soul		

⏥	E2 b	Pot possibly used as lamp, means soul	BA	(Ba)t, a(ba)ck, canni(ba)l, (ba)rrier, (ba)g, sam(ba), arm(ba)nd, ala(ba)ster, (ba)r(ba)rian, (ba)rrage (ba)lloon
🐦	E7 ~	Human headed bird preceeded by bowl for incense with smoke rising from it.		
⌒	E1 C	Basket with handle	C/k	(C)all, (c)opy, (c)at, la(ck), bas(k)et
⌒	E1 t	Rope for teathering animals; hobble rope	CH/ tch	(Tu)ne, (ch)ew, (ch)ildren, cat(ch), (ch)eese, pic(tu)re, (ch)oice, (tu)lip, (ch)urch
⊖	E1 c	Ball of string, placenta	CKh	(Ck) as in Scottish lo(ch), an(ch)or, lo(ck), ro(ck), mo(ck), so(ck), (c)or(k)
⌂	E2 C	Butchers block	CR	A(cr)e, a(cr)ylic, (cr)aft, aristo(cr)acy, bureau(cr)ats, ban(kr)upt, co(ckr)oach, da(rk)room, (kr)ypton, mu(ckr)ake
✋	E1 D	Hand	D	(D)og, (d)rea(d), (d)umb, (d)oubt, (d)u(d), (d)onkey, (d)a(d).
△	E4 -	Bread mold. Means give.		
🏹	E2 D	Reed-floats used in fishing and hunting the hippopotamus	DBA	Fee(dba)ck, han(dba)g, har(dba)ck, san(dba)nk, threa(dba)re, win(dba)g

Hieroglyphs and Arithmetic of the Ancient Egyptian Scribes   69

Glyph	Code	Description	Sound	Examples
★	E2 d	Star	DWA /sba	Ban(dwa)gon, bir(dwa)tcher, (dwa)rfish, (dwa)rves, win(dwa)rd, E(dwa)rdian, floo(dwa)ter, lan(dwa)rds
⏐	E1 E	Flowering Reed (approximation)	E/i	(Eh), soft (e) almost silent, p(e)g, m(e)n, l(e)mon. More like b(i)t, s(i)t
⟋⟋	E2 E	Pair of strokes, abbr' for two-flowering reeds	EE/y	L(ea)d, s(ea), fl(ea), str(ee)t, fl(ee)t, Mar(y), Henr(y)
⏐⏐	E1 e	Two-flowering reeds		
	E2 e	Pair of crocodiles, represents King or sovereign	ETY	Very weak 'I' or weak 'E' sound. spagh(etii),—(ity),—(ety),
	E1 F	Horned viper	F/v	(F/fu/v/vu), (f)it, (f)lower, (f)ish, (ph)one, tou(gh), (fu)lcrum, (fu)rniture, (fe)rry
	E1 G	Pot/Jar Stand		
	E1 g	Seat	G	(G)et, (g)ap, (g)ot, (g)ust, lo(g)(g)in(g), di(g)(g)in(g)
	E2 G	Red Pot		
⋈	E2 g	Deformed-granite bowl, represents town of Elephantine	GAW	(Gaw)k, (gaw)kily, me(gaw)atts, (gow)n, de(gau)ss, (gau)che, (gau)ds, (gau)dy, (gau)ntlet, (gau)ze,

	E3 G	White-fronted goose, means Earth God Geb,	GB	Fo(gb)ound, lo(gb)ook, pe(gb)oard
	E1 F	Horned viper	GH	Trou(gh), lau(gh), cou(gh), curra(gh)s, drau(gh)ts, enou(gh), rou(gh), sloughs, tou(gh)en
	E3 g	Black ibis, means find, look at	GM	-d(gm)ent, asti(gm)atism, acknowled(gm)ent.
	E3 ?	Depiction uncertain. Thought to be body part such as shortened pair of ribs.	GS	Lo(gs), clo(gs), alon(gs) ide, amon(gs)t., an(gs) trom, do(gs). Also represents the fraction ½
	E1 H	Reed shelter floor plan	H	(H)ome, (h)en, (h)elp, (h)ouse, (h)e, (wh)o
	E1 h	Wick of twisted flax	H	Emphatic h, (Ha!); back of the throat (harh!), (eh!); (h)eh!
	E2 H	Lion head with paw, means front or Prince	HAT/at	Short back of the throat (haa) with (t); weak H; (hat)ch—*aatch*, (hat)—*aat*
	E2 h	Basin with canopy, means festival	HB	Nei(ghb)our,—(ghb)-, moth(b)all, tooth(b) rush,—th(b)-
	E3 H	Alabaster basin		
	E3 h	Club used by fuller who dyed, beat, and processed cloth	HM	Algorit(hm), arit(hm)etic, birt(hm)ark, rhyt(hm), bra(hm)an

Hieroglyphs and Arithmetic of the Ancient Egyptian Scribes 71

⌂	E4 H	Receptacle	HN	Demijo(hn), dou(ghn)ut, tou(ghn)ess,—(ghn)-, Smooth(n)ess, eart(hn)ut, et(hn)ography,—t(hn)-
∩	E4 h	Unknown symbol, means prepare	HR	Th(r)oat,—th(r)-, th(r)ower, c(hr)ysalis, diaph(r)agm,—ph(r)-, fa(hr)enheit, ac(hr)omatic, C(hr)ist, c(hr)onic
👤	E5 H	Face means ON, added to; prepare or bitter		
🏺	E5 h	Water pot	HS	Aftermat(hs), clot(hs),—t(hs)-, barograp(hs), calip(hs),—p(hs)-,—(ghs)-borou(ghs), bou(ghs),
👁	E1 i	Decorated eye relates to actions etc of eye.	I	M(i)te, s(i)te, br(i)ght,—(i)ne k(i)te,—(i)de,—(i)fe,—(i)se,—(i)ze,—(i)ke,—ph(i)le, w(i)se. (subsitute, approximation)
🌾	E1 I	Flowering Reed	I /e	(Ih), h(i)m, h(i)d, b(i)t, p(i)ll, gr(i)lled, (i)ll. (approximation)
⛃	E2 I	Cup or mistress	IAB	Am(iab)le,—(iab)le, l(iab)le, certif(iab)le, d(iab)etic, d(iab)olical,—(iab)ly
🐐	E2 i	Kid, small cattle, goat	IB	-(ib)ly,—(ib)le, l(ib)erty, aud(ib)le, attr(ib)ute, amph(ib)ian, d(ib)-d(ib)
⬭	E3 I	Draughts-piece	IBA	Cann(iba)l, cel(iba)cy, cr(ibba)ge, l(ibe)rty,—(ib)le, cal(ibe)r, del(ibe)rate, d(ibbe)r, g(ibbe)rish, aud(ib)le

⌣	E3 i	Bandage in basin; means bind, bandage	IDR	M(idr)iff
⌒	E4 I	Pair of ribs	IM	(Im)possible, (im)port, tr(im), acr(im)ony, an(im)al, bl(im)p, br(im)stone, ch(im)p, compl(im)ent
⌒	E4 i	Part of a body	IM	(Im)possible, (im)port, tr(im), acr(im)ony, an(im)al, bl(im)p, br(im)stone, ch(im)p, compl(im)ent
⌒	E5 I	Means doubtful. Depiction uncertain, Thought to be pair of ribs.		
✢	E5 i	Two planks crossed and joined; means who is in.	IMI	An(imi)st, ass(imi)late, cr(imi)nal, del(imi)t, d(imi)nution, discr(imi)nate, d(imi)nish, el(imi)nate, facs(imi)le
◯	E2 -	Bowl, pot	IN/ nw	Abst(in)ence, bas(in),—(in),—k(in), adm(in)-, s(in)ister, res(in), glut(in), backsp(in), abom(in)able, aborig(in)al,
⊼	E2 >	Bowl with legs	INI	Adm(ini)stration, cl(ini)c, aff(ini)ties, alkal(ini)ty, s(ini)ster, def(ini)tion, -(ini)ty,—(ini)st

Hieroglyphs and Arithmetic of the Ancient Egyptian Scribes

Hieroglyph	Key	Brief Description	Sound	Examples of Usage
👁	E2 [	Eye, means see; look	IR	Adm(ir)al, aff(ir)m, c(ir)cle, b(ir)d, persp(ir)ant, b(ir)th, resp(ir)ation, g(ir)l, b(ir)ch, besm(ir)ched, sh(ir)t
𓇋	E2]	Bundle of reeds	IS	M(is)t, l(is)t, gr(is)t, f(is)t, ar(is)tocrat,
🐄	E2 =	New-born calf, means conceive, inherit	IW	Gol(iw)og, per(iw)ig, hand(iw)ork
𓆙	E1 J	Cobra snake	J	Like French (di)eu; (j)oke, soft G; (g)enerous, (j)elly, a(dj)ust, a(dj)oin, (g)em
𓂡	E2 J	Fire-drill, a bow and string used to twizzle stick on wood block	JA	(Ja)ck, (ja)bbed, (ja)m, ad(ja)cent, hi(ja)ck, (ja)cket, (Ja)nuary, a(ja)r, py(ja)mas
𓂡	E2 j			

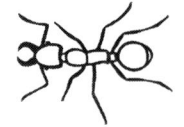

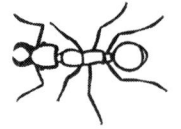

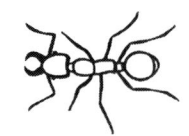

 ✶	E3 J	Sceptre	JAM	Door(jam)b, en(jam)bments, (jam)boree, py(jam)as, wind(jam)mer, (jam) (Jam), (jam)b
 ✶	E1 j	Represents Electrum, an alloy of gold and silver used in jewellery		
 ✶	E1 k	Animal belly with tail	K(i/u)	Ck as in German i(ch), (C)uthbert, (K)ilmarnock
 ✶	E1 K	Basket with handle	K/c	(K)it, (k)ettle
 ✶	E 41-E49	Leaf, stalk, and rhizome of lotus plant, represents one thousand.	KA	(Ca)t, Afri(ka)ans, al(ka)li, Bal(ka)n, ban(ka)ble, ban(ker), (ka)put, blo(cka)ge, brea(ka)way, che(cka)ble. Al(ka)line, brea(ka)ge, (ca)p, ice(ca)p, attac(ka)ble,
 ✶	E2 K	Oxy-rhynchus fish		
 ✶	E2 k	Arms raised, means soul or spirit		

Hieroglyphs and Arithmetic of the Ancient Egyptian Scribes 75

⌒	E3 K	Sunrise above hills	KA	Al(ka)line, (ca)t, attac(ka)ble, bal(ka)n, (ca)p, ban(ka)ble, brea(ka)ge, icecap.
⌒ / ⬭	E3 k / E4 K	Censer, means fumigate; harim; nursery	KAP	(Kap)ok, (kap)ut, (cap)ital, de(cap)itate, handi(cap), ice(cap), (cap), knee(cap)
⬚	E4 k	Flaming charcoal, means black	KM	Blac(km)ail, boo(km)ark, che(ckm)ate, sto(ckm)an, emban(km)ent, mil(km) aid
⬤⬤	E3 "	Two fossil belemnites. Emblem of god of Panopolis	KM	
𓂝	E5 K	Arms rowing, means row; turmoil	KN	-ac(kn)-, ac(kn)owledge, -(kn)ess-, sickness, quic(kn)ess
𓅭	E5 k	Bird taking flight, means alight and halt	KN	Ck as in Scottish lo(ch), bla(ckn)ess, a(ckn)owledge.
🐐	E2 <	Hide of goat	KN	Fran(kn)ess, sic(kn)ess, ban(kn)ote, coc(kn)ey
│	E2 \	Ships oar	KRw	Ck as in Scottish lo(ch) and trilled (r), ban(kr)upt, (cr)umbs, cloa(kr)oom, co(ckr)oach, mu(ckr)ake

	E5 t	Harpoon-head of bone. Unit of measure the Pole	KS	'K' as in Queen; Du(cks), chu(cks), bu(cks), pu(cks), ru(cks), su(cks), tu(cks).
	E2 /	Wood or tree branch	KT	Ba(ckt)rack, bu(ckt) eeth, co(ckt)ail, di(kt)at, abdu(ct), abstra(ct),—a(ct),—e(ct), -o(ct),—i(ct),—u(ct)
	E1 L	Recumbent lion	L	(L)isp, hi(ll), lo(l)(l) ipop, (l)ion, bu(l)(l)ion, a(ll), ha(l)(l)ows, a(l)(l) egorica(l), e(ll)iptica(l)(l)y, bi(l)(l)y
	E1 M	Owl. Means IN	M	(M)ouse, (m)at, co(m)(m)it(m)ent, aco(m)(m)odation, a(m)(m)oniu(m),—(m)ent, co(m)-(m)and(m)ent
	E1 m	Owl with forearm offering loaf, means be neglectful	M	(M)ouse, co(m)(m)it(m)ent, aco(m)(m)odation, (m)at,—(m)ent, a(m)(m)oniu(m), co(m)(m)and-(m)ent
	E2 M	Owl with forearm, means be neglectful		
	E2 m	Sickle	MA	(Ma)ck, (ma)ths, sea(ma)n, (ma)t, aro(ma), ad(ma)n, after(ma)th, abys(ma)l, (ma)ps, (ma)rker, ani(ma)l
	E3 M			
	E3 m	Vulture and sickle, means renew		

Hieroglyphs and Arithmetic of the Ancient Egyptian Scribes

Glyph	Code	Description	Translit.	Examples
	E5 M	Sickle with plinth, meaning truth	MAa	Long (a), market, abnor(ma)l, a(ma)lga(ma)ted
	E5 m			
	E2	Statue plinth or platform, means truth		
	E1			
	E1	Granite bowl; Elephantine was source of the red granite	MAT	Achro(mat)ic, affir(mat)ive, a(mat)eure, gram(mat)ist, aro(mat)ize, auto(mat)ic, (mat), co(mat)ose, for(mat), der(mat)o-, diplo(mat)
	E2	Quail chick and sickle, means anew	MAW	(Maw)s, (maw)kish), mortal,—(more)-, (ma)ll
	E3	Walking stick or staff	MD	Du(md)um, hu(md)rum
	E4 M	Whip, means the coiled one	Mh	Makes some cardinal numbers ordinals. Ar(mh)ole, far(mh)ouse, dru(mh)ead.
	E3	Milk-jug in net means milk;	MI	Abo(mi)nable, (mi)nd, ad(mi)n, alar(mi)sts, (mi)ll, che(mi)st, s(mi)th, ato(mi)c, (mi)nt, bes(mi)rch, (mi)lk

Hieroglyph	Key	Brief Description	Sound	Examples of Usage
	E3 }	Hobble for cattle with cobra, means stable or cattle stall	MJ	Ra(mj)et, ji(mj)ams
	E3 ~	Two owls	MM	Aco(mm)odate, a(mm)o, co(mm)odore, a(mm)eter, ga(mm)on, co(mm)erce
	E3 !	A gaming board (draughts), represents the God, Anum	MN	Colu(mn), alu(mn)i, a(mn)esty, Autu(mn), chi(mn)ey, da(mn), gy(mn)ast, (mn)emonic
	E3 $	Hoe, means hack up or cultivate	MR	Co(mr)ade, pri(mr)ose, ra(mr)od, sha(mr)ock, stea(mr)oller, Cy(mr)u
	E3 &			
	E3 %	Plan of street		
	E3 *	Channel or canal		
	E3 a	Chisel, means be ill or friend	MR/ ab	Co(mr)ade, pri(mr)ose, ra(mr)od, sha(mr)ock, stea(mr)oller, ky(mr)ic

Hieroglyphs and Arithmetic of the Ancient Egyptian Scribes

🪡	E3 -	Apron of three-fox skins	MS	Acclai(ms), ai(ms), al(ms), ato(ms), botto(ms), bu(ms), bri(ms)tone, broo(ms)tick
〰️〰️〰️	E3 ,	Group of water ripples, summer	MW	Di(mw)it, banta(mw)eight, tea(mw)ork, tra(mw)ay, wor(mw)ood
⌒⌒	E3 ⌐ Alt Gr	Arms in gesture of negation. Used with 〰️〰️〰️ means 'No'.	N	(N)et, (n)one, a(n) te(n)(n)a, i(n) terco(n)—(n) ectio(n),—i(n), bice(n)te(n)(n) ials,—tio(n),—e(n), -(n)ess, ru(n)(n)er,
♕	E1 n	Red royal crown of lower Egypt and same in a basket		
♕	E2 n			
〰️〰️〰️〰️	E1 N	Ripple of water		
⌣	E2 N	Basket without handle	NB	Bea(nb)ag, bo(nb)on, canno(nb)all, cra(nb)erry, fi(nb)ack, gu(nb)oat, he(nb)ane, hor(nb)ill, i(nb)red
⌐	E3 ⌐	Pennant, means God	NchR	Lu(nchr)oom, pa(nchr)omatic, sy(nchr)o-, sy(nchr) otrons

✝	E4 N	Unknown article, means ask; enquire	NdJ	Wi(ndj)ammers, Ba(nj)o, co(nj)ecture, co(nj)oin, co(nj)ure, co(nj)ugate, e(nj)oy, fa(nj)et, i(nj)ect, i(nj)ustice
♁	E4 n	Heart and windpipe, means good. Also substituted for zero.	NFR	Co(nfr)ont, i(nfr)a-, u(nfr)ock i(nfr)equent, i(nfr)inge, u(nfr)iendly
🐦	E3 N	Guinea-fowl, means prey and eternity	NH	A(nh)ydrous, butto(nh)ole, disi(nh)erit, dow(nh)ill, e(nh)ance
🔪 /)	E3 n / E5 N	Butchers knife, means orphan	NM	Ador(nm)ent,—(nm)ent, e(nm)esh, gu(nm)an, no(nm)-, no(nm)etal, u(nm)-, u(nm)arked
↡↡	E5 n	Rushes	NN	A(nn)ex, a(nn)eal, ca(nn)on, a(nn)iversary, a(nn)ounce, ma(nn)ered, begi(nn)er, wi(nn)er, bu(nn)y, di(nn)er

HIEROGLYPHS AND ARITHMETIC OF THE ANCIENT EGYPTIAN SCRIBES   81

⌐	E3 <	Ox tongue	NS	Tur(ns), acor(ns), co(ns)-, agai(ns)t, a(ns)wer, i(ns)-asce(ns)ion, tra(ns)-
⌐ / ⌐	E4 ! / E4 $	Adze, means cut or chop	NW	Brai(nw)ashing, chi(nw)ag, ru(nw)ay,—u(nw)-,—(nw)ard, u(nw)anted, iro(nw)ork, gu(nw)ale
○	E2 -	Bowl, pot	NW/ in	Brai(nw)ashing, chi(nw)ag, ru(nw)ay,—u(nw)-,—(nw)ard, u(nw)anted, iro(nw)ork, gu(nw)ale
ƒ	E1 O	Lasso (common approximation)	O	L(o)t, bl(o)t, cl(o)t, d(o)t
🐦🐦	E1 o	Two quail chicks	OO	B(oo)ks, bl(ue), r(u)de, w(oo)d, t(oo), t(o), m(oo), t(oo)k, sh(oo)k, t(wo),
🐦ƒ	E2 O	Lasso and quail chick	OU	B(oa)t, afl(oa)t, appr(oa)ch

 ▦	E1 P	Stool of reed matting.	P	(P)et, (p)retty, flo(p) (p)ed, A(p)(p) roximate, a(p)(p)le, a(p)(p)erce(p)tion, gallo(p), cli(p)(p)ing, abru(p)t
 🦆	E2 P	Duck in flight	PA	(Pa)t, (pa)th, al(pa)ca, (pa)thetic, car(pa)l
 ⌒	E2 p	Round loaf, means beginning of time, antiquity	PAT	(Pat)ch, a(pat)ite, s(pat)ter, cha(pat) is, ex(pat)riate, (pat) tern, com(pat)ibility, (pat)ronize, s(pat)ula, pita(pat)
 ⌣	E3 P	Bow consisting of oryx horns joined by wooden centre-piece	PD	Lapdog, slapdash, snapdragon, update, trapdoor. Old Kingdom used (pj) fla(pj)ack, pro(pj)et,
 🐍	E1 F	Horned viper	PH	-gra(ph),—(ph) ile,—(ph)on-,—(ph) ob-,—o(ph),—tro(ph) ic-, al(ph)a, am(ph) ibian, sul(ph)ide, (ph)iloso(ph)y, (ph) otogra(ph),

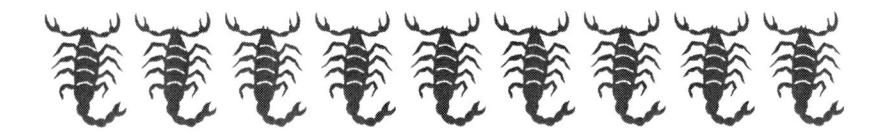

Hieroglyphs and Arithmetic of the Ancient Egyptian Scribes

	E4 P	Hind-quarters of lion	PH	Loo(ph)ole, pee(ph)ole, sla(ph)appy, u(ph)olster, u(ph)eave, u(ph)eld, u(ph)ill
	E4 p	Plan of house	PR	(Pr)ism, (pr)ank,—(pr)oof, (pr)int, ap(pr)ox, A(pr)il, a(pr)on, ap(pr)aize
	E1 p	Sun and moon were eyes of Falcon God Horus; means view.	PTR	Cla(ptr)ap, dio(ptr)e, com(ptr)oller, sce(ptr)e, scul(ptr)ess
	E1 Q	Hillside; slope	Q	(K)oran; (Qu)ran, K made back of throat, (k)ind, pi(ck), (Ch)ristmas
	E1 q	Basket with handle and a quail chick	QU	(Qu)ail, (qu)een, (qu)ack, ac(qu)aint, ac(qu)ire, ade(qu)ate, a(qu)aplane, a(qu)a-, ban(qu)ette, che(qu)e
	E1 R	Mouth	R	(R)ed, disticly trilled as in Scottish pronounciation of (R), (r)ough, (r)ugged
	E2 R	Horus eye, sun symbol, changed its meaning over the millennia	RA	(Ra)madam, dio(ra)ma, ab(ra)cadab(ra), algeb(ra), amo(ra)l, d(ra)ma, ampho(ra)

⊙	E2 r	Sun	RA	(Ra)madam, dio(ra)ma, ab(ra)cadab(ra), algeb(ra), amo(ra)l, d(ra)ma, ampho(ra)
∩	E1 S	Folded linen cloth	S	Soft S; mi(ss), hi(ss), li(c)e, li(c)ence, (sc)ien(c)e, ni(c)e, (c)ircus
⎯∞⎯	E1 s	Door bolt	S/z	Hard (s), soft (z), closer to (z); (s)and, sci(ss)ors, (s)ex, fi(ss)ile, lo(z)enge,—(s)ive-, abra(s)ive, (z)ap, Au(ss)ie, canva(ss)
🪷	E2 S	Lotus pool	SA	(Sa)p, (sa)ck, as(sa)ssin, amper(sa)nd, (Sa)xons, (sa)nk, de(sa)linate,—(sa)ur, -(sa)urus, (sa)nds,—(sa)ble
🦆	E2 s	Pintail duck		
	E3 S	Cattle hobble		
	E3 s	Rolled up herdsman's shelter of papyrus, means protection	SA	(Sa)p, (sa)ck, as(sa)ssin, amper(sa)nd, (Sa)xons, (sa)nk, de(sa)linate,—(sa)ur, -(sa)urus, (sa)nds,—(sa)ble
	E4 S			
	E4 s	Bird leg and foot, means the land of Shat		
	E4 &	Vertebrae, means back of something		

★	E2 d	Star	SBA/ dwa	Hu(sba)ndry, Ca(sba)h, cro(ssba)r, di(sba)nd, di(sba)r, ga(sba)g
	E4 .	Bolt with rope for drawing it. Means drag or draw (pull)	SCHa	Di(scha)rge, e(scha)tology, mi(scha)nces, Pa(scha)l
	E4 /	Tail	SD	Wedne(sd)ay, di(sd)ain, doom(sd)ay, eave(sd)rop, juri(sd)iction, mi(sd)eed, mi(sd)emeanor, tran(sd)uce, wi(sd)om
	E4 :	Fold of linen and horned viper, means yesterday	SF	Bli(ssf)ul, tran(sf)usion, colt(sf)oot, tran(sf)er, cro(ssf)ire, di(sf)igure, kin(sf)olk, mi(sf)it

▭	E4 ;	Garden pool, sign for irrigated land	SH	(Sh)ip (s)ugar, mi(ss)ion, ma(ch)ine, (sh)ower, pu(sh), wor(sh)ip,—(sh)ip, (sh)rimp, mu(sh)room, a(sh)es
⬡	E4 ∨	Garden pool with sloping sides, sign for irrigated land		
▬	E4 =	Garden pool full of water, sign for irrigated land		
🏠	E4 >	The divine shrine	SH!	Fric(tio)n, dic(tio)n,—(tio)n, abduc(tio)n, ac(tio)n
🫗	E4 ?	Water-skin	SHD	(Should), (shud)der, (shad)ow, (shad)s, rough(shod), slip(shod), aboli(shed), burni(shed)
⟋	E4 @	Thought to be a knife sharpener and same with legs, means guide, lead	SHM	Aba(shm)ent,—i(shm)ent, fi(shm)onger, mar(shm)allow
🚶	E4 [			Not verified, Aba(shm)ent,—i(shm)ent, fi(shm)onger, mar(shm)allow

⚲	E4 \	Twisted cord, means encircle	SHN	Boori(shn)ess, boyi(shn)ess, bracki(shn)ess,—i(shn)ess-, flu(shn)ess, lu(shn)ess, har(shn)ess
⚭	E4]	Twisted cord or rope	SHS	Wa(shs)tand, di(shs)tand
♆♆♆♆♆ / ♆♆♆♆	E4 < / E4 ⌐	Short vertical fence and same leaning, means receive	SHsP	Sound of unscrewing fizzy pop bottle; fi(shp)late, fle(shp)ot
⌇	E4 ~	Feather	SHW	Bru(shw)ood, fi(shw)ife, fre(shw)ater
≡▭	E4 ~	Piece of cloth with fringe	SIA	Quas(sia)s
←∝	E5 &	Horizontal arrow	SIN	(Sin), ab(sin)th, re(sin), (cin)ema, (sin)ister, ba(sin), (sin)k, cou(sin), di(sin)-,—i(cin)e, di(sin)cline, (cin)der, medi(cin)e, (cin)ch

Hieroglyph	Key	Brief Description	Sound	Examples of Usage
	E2 w	Fibre swab, means perish	SK	A(sk), a(sk)ew, ba(sk)ing, ca(sk), whi(sk)er, (sk) in, di(sk), hu(sk), ma(sk), riskier, tu(sk)er, whi(sk)er
	E4 ¿	*Aba*-sceptre	SKM	Ta(skm)aster, ta(skm)an, mu(skm)elon
	E5 S	Unknown symbol, means smite	SKR	Mu(skr)at, San(sk)rit, (scr)ew, a(scr)ibable, con(scr)ipted, de(scr)ibe, cri(sscr)oss, di(scr)edit, mi(scr)eants
	E5 s	Means Upper Egypt	SMA	Chari(sma), aby(sma)l, draft(sma)n, di(sma)l, (sma)sh, out(sma)rt
	E5 $	Lungs and windpipe, means unite		
	E5 !	Folded linen cloth & sickle. Phonogram not verified.	SMa	(Sma)rt, (sma)sh, (sma)ck, band(sma)n

↓	E5 %	Two-barbed arrow head, represents two	SN	(Sn)ow,—(sn)ess, par(sn)ip, artles(sn)ess, (sn)ap, (sn)ipe, (sn)ake, (sn)orkel
	E4 0	Unknown item, the two barbs represent value of two		
⊙	E5)	Threshing floor	SP	(Sp)oon, (sp)ice, air(sp)eed, (sp)irit, a(sp)ect, a(sp)idistra, (sp)ider, su(sp)icious
⌒	E5 *	Rib	SPR	(Spr)ing, bed(spr)ead, bow(spr)it, (spr)out, e(spr)it, di(spr)oportion, hair(spr)ing, new(spr)int, well(spr)ing

⌐	E5 +	A Throne, represents the god Osiris and goddess Isis	ST	(St)ring, (st)rong,—e(st), —i(st), —i(st)ic,—logi(st), —(st)er, —(st)at, abrea(st), a(st)ro-, barri(st)er, Chri(st)mas
⚭	E4 +	Shoulder knot		
⚔	E5 ,	Cow's skin pierced by arrow		
⌐	E5 -	Cut-up ox, means choose	STP	Brea(stp)late, du(stp)an, po(stp)one, ru(stp)roof
⚘	E5 .	Sedge plant	SW	(Sw)an, (sw)itch, (sw)ill, (sw)im
⌒	E1 T	Bun; half loaf of Egyptian bread	T/th	(T)alk, (t)ub, bi(t), (t)ank, mis(t), Bu(t)(t)er
⌒	E2 T	Kiln, represents hot	TA	(Ta)p, acquat(ta)l, s(ta)ic, at(ta)ch, admit(ta)nce, (ta)x, me(ta)l
—	E2 t	Flat-alluvial plain and same with grains of sand.	TA!	Abore(ta), bo(ta)nic, (ta)r, (ta)ckle, capi(ta)l, crys(ta)l, den(ta)l, (ta)x, dic(ta)phone.
⋯	E3 T			
⋈	E3 t	Girdle knot	TCHs	Very short (Ch)oose, tren(chs), tou(chs)tone
⚱	E2 o	Bolt supported by walking legs	TH/z/s	In very old texts sounds like; (th), (th)at, (th)em. in modern texts sounds like, (zs), (Zzzth), (ze)bra.

Hieroglyphs and Arithmetic of the Ancient Egyptian Scribes

(hobble rope)	E2 c	Hobble rope for tethering with diacritical tick.	th/ tch /ch	Pic(tu)re, (chu)rn, (th)ink, ma(th)s, (th)is, (th)at, fa(th)om.
(hand)	E1 D	Hand (approximation)	TH/d	Closest match is (d) sound (du)ll sometimes substituted for (th), as in (th)em.
(duckling)	E4 T	Duckling, nestling (Approximation)	THA	(T) like (t)une, (tch-ha); betro(tha)l, e(tha)nol, (tha)t, le(tha)l, (tha)nk.
(pestle)	E4 t	Pestle of red granite	TI	(Ti)m, (ti)ck, (ti)ll,—is(ti)c-, ar(ti)s(ti)c,—i(ti)s-, analy(ti)c, semi(ti)sm,—ly(ti)c-, (ti)p, paraly(ti)c
(sledge)	E5 :	Sledge	TM	Abu(tm)ent, adjus(tm)ent, ca(tm)int, Chris(tm)as, apar(tm)ent,—(tm)ent.
(symbol)	E5 ;	Unknown symbol, also represents to lesser extent phonogram (chma)	TMA/ chma	Boatman,—(tma)n, Chris(tma)s, ou(tma)tch, foo(tma)rk, nigh(tma)re, toas(tma)ster; also (chma) hen(chma)n, mat(chma)ker

🗿	E5 <	Head in profile, means UPON; Chief or first	TP	Breas(tp)late, dus(tp)an, foo(tp)ad, ho(tp)ot, ho(tp)late, marke(tp)lace, ou(tp)lay, ou(tp)ut, pos(tp)one,
🦅	E5 =	Buzzard	TW	Be(tw)ixt, be(tw)een, car(tw)heel, en(tw)ine, ers(tw)ile
🌾🐦	E1 u	Reed + quail	U	Long U as in r(u)le, r(u)de, bl(ue), fl(u)
ℯ	E1 U	Abbr' for quail chick (Phonogram approximation)	U/w	Sounds like short (ouw)!, l(u)ll, c(u)t, (u)gly, m(u)ll
🐦	E2 U	Quail chick (Phonogram approximation)		
🐍	E1 V	Horned viper	V/f	(F/fu/v/vu), con(vu)lsi(v)e, di(vu)lge, (vu)lnerable, li(ve)ly, (ve)ry, le(ve)l, semper(vi)(vu)m, vulcanite,—i(ve)-
🐦	E1 W	Quail chick (Phonogram approximation	W/u	Sounds like (ouw)!, (w)et, (w)ind, (wh)at, co(w), mo(w), se(w)
ℯ	E1 w	Abbr' for quail chick (Phonogram approximation)		

Hieroglyphs and Arithmetic of the Ancient Egyptian Scribes

Glyph	Code	Description	Sound	Examples
|	E11-E19	Single vertical stroke. Also represents one	WA	(Wha)t, (wa)nd, (wa)ck. Often used in conjuction with ideograms
←—	E2 W	One-barbed harpoon, represents one	WA!	(Wa)ter, (wa)tt, (wa)nt, (wa)tch, (wa)x, (wa)g, s(wa)t, (wa)ttle, s(wa)g, (wa)cky, (wa)gon, th(wa)ck
⚱	E2 w	Fibre swab, means place, endure	WAH	S(wah)ilian, (wa)nd, allo(wa)nce, s(wa)n, (wa)nner, ro(wa)n, (wa)ffle
⚚	E3 W	Sceptre	WAS	(Was)twater, sh(was), (was)p, (was)pish, s(was)tika, (was)sail
🐦	E3 w	Forearm crossing quail chick, means soldier	WE	(We)dnesday, (we)b, (we)d, (wai)r, be(wa)re, (wea)ther, (wai)n, a(wa)re
⦶ / ⦶	E5 W / E5 w	Cord wound on stick and with an end visible, means command	WJ	Sho(wj)umping
✤	E5 >	Flower. Means be young	WN	Blown, do(wn), bra(wn), bro(wn), (win)dow
🐇	E5 ?	Desert hare		

⌣	E5 @	Horns of ox	WP	Blo(wp)ipe, co(wp)ox, ga(wp), sho(wp)iece, sno(wp)lough, to(wp)ath
🐦	E5 }	Fork-tailed swallow	WR	Arro(wr)oot, co(wr)y, do(wr)y, elbo(wr)oom, a(wr)y, Je(wr)y, j(ur)y, lo(wr)y, to(wr)ope
🐦	E4 W	House martin—Hirundidae, means great; anoint		
⌐	E4 w	Seat of Osiris	WS	Aircre(ws), scre(ws), arro(ws), la(ws), bro(ws)er, co(ws)lip, dowsing,—(ws), dro(ws)y, ha(ws)er, miao(ws)
⌒∞	E1 X	Basket with handle + door bolt	X	Actually (KS); e(ks)tra, fo(x), fi(x), ma(x)imum, a(x)es, ta(x)i, mi(x)ture, e(x)citement, e(x)plain, matri(x), an(x)ious
⌒∣	E1 x	Basket with handle + linen-folded cloth		
∥∣	E1 Y	Pair of strokes + one addional reed	Y	(Y)ellow, (y)oke, (y)acht, (y)ardstick, (y)ear, (y)es, (Y)in and (Y)ang, (Y)olk, (y)onder, (y)oung, (y)okel

Glyph	Code	Description	Sound	Examples
	E2 y	Eye weeping, means weep Substitute, approximation	Y	B(y)te, b(y)e, sk(y), t(y)re, (eye),—ps(y) cho-,—h(y) per-,—h(y) d-,—ph(y)t-,—p(y) ro, p(y)ri, p(y)rex, pap(y)rus
	E2 Y	Two-flowering reeds + one addional reed	Y	(Y)ellow, (y)oke, (y)acht, (y)ardstick, (y)ear, (y)es, (Y)in and (Y)ang, (Y)olk, (y)onder, (y)oung, (y)okel
	E3 Y	Pair of strokes abbreviation for two-flowering reeds	Y/ee	Sounds like (ee); an(y), penn(y), Mar(y), Henr(y), discover(y)
	E1 y	Two flowering reeds		
	E1 N	Arm holding a wand; means holy	Z	Hard Z; (Dz); (z)ebra, (x)ylophone, (z)oo, (cz)ar, ad(z)e
	E1 z	Door bolt	Z/s	Soft (z), hard (s); dog(s), cog(s), u(se), ey(es), die(s), (z)ap, bra(ss)ier, la(s)er, sewer(s), (jz)tice,—(s)ive-, la(z)y, ha(z)y

1.13.0 Main Egyptian Hieroglyphs for Whole Numbers

1.13.1 Rope, Fingers, and Polliwogs

Hieroglyph	Key	Brief Description	Value	Examples of Usage
1	E11-E19	Symbol used to maintain symmetry and also represents one	1	Keys provide 1 to 9 in sequence. ||||/||| = 7
∩	E21-E29	Hobble for cattle, means a stable.	10	Keys provide 10 to 90 in sequence. ∩∩/∩ = 30
@	E31-E39	Coil of rope, means to tie.	100	Keys provide 100 to 900 in sequence. @@/@@@ = 500

Hieroglyph	Key	Brief Description	Value	Examples of Usage
(lotus)	E41-E49	Leaf, stalk, and rhizome of lotus plant,	1000	Keys provide 1000 to 9000 in sequence. = 9000
(finger)	E30	Finger.	10000	||| = 30,000

Hieroglyphs and Arithmetic of the Ancient Egyptian Scribes

𓆐	E1 (	Tadpole, sometimes called a polliwog.	100,000	𓆐𓆐𓆐𓆐 = 400,000
𓁨	E1)	God Heh; means one million or many	1000,000	𓁨 𓁨 = 2,000,000
𓆈	E1 *	Lizard with 3 strokes represents many millions.	10,000,000 or >	For very large numbers. For example, amount of corn needed by the king in the afterlife

§ 1.13.1 Notes of Interest

The idea that the ancient Egyptians regularly had incestuous relationships was only true for royal families, otherwise it was completely taboo. These types of marriages were usually between brother and sister. Princesses were not allowed to marry outside the royal family except on rare occasions. Their marriages could even be with their father or grandfather and even produce children to them.

2.0.0 CHAPTER TWO

ANCIENT EGYPTIAN ARITHMETIC

AND

UNITS OF MEASURE

> § 2.0.0 Notes of Interest
>
> Each of the four hieroglyphs above, represent a god of the wind; starting at the top in a clockwise direction, we have the Northern, Eastern, Southern and Westerly winds.

2.1.0 COUNTING WITH HIEROGLYPHIC NUMBERS

2.1.1 THE DEVELOPMENT OF NUMBER SYSTEMS

Most ancient civilizations developed some sort of denary numbering system, that which is based on 10, no doubt because humans have ten fingers. This is why we use the term digits for numbers, and sometimes to mean fingers as well.

Denary means counting in multiples of 10; the decimal system is similar but not the same. The decimal system uses a point or decimal point to separate base 10 integers on the left from base 10 fractions on the right.

Some civilizations counted in groups of 5; some 20 like the Mayans. The Romans used 12, which we adopted for our old coinage system, and the ancient Babylonians used a numbering system based on 10 and 60.

The ancient Egyptians had hieroglyphic words for a very wide range of numbers, but it was obviously more convenient for them and easier to remember a simpler system using lines or marks. Therefore they normally wrote numbers with numerical symbols rather than spelling out the words for each number.

Instead of using a different symbol for each number from 1 to 9 as we do today, the ancient Egyptians adopted a system of repetition to represent each number. For example, they would have represented the number five as (|||||).

The ancient Egyptians had a series of different hieroglyphs that represented units, tens, hundreds, and the higher orders of magnitude of base ten, and used multiples of these hieroglyphs to construct their numbers. A particular column did not distinguish between the units, tens, hundreds, and the higher magnitudes. They could not look at a single symbol as part of a series of numeric symbols as we do today and say 'that symbol represents eight hundred'.

However, they did keep the hieroglyphs in order depending upon the size of the value they stood for.

The earliest ancient Egyptian hieroglyphs used to represent numbers can be seen in the following tables.

2.1.2 Hieroglyphs For Numbers From 0 to 9

Denary	Egyptian	Denary	Egyptian
Depleted, nothing left.	⚱	5	|||||
1			6							
2				7								
3					8									
4						9										

The ancient Egyptians had no concept of a numerical zero, even when the results of a calculation involving subtraction resulted in zero. Instead they just left a space meaning there was nothing left or they used a heart and windpipe hieroglyph (⚱).

This symbol meant the results were depleted or nothing was left. This was not the same as the concept of zero because this symbol never became part of any arithmetic calculations or their results.

2.1.3 Hieroglyphs For Numbers In Multiples Of 10

Denary	Egyptian	Denary	Egyptian
10	∩	60	∩∩∩ ∩∩∩
20	∩∩	70	∩∩∩∩ ∩∩∩∩

30	∩∩∩	80	∩∩∩∩ ∩∩∩∩
40	∩∩ ∩∩	90	∩∩∩∩∩ ∩∩∩∩
50	∩∩∩ ∩∩		

2.1.4 Hieroglyphs for Numbers in Multiples of 100

Denary	Egyptian	Denary	Egyptian
100		600	
200		700	
300		800	
400		900	
500			

2.1.5 Hieroglyphs for Numbers in Multiples of 1000

Denary	Egyptian	Denary	Egyptian
1000		6000	
2000		7000	
3000		8000	
4000		9000	
5000			

2.1.6 Hieroglyphs for Numbers Greater Than 1000

Denary		Egyptian
10,000		
100,000		
1,000,000		
10,000,000	Many millions; ∞	

2.1.7 Keyboard Locations of Hieroglyphic Numbers

Main Egyptian Hieroglyphs for Whole Numbers			
Hieroglyph	Key	Brief Description	Value
|	E11 - E19	Symbol used to maintain symmetry and also represents one	1
∩	E21 - E29	Hobble for cattle, means a stable.	10
@	E31 - E39	Coil of rope, means to tie.	100
	E41 - E49	Leaf, stalk, and rhizome of lotus plant.	1000
	E30	Finger.	10,000

Hieroglyph	Key	Description	Usage
	E1 (	Tadpole, sometimes called a polliwog.	100,000
	E1)	God Heh; means one million or many	1,000,000
	E1 *	Lizard with three strokes represents many millions.	10,000,000

2.1.8 Ad Hoc Numbers

Hieroglyph	Key	Description	Usage
	E10	Heart and windpipe, means good and related words.	This symbol or a space was used when subtraction resulted in zero.
	E2W	One-barbed harpoon.	One
	E5%	Two-barbed arrow head.	Two
	E40	Unknown item, the two barbs represent two.	Two
	E1?	Shen Ring—original style of cartouche. In calculations means infinity.	All that is (the entire region ruled over by the sun). Holds a name.

> § 2.1.8 Notes of Interest
>
> The priesthood of Amun at Karnak during the reign of Ramses III owned approximately 1,500 square kilometres of farming land, vineyards, mines, quarries, and both sea-going ships and riverboats. An income was derived from the land by renting it to peasant farmers for a third of their harvest. Eventually, the priesthood's power grew until it rivalled that of the kings. The fact that each king after his death was buried with hordes of treasure probably did not help the financial situation of the new king assigned to the throne.

2.2.0 Big Number Examples

2.2.1 Repetition Method

Denary	Ancient Egyptian Numbers
10,039 =	
1953 =	
1066 =	
2010 =	

In English and other European languages, we read and write words from left to right; the text is normally left justified. We might read and write numbers from left to right but the number values are in a right to left order and are right justified. We also manipulate numbers in calculations on a right to left basis; we add up and subtract the unit's column first.

As the ancient Egyptians carved or painted most of their hieroglyphs from right to left just as the Hebrews did and the Arabs read and write today, it is not surprising their numbers look back to front as well.

For convenience, it is an accepted convention that during translation into English or other European languages that the directions of the text are reversed. Therefore one must be careful to note whether or not this convention applies before studying any translations. Also it must be remembered that the ancient Egyptians were great believers in symmetry.

For example, where two pillars of stone supported a roof, the writings on one pillar would be the mirror image of the writings on the opposite pillar. Consequently the hieroglyphs and if there were any numbers, would have to be read in different directions on each pillar.

For example if a text must be read from left to right and a number is encountered, that number is read the same way as in English; thousands, hundreds, tens and units:

Battle of Hastings 1066

If a number is encountered and text must be from right to left, the usual direction of reading a hieroglyphic carving, then the number would be back to front for us:

6601 sgnitsaH fo elttaB

Fortunately, if you are writing a line of text phonetically from left to right, just write out the number with the appropriate symbol combinations as you would in English. For 1066, this would be:

2.2.2 MULTIPLICATION METHOD

As well as using the repetition method to describe numbers, the ancient Egyptians also adopted a true multiplication system for numbers above

10,000. By placing lower denominations of numbers below higher values, they could describe multiples of the higher value.

Consider the following examples:

Egyptian	Denary	Egyptian	Denary
||||	4	300 spirals	300
staff	10,000	tadpole	100,000
staff over ||||	40,000	tadpole over 300	30,000,000

Therefore, given that . . .

$$\text{(symbols)} = (1000 \times 3) + (100 \times 2) + (10 \times 3) = 3{,}230 \text{ and this} \ldots$$

$$\text{(symbols)} = (100 \times 3) + (10 \times 1) + (1 \times 5) = 315$$

. . . You should now be able to see more easily how 3,230 and 315 are integrated into large numbers in the table that follows.

Egyptian	Denary
(symbols)	3,230

𓅆	100,000
𓆼𓍢𓎊𓏤𓏤𓏤𓏤𓏤	315
𓁨	10,000
𓁨𓁨𓁨𓎉𓎉	323,000,000
𓁨𓆼𓍢𓎊𓏤𓏤𓏤𓏤𓏤	3,150,000
𓁨𓁨𓁨𓎉𓎉𓁨𓆼𓍢𓎊𓏤𓏤𓏤𓏤𓏤	326,150,000

2.3.0 CARDINAL NUMBERS

2.3.1 MASCULINE OR FEMININE

Cardinal numbers, also known as counting numbers, are those which represent quantity as opposed to ordinal numbers which define the position of something in a series.

In ancient Egyptian, cardinal numbers are normally indicated in hieroglyphs by numerals rather than by words. Other than number one, it is unusual to find numbers written in words.

An interesting point about these written numbers is that in the early history of the Egyptians, it was common to use either masculine or feminine forms for these numbers. Most of these numbers had just masculine forms but a few had both masculine and feminine forms and some had only feminine forms such as one hundred and two hundred.

Except for one hundred and two hundred, all the cardinal numbers beyond thirty were purely masculine.

Usually a number in word form was identified as masculine if it ended with a quail chick (🐦) or its equivalent. If it ended with a loaf of bread (◠) or its equivalent, it was feminine. In some instances, additional symbols were associated with these gender symbols as well. Eventually nearly all the symbols describing the gender of written numbers fell away at different times, mostly early on.

Denary	Feminine
100	
200	

An exception to this gender rule applies to the numbers which are not listed in the following table. The hieroglyphs for the cardinals which are excluded from the next table are formed by combining two or more single word cardinals, similar to how it is done in English.

For example, in English we would say four hundred and fifty. Also, when a series of cardinals are chained together, the first cardinal whenever possible is always masculine and the latter parts can be either masculine or feminine.

2.3.2 COMMON CARDINAL NUMBERS

Cardinal	Masculine	Feminine	Later Use
1			
2			
3			
4			

Hieroglyphs and Arithmetic of the Ancient Egyptian Scribes

5			
6			
7			
8			
9			
10			
20			
30			
40		N/A	
50		N/A	
60		N/A	
70		N/A	
80		N/A	
90		N/A	

2.3.3 GENDER EXCEPTIONS

Remember numbers above thirty with the exception of one hundred and two hundred were always masculine, this rule applied to very large numbers as well.

Cardinal	Masculine
1000	
10,000	
100,000	
1000,000	

2.4.0 ORDINAL NUMBERS

2.4.1 ORDER IN THE RANKS

Words which are used to indicate the numerical order of things in a series, set of items or indicate the rank or position of items in a list are ordinal numbers. For example; first, second, and third. Ordinal numbers do not show quantity.

To form ordinal numbers in English, we simply add 'th' to the end of the cardinal name except for first, second and third which are special words. In ancient Egyptian only 'first' was a special word.

The ordinals for 2 to 9 are formed by adding either (○) for masculine or (○△) for feminine to the end of the root cardinal name or the end of the actual numerals themselves, which was more common. For example masculine 5th (||||| ○).

The rest of the ordinals from tenth upwards are formed by adding the appropriate prefix. A prefix of a whip (⌐) converts the cardinal to a masculine ordinal, while a prefix of a whip and loaf (🪒) converts the cardinal to a feminine ordinal. If you require access to these hieroglyphs displayed in the table below with your PC or laptop, refer to Section 1.12.2 for an explanation of how to do this.

Hieroglyph	Key	Hieroglyph	Key
	E4 M		E4 m

2.4.2 COMMON ORDINAL NUMBERS

Ordinal	Masculine	Feminine
1st		
2nd		
3rd		
4th		
5th		
6th		
7th		
8th		
9th		
10th		

11th	𓏺𓈖𓏏	𓏺𓈖𓏏𓂂
200th	𓆼𓊃𓊃	𓆼𓊃𓊃𓂂

2.5.0 Fractions

2.5.1 The Mouth Hieroglyph

The commonest method the ancient Egyptians employed for expressing fractions was by writing the hieroglyph R (Egypt1 font, keyboard character R), the mouth hieroglyph above a numeral, the denominator.

2.5.2 R-Notation Fractions

Hieroglyph	Fraction	R-notation
𓂋𓏺𓏺𓏺𓏺𓏺	1/5	r-5
𓂋𓏺𓏺𓏺	1/7	r-7
𓂋𓎆𓏺	1/30	r-30
𓂋𓎏𓏺𓏺	1/62	r-62

Using an 'r' in front of a number to represent the mouth over a number is known as the r-notation to represent r-fractions. When there is no need to draw complete hieroglyphs, the r-notation can be very convenient.

All these r-type fractions had a numerator of one except for ☐, ¾. The r-type fraction for ☐ is also peculiar, in that its denominator is one and not three.

2.5.3 R-Fraction Exceptions

Hieroglyph	Key	Description	Value
⬭	E1 R	Mouth; represents the unit ro = 1/320 part of a Hekat (Heqat)	1 ro was the smallest named unit for grain.
⬭ with one stroke	E1 ^	Mouth with one stroke. A fraction not used for measuring grain as the ro was already 1/320 part of a Hekat.	1/3
⬭ with two strokes	E1 [	Mouth with two strokes. A fraction not used for measuring grain as the ro was already 1/320 of Hekat.	2/3
⬭ with three strokes	E1]	Mouth with three strokes. A fraction not used for measuring grain as the ro was already 1/320 of Hekat.	3/4

Fractions with a numerator of one are known as unit fractions or aliquot fractions. Apart from the exceptions mentioned above, all fractions were described in a unit form. Even though the ancient Egyptians had a symbol for ¾, they tended to write ½ + ¼ which is the same value. When writing from left to right the largest fraction is always written first and vice versa; a half is a larger fraction than a quarter!

When the denominator became too large to physically fit beneath the mouth hieroglyph, the rest of the number was written to the side. No matter how large a denominator became, the rules of largest number to the left were still maintained.

2.5.4 Bulky Fractions

Hieroglyph	R-notation
	r-69
	r-85
	r-633
	r-5833

> § 2.5.4 Notes of Interest
>
> Not many people know the names of all the parts of a fraction. If you didn't know before, you do now!
>
> $$\frac{3}{7}$$
>
> 3 — Numerator
> — Vinculum
> 7 — Denominator

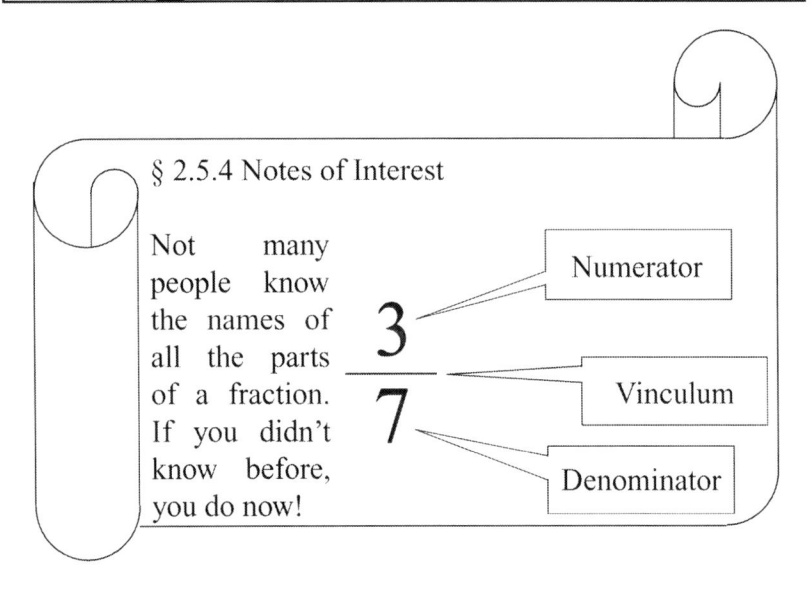

When reading from left to right, any whole number along side the fraction also obeys the rule 'largest number left', the same as numbers within a fraction. Consider the following, bearing in mind the ancient Egyptians loved to make things look very neat and pretty.

$$7290 \; \frac{1}{5634} \; or \; 7290\,r-5634$$

In an ancient papyrus known as the Rhind Papyrus, a fraction of 2/61 was expressed as 1/40 + 1/244 + 1/488 + 1/610. In hieroglyphs this looks rather complicated as follows:

2.5.5 THE PARADOX OF AN ORDINAL FRACTION

The word 'mouth' in the r-fraction system meant 'part', thus r-6 meant part-6 which was equivalent to our fraction of 1/6. In the mindset of the ancient Egyptians, the number following the word 'r' had an ordinal meaning not a fractional meaning. For example, to an Egyptian scribe part-6 meant the final 6th part completing a sequence of 6 equal items. It would have made no sense to an ancient Egyptian to express a fraction as 4/9. This is because to them, in a series of nine equal items, only one item could be the ninth, namely that which occupied the last and ninth place.

Therefore, the Egyptian scribe would not even express a fraction of 4/9 as r-9 + r-9 + r-9 + r-9 because as explained earlier, there can only be one ninth item. Instead of 4/9, they would have used r-6 + r-9 which is 1/6 + 1/9 in our nomenclature. Some complex fractions were made up from a combination of up to five different r-fractions all with one as the numerator.

§ 2.5.5 Notes of Interest

It is a well-known fact that the ancient Egyptians had a very strong belief in the afterlife. They believed that death was merely an interruption to an existence that continued beyond the grave for eternity, this existence being similar to that which they had experienced in life.

The ancient Egyptians also believed that the human body was a receptacle for three main spirits that were released when a person died. These spirits were the ka, the ba, and the akh. The ka was a person's life force, a sort of spirit-double, represented by a pair of up stretched arms (⊔).

The ba was a wandering sole that resembled a spirit bird with a human head (𓅐). The jabiru (𓅡) stands for soul in bird form. Both these hieroglyphs each represented the ba. The akh was a type of ghost that was represented by a crested ibis (𓅂) which returned to the stars after death. A crested ibis means spirit or spirit-like nature. As it was believed that the ka and ba relied on the body for their existence, it was essential that the corpse was preserved to ensure life was to continue after death.

HIEROGLYPHS AND ARITHMETIC OF THE ANCIENT EGYPTIAN SCRIBES

2.5.6 COMMON ARITHMETIC HIEROGLYPHS

North Wind	Arithmetic Symbols	South Wind

Hieroglyph	Key	Brief Description	Examples of Usage
	E11	Heap of corn; quantity not known; algebraic X, or missing number.	Therefore find remainder **X**
	E1 M	Owl. Means (=) or namely, when used in calculations.	2/3 X 6 = 4
	E5 H	Face above a stroke. Means; Added to, in arithmetic operations.	4 + 6 = 10
	E3 r	Ball of string & mouth. In math's means Therefore; in dates, means Under.	Therefore find remainder 10

Symbol	Code	Description	Meaning
(black ibis)	E3 g	Black ibis. Means find	(ibis + speckled shape) Find unknown quantity **X**.
(fire drill, loaf, bars)	E2 $	Fire drill, loaf, and three bars. Means Remainder or Balance.	Remainder one half
(papyrus scroll)	E2 %	Papyrus scroll. Means Total in calculations.	Total seven
(rosette with two bars)	E1 b	Times by 2 or twice.	In writing it can be used as a 'ditto' sign to mean the previous word is repeated.
(rosette with two bars)	E1 r	Times by 2 or twice. To be read from left to right.	In writing, it can be used as a 'ditto' sign to mean the previous word is repeated.
(legs walking)	E6 {	Legs walking forward, when reading from left to right.	Means come, go, stop, and approach. Used as Addition symbol.
(legs walking)	E6 }	Legs walking backwards, when reading from left to right.	Means backwards, turn back, cause to retreat, reverse. Used as Subtraction symbol.
(ripple)	E1 N	Ripple of water.	Means of or times in calculations.
(horned viper)	E1 F	Horned viper.	Used at end of calculation means of it

Glyph	Code	Description	Meaning
⬭	E1 R	Mouth; Means by in arithmetic operations.	⟅ ||| ⬭ ⟅ |||| 6 palms by 5 Palms
⟅	E4 O	Palm without thumb. Unit of measure Palm width, equals 7.5 cm	⟅ = 4 fingers = 1/7 cubit
⌒	E4 Q	Crescent moon. Unit of measure 7.5 cm. Equivalent to Palm measure	⌒ = 4 fingers = $\frac{1}{7}$ cubit
◣	E5 I	Tongue of land. When added to other glyphs means fields, earth, river banks, or towns	Used in some units for land measure, such as the— 'Unit River' = 20,000 Cubits.
⊏	E3 ?	Thought to be a shortened pair of ribs.	½
✕	E3 \	Two sticks crossed; count, tally or break	Divide or Subtract
X	E3 /	Two sticks crossed; count, tally or break.	Divide or subtract. Often used to represent 1/4 of measures of length or area.
🦆	E2 s	Pintail duck	Often used to represent 1/8 of measures of length or area.
	E8 k	Knotted strips of cloth, papyrus rolled up, tied and sealed, and a hand.	Total. The papyrus may be vertical within group.

2.5.7 Simple Arithmetic Examples

The following have been discovered in ancient papyri:

$$1/9 \quad \text{of} \quad 18 \quad = \quad 2$$

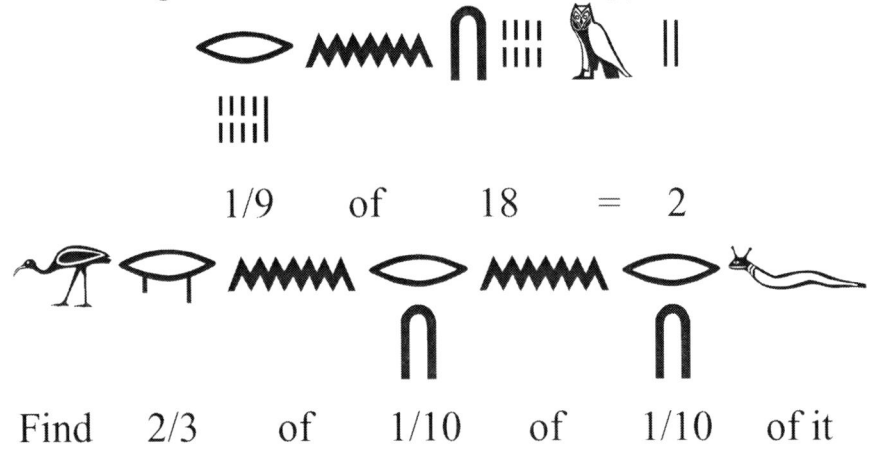

Find 2/3 of 1/10 of 1/10 of it

2.6.0 The Eyes of Horus

2.6.1 Belief Development with Time

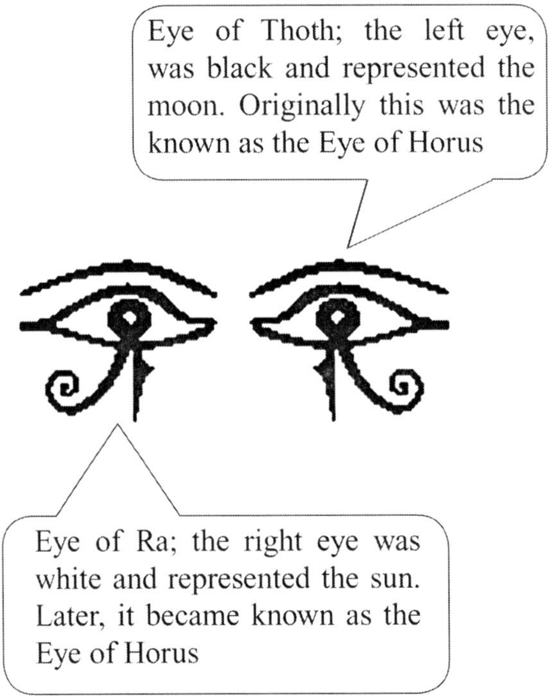

> Eye of Thoth; the left eye, was black and represented the moon. Originally this was the known as the Eye of Horus

> Eye of Ra; the right eye was white and represented the sun. Later, it became known as the Eye of Horus

As with many ancient Egypt beliefs, the meaning of symbols, traditions, and myths changed over time. What the eyes of Horus represent and the myths associated with them have also changed over the millennia.

The falcon-god Horus was an ancient sky god whose eyes were said to be the sun and the moon. The right eye was white and represented the sun and the left eye was black and represented the moon.

Later, however, Horus chiefly became associated with the sun, while the ibis god Thoth was associated with the moon.

Originally what was called the Horus eye, for most of the time was the left eye. It was painted on doors and boats and frequently used in jewellery. The Horus eye acted as a symbol of protection to everyone and everything near to it.

The ancient Egyptians believed that the Horus eye would ensure the safety and health of the bearer and provide wisdom and prosperity for them. Many people still believe this to be true today.

The right eye was known as the 'Eye of Ra' or 'Re', a powerful destructive force linked with the fierce heat of the sun. In the later history of the Egyptians, the 'Eye of Horus' became accepted and synonymous with the 'Eye of Ra' the right eye. The left eye became better known as the 'Eye of Thoth'.

2.6.2 THE WADJET EYE

The 'Eye of Horus', also known as the Wadjet or Ujat eye, means 'Whole One' or 'The Sound Eye'. Initially the left eye was recognized as the Wadjet eye, but in many ancient Egyptian murals and sculptures the right eye became known as the 'Eye of Horus'. Consequently it followed that the right eye was also recognized as the Wadjet or Ujat eye.

The reason for some of the confusion is because the moon is sometimes classed as a nightly sun. This is why sun deities that should be shown pushing the sun are seen pushing the moon instead.

Museums all over the world contain broaches and amulets of both the left and right eye of Horus. The high quality of workmanship of many

2.6.3 THE MURDER OF OSIRIS

An ancient myth describes how Osiris, the father of Horus, was murdered by his father's brother, the god Seth. Horus fought with his wicked uncle, the god Seth, for the throne of Egypt.

In the battle, Seth was castrated, but he managed to tear out the left eye of Horus and break it into fragments. Horus eventually won the battle with the help and support of the other gods. The eye was magically restored to Horus by Thoth at which point it was given the name 'Wadjet', and it became a powerful symbol of protection for the ancient Egyptians. After this battle, Horus was chosen to be the ruler of the world of the living.

The restored eye became emblematic of the re-establishment of order from chaos. Horus made a gift of the eye to his father Osiris to help him rule the Netherworld. Osiris ate the eye and was restored to life. As a result, it became a symbol of life and resurrection. Offerings are sometimes called 'The Eye of Horus' because it was thought that any goods offered became divine when presented to a god.

The Eye of Horus was used as a notation for measuring corn, ingredients in medicines, and pigments. The symbol was divided into six parts, representing the shattered pieces of the Wadjet eye. As you will see in the table that follows, each piece was associated with a specific fraction and, for some mystical reason, each of the six senses.

§ 2.6.3 Notes of Interest

People from the South of Egypt had darker skins than those from the North of Egypt. The reason for this was that the origins of those from the South were closer to Nubia, those from the North were paler because their origins were in the Near East.

2.6.4 THE CORN-MEASURE

The individual symbols employed to make up the following hieroglyph, the Wadjet eye, represent fractions of a Hekat (Heqat) for measuring corn.

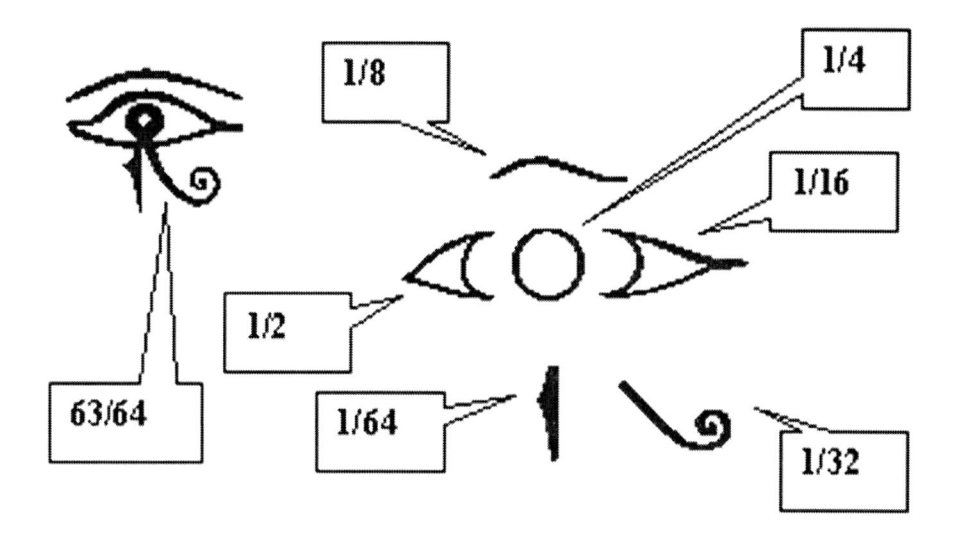

A Hekat was approximately 4.8 litres in volume. The Corn-Measure system was also used to share out dry portions of other materials, such as medicines, dyes, etc. The eye is supposedly decorated with the markings that adorn the eyes of hawks.

Sometimes the parts of the right eye are used to represent fractions of a Hekat. This does not cause any problem as the images maintain the same value as their counterparts in the alternate eye. As parts of either eye can be used to represent fractions, a little extra attention must be taken when dealing with the white of the eyes: (◁) and (▷).

2.6.5 Hekat Fractions and Ro

Hieroglyph	Key	Description	Fractions of Hekat	Ro	Sense
◁	E3<	White of Horus eye, right corner.	1/2	160 Ro	Smell
○	E3(	Pupil of eye of Horus.	1/4	80 Ro	Sight
⁀	E3)	Eye-brow of Horus eye.	1/8	40 Ro	Thought
▷	E3>	White of Horus eye, left corner	1/16	20 Ro	Hearing
↙	E3]	Paint mark on Horus eye.	1/32	10 Ro	Taste
		E3[	Paint mark on Horus eye.	1/64	5 Ro	Touch
↱	E1{	Combination of eye fractions.	3/64	15 Ro	/
𓂀	E1{	Left eye of Falcon God, Horus, represents moon.	63/64	315 Ro	/

In some texts, the word 'Hekat' is spelt with a 'q', for example, 'Heqat'.

2.6.6 Eye-Part Combinations

More complex fractions were created by adding the symbols together. It is interesting to note that if all the pieces are added together, the total is 63/64 not 1. The fact that the pieces did not total one is probably related more to the simplicity of the system rather than for any other reason.

Perhaps, the missing 1/64th was magically supplied by Thoth. Some examples of eye-part combinations:

⟨👁 1/2 + 1/4 = ¾

◠▷ 1/8 + 1/16 = 3/16

𝈀 1/32 + 1/64 = 3/64

◠👁▷ 1/2 + 1/4 + 1/8 + 1/16 = 15/16

This system allowed the ancient Egyptians to deal with common fractions quickly. The missing 1/64 was not a problem; after all, they already had quite a number of symbols that could represent the number one. As we shall see later, they had other numerical notations available when they needed to express smaller or a wider range of fractions.

2.7.0 THE RO-MEASURE

2.7.1 A MOUTHFUL OF GRAIN

The Ro was the smallest unit for grain by definition 320 Ro = 1 Hekat. The symbol for the Ro is the mouth. In volume it was about one tablespoon full of grain, basically it represented a mouthful. Strokes above the mouth provided a means of multiplying up a number of Ro.

The Horus Eye fractions were the only means of dividing a Hekat into smaller portions. Therefore a ◡ of a Hekat contains 10 Ro.

2.7.2 RO EXPRESSED AS FRACTIONS OF A HEKAT

Hieroglyphs	Key	Multiples of Ro	Fractions of Hekat
⬯	E1R	1 Ro	1/320

𓏻 (𓂝)	E3£	2 Ro	1/160
𓏼 (𓂝)	E4"	3 Ro	3/320
𓏽 (𓂝)	E4|	4 Ro	1/80
𓏾 (𓂝)	E4£	5 Ro	1/64

It is interesting to note that both (|) and (𓂝 with 𓏾), are equal to 5 Ro.

2.8.0 THE SACRED RATIO

2.8.1 NATURAL FORM

The ancient Egyptians found some natural shapes and forms pleasing to the eye such as the swirls of shells, crystal structures, and flowers. They also realized things more pleasing visually and easier to build if all the dimensions were kept to these natural proportions.

All these natural structures and more including snow flakes, obey mathematical formulas and laws which can be expressed as ratios between the lengths and other elements of geometric shapes. These mathematical ratios we collectively call the 'Golden Ratio'. The golden ratio has fascinated intellectuals of diverse interests for at least 3000 years.

2.8.2 DIVINE PROPORTION

During Medieval and Renaissance times, a number of painters including Leonardo da Vinci laid out their paintings according to this golden ratio to achieve balance and beauty. In 1509, the treatise '*On the Divine Proportion*' by Luca Pacioi, Leonardo da Vinci illustrated the golden ratio in polyhedra and the make up of the human body. This has lead some scholars to speculate that Leonardo incorporated the golden ratio into his sculptures; the statue of David is a particularly good example of a construction employing the golden ratio. Even his paintings, such as his Mona Lisa, embodies the golden ratio as some suggest; although no documentation exists to indicate that he consciously used the golden ratio in any of his compositions. The use of the golden ratio or golden mean in art has become known as the technique of dynamic symmetry.

The ancient Egyptians derived these same ratios by observing the natural world. They realized that this mathematical ratio was so ingrained into the fabric of the universe that it must have had magical properties.

This ratio was so important to them that they called it the 'Sacred Ratio' and even made it part of their religion.

They used this ratio when building temples and places for the dead. It was believed that if the proportions of their buildings were not built according to the Sacred Ratio, the deceased might not make it to the afterlife or the temple would not please the gods.

2.8.3 PHI (ϕ)

The Golden Ratio can be expressed as a mathematical constant, usually denoted by the Greek lower case letter phi (ϕ), which has a value of approximately 1·618. Phi is classed as an irrational number, the same as pi (π), because their fractional decimal part goes on forever. Egyptian mathematics did not include the notion of irrational numbers. No doubt their cumbersome approach to handling fractions was of little help in this area.

The Ark of the Covenant is a Golden Rectangle because its rectangular shape is in the proportions of the Golden Ratio. In Exodus 25:10, God commands Moses to build the Ark of the Covenant saying, 'Have them make a chest of acacia wood—two and a half cubits long, a cubit and a half wide, and a cubit and a half high'. The ratio of 2.5 to 1.5 is 1.666, which is as close as you can get to the golden ratio (phi) using such simple numbers; the tiny inaccuracy would certainly have not been visibly to the naked eye.

For the mathematic boffins, the golden ratio can be expressed algebraically as follows: a/b = (a + b)/a, where a > b. The golden ratio approximates to 1.6180339887. In fact, the value is: 1.61803398874989484820 . . . and it keeps going on, and on and on, without any pattern. This is why it is an irrational number.

You may care to evaluate the following quadratic equation if you are feeling up to it:

$$\phi^2 - \phi - 1 = 0$$

The correct answer provides you with a value for the Golden Ratio, incidentally capital phi (Φ) represent the inverse of phi (ϕ).

2.8.4 Golden Pyramids

In the Rhind Papyrus, an ancient Egyptian mathematical manuscript, a pyramid shape is defined with its dimensions based on a 3:4:5 triangles. The dimensions of this particular pyramid are an excellent example of the use of the Golden Ratio. Pyramids which incorporated in their design the Golden Ratio or Sacred Ratio as the ancient Egyptians called it are known as golden pyramids.

The Great Pyramid of Giza (also known as Cheops or Khufu) is extremely close to being a golden pyramid. The slope of each side is less than ½ a minute of a degree out from being a perfect theoretical golden pyramid. Bearing in mind, that a minute is only one sixtieth of a degree, this is quite remarkable. Other pyramids at Giza, such as Chephren and Mycerinus, are very close contenders being less than a degree out. Several other Egyptian pyramids are extremely close to the Golden Ratio as well.

Even though, there is an abundance of evidence that the ancient Egyptians used either pi (π) or phi (ϕ) or both in the design of their pyramids and most other structures, there remains a lot of doubt about their use of the golden ratio. It is a fact that many pyramids fit the criteria to be classed as golden pyramids. However, sceptics remain unconvinced that the ratios have mystical connotations, and, to them the matter must remain controversial.

2.9.0 MEASURING LENGTH

2.9.1 THE CUBIT

The ancient Egyptians used as their standard unit of measurement for small items the cubit, the length of a forearm, from the elbow to the tip of the middle finger.

Of course, this distance varied between different individuals, therefore in order to try and standardise, the ancient Egyptians used either wooden, metal, or stone rulers.

Two standard units came into use, the 'Royal Cubit' (7 Palms) which was about 523 mm and the 'Short Cubit' (6 Palms) which was about 450 mm. The royal cubit became used the most and therefore when 'cubit' is mentioned, it is normally accepted that we mean the Royal Cubit. Usually, it is specifically stated when the short cubit is being used.

The Remen consisting of 5 Palms was another important unit of measure. For example two Remen, the Double-Remen was equal to the diagonal of a square having sides of 1 cubit.

It is thought that the Double-Remen was used in land measurement because it allowed the scribes to easily halve or double areas of land without altering the shape of the area of land being measured.

A note of caution, the Remen is also the name for a unit of area. When the Remen is used as a unit of area, it does not represent the length-Remen squared, it is in fact a different unit with the same name. So in other words, if a length-Remen is squared, it does not equal the Remen used as a unit of area.

We have the same problem with the cubit. The cubit can be used as a unit of area as well as length. When the cubit is involved in measures of land area, it represents a strip of land 100 cubits long by 1 cubit wide, 1/100 of Aroura. To avoid confusion, this cubit area unit is called a Centaroura.

It may be a mystery of how the ancient Egyptians managed to build such massive monuments that were not skewed in shape. It is highly probable that any team of architects or designers working on a structure would all work to the same standards of their school.

Therefore, you must check on the context in which units of length are being used before deciding on whether they really represent length or area. For example, a unit of area would never be multiplied by a unit of length unless the expected result was meant to be a volume.

2.9.2 Ancient Egyptian Units of Length

Hieroglyph	Key	Description	Approx. Metric length & Equivalent
❘ or \	E30	Finger or back stroke. Finger (width)	1.87 cm, 1/28 Cubit
⌐ or ⌒	E4O E4Q	Palm (breadth) Thumbless Hand, alternatively; crescent moon.	7.47 cm, 4 Fingers

Glyph	Code	Description	Equivalent
	E1 D	Hand (breadth) showing all fingers.	Hand equivalent to 9.34 cm, 5 Fingers
	E5 D	Clenched fist	Fist = 6 Fingers = 11.21cm,
	E1 S P D	Span also called Small Span	Span = 3 Palms, 22.41 cm
	E1 B	Foot	Foot = 4 Palms, 29.89 cm
	E4 V	Whip above arm. Cubit or Royal Cubit. (Palm down)	Cubit = 7 Palms, 52.3 cm
	E5 J	Bent arm means bend. (Palm down)	Remen = 5 Palms 37.36cm Also unit of area, ½Aroura
	E1 2 E5 J	2 Strokes & bent arm; palm down. Double-Remen	Double-Remen = 10 Palms, 74.71 cm

⌐	E5 L	Abbr. for above; cubit or royal cubit. (Palm down)	Cubit = 7 Palms, 52.3 cm. (Warning, cubit also used for area)
〰〰	E4 *	Water, Leg, reed, abbr' quail chick, harpoon-head of bone.	Pole = 1¼ Cubits, 1 cubit 7 Fingers.
	E8 @	Branch, loaf, and stroke. A Rod	1 Rod or 1 Khet = 100 Cubits, 52.5 m
	E2 / 1	Branch. This example = 10 Rods	
	E1 k T	Animal's belly and loaf	Khet = 100 Royal Cubits
		E5o	River = 20,000 Cubits, 10.5 Km.

2.9.3 Multiples of Units

By placing a specific number after the unit of measure, any quantity of units can be expressed. For example:

267 Cubits and 5 Palms

A further example:

A Field   of   41 Rods by   50 Rods 5 Palms

The following example may take a few moments to follow:

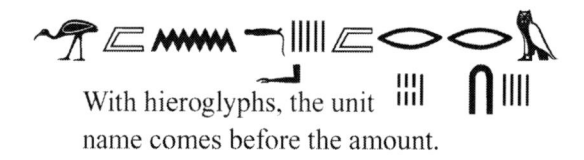

[hieroglyphs]
With hieroglyphs, the unit name comes before the amount.

Find 1/2 of Cubits 5 + 1/2 + 1/7 + 1/14 =

[hieroglyphs]

Cubits 2 + ½ + 1/4 + 1/14 + 1/28

Basically the whole of the above amounts to:

1/2 of $5\frac{5}{7}$ Cubits = Cubits = 2 Cubits 6 Palms

Bearing in mind that a Golden Triangle has sides in the ratio of 3:4:5, the Remen, as a unit of length, had a particular use in geometry. A right-angled triangle constructed with the sides consisting of the units 1 Span for the opposite and 1 Foot for the adjacent, provided a hypotenuse of 1 Remen.

Some would say that as these proportions are in the ratio of 3:4:5, they demonstrate how the ancient Egyptians endeavoured to obey the rules of their Sacred Ratio as much as possible. These units would certainly have been a bonus when constructing buildings that employed the Sacred Ratio.

2.10.0 MEASURING AREA

2.10.1 ANCIENT EGYPTIAN UNITS OF AREA

The basic unit of area used by the ancient Egyptians was the Greek Aroura. This was a measure of 1 square Khet or 100 cubit Strips, roughly ⅔ of an acre.

The Egyptian Scribes not only managed to confuse everyone in their time, but they have managed to confuse a few authors today as well. As mentioned earlier, the word 'Cubit' when referring to length is 7 Palms, when referring to area; it is a narrow rectangle, 1 cubit wide by 100 Cubits long. For reasons of clarification, this text refers to 'Cubit Strip' when appropriate.

Hieroglyph	Key	Description	Area & Equivalents
(Not confirmed)	E5 x	Square Cubit. (Not to be confused with the cubit strip or linear cubit)	square cubit = 7 by 7 Palms cubit^2 = 52.3 cm^2
	E5 L	Forearm, upper arm straight. Means a strip of land 1 by 100 Cubit. (Palm down)	Centaroura (cubit strip) = 1/100 of Aroura, 273.5 m^2.
	E5 J	Bent arm. (Palm down)	1/2 of an Aroura. (Warning, this glyph also used for length)
	E6 ~	Pool (followed by qty of Aroura). Area of land 100 by 100 Cubits or equivalent.	Aroura = 1 Khet^2 = 1 Setat = 100 cubit Strips, 2735 m^2
	E8 n	Door bolt and two loaves.	
	E5 #	Oval represents a sandy tract.	
	E4 < E11	Garden pool (followed by number of Setat). Area of land 100 by 100 cubits or equivalent.	1 Setat = 100 cubit strips = 1 Khet^2

Glyph	Code	Description	Value
 (lotus leaf, stalk, rhizome with stroke)	E6 >	Lotus leaf, stalk, and rhizome; alluvial plain with grains of sand; irrigated land and stroke.	Decaroura = 10 times Aroura = 1000 square Cubits, 27,350 m²
 (lotus)	E4 l	Lotus leaf, stalk, and rhizome. Multiples used to scale up quantity.	
|	E1 l	Single stroke used as abbreviation for lotus leaf, stalk, and rhizome. Multiples used to scale up quantity.	Decaroura = 10 times Aroura = 1000 square Cubits, 27,350 m²
 (duck)	E2 s	Pintail duck.	1/8 of an Aroura.
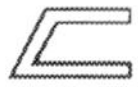 (ribs)	E3 ?	Thought to be shortened pair of ribs.	General representation of half
X	E3 /	Two sticks crossed.	Usually means a ¼. Can mean multiply or add.

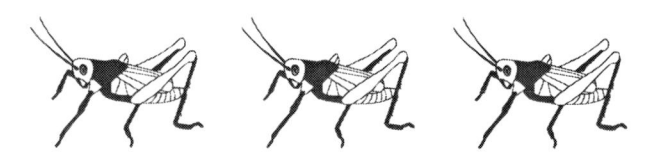

2.10.2 REFERENCES TO CENTAROURA AND DECAROURA

The unit names 'Centaroura' and 'Decaroura' seem to be used mainly in Italian and French texts. These terms are useful because they help to clarify the confusing multiple use of some hieroglyphs.

Even though the unit name 'Cubit' usually measures length, or sometimes represents area in the case of the cubit strip (Centaroura), we can still square a length cubit of 7 Palms. This gives us an area of 49 Square Palms (Cubit²).

Remember, whatever units you are working with, there is a difference between area (A) of 100 units squared and area (B) of 100 square units. Area (A) contains 10,000 square units and area (B) contains 100 square units.

2.10.3 Examples of Adding Areas

A Field of 4 Decarouras, 3 Arouras = 43 Arouras

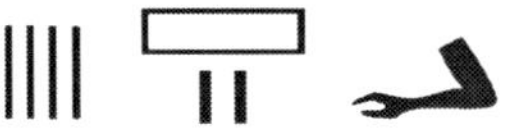

= 42 1/2 Arouras

4 Decarouras + 2 Arouras + 1/2 Aroura

Arouras   (Add)   cubit strips

Find 8, 1/2, 1/4, 1/8 added to 10, 1/2, 1/4

88,750 square cubits plus 1,075 square cubits

Square Cubits

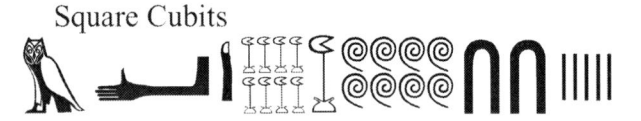

= 89,825 square cubits

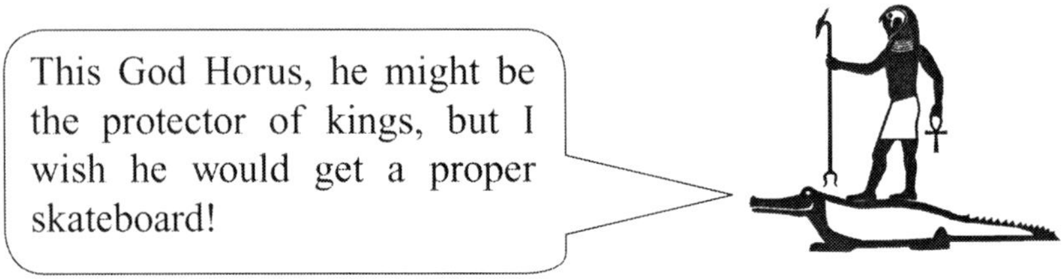

> This God Horus, he might be the protector of kings, but I wish he would get a proper skateboard!

2.11.0 MEASURING VOLUME

2.11.1 ANCIENT EGYPTIAN UNITS OF VOLUME

The ancient Egyptians employed different units for measuring liquids compared to the measurement of solids. Liquids such as beer and wine were measured in various jars and jugs.

The most common standard unit for volumetric dry measure was the Hekat (Heqat). There were a large number of hieroglyphs that represented the Hekat measure or its multiples. Most of them looked like one or more barrels with other hieroglyphs attached or nearby.

The corn-measure rule (Eye of Horus) was used for fractions of 1/2, 1/4, 1/8, 1/16, 1/32 and 1/64 of a Hekat.

Hieroglyph	Key	Description	Unit and Equivalent
	E8 A	Hekat corn measure with grain.	1 Hekat = 1/30 cubic royal cubit (1/30 cubit³)
	E8 B	Hekat corn measure with grain beneath 3 grains.	
	E8 C	Hekat corn measure with grain and crook.	
	E8 D	Hekat corn measure with grain and finger.	

Hieroglyph	Key	Description	Unit and Equivalent
	E8 E	Hekat corn measure with grain, crook, hill, and loaf.	1 Hekat = 1/30 cubic royal cubit (1/30 cubit³)
	E8 F	Hekat corn measure with grain and throw stick.	
	E8 G	Hekat corn measure with grain, loaf, and stroke.	
	E8 H	Double Hekat	2 Hekat = 1/15 cubic royal cubit
	E8 I		
	E8 J		
	E8 P	Hinu; for measuring beer, milk, honey, grain, and scent.	1 Hinu (Hin) = 1/10 Hekat (Heqat) Liquid and grain measure.
	E8 K	Quadruple Hekat or Oipe	1 Oipe = 4 Hekats
	E8 L		
	E8 M		
	E8 N	4 Quadruple Hekats (Was originally 5 Quadruple Hekats)	Sack = 4 Oipes (4 Quadruple Hekats) = 16 Hekats (Approx. 76.88 L)
	E8 O		

⟨hieroglyph⟩	E8 o	Khar	1 Khar = 20 Hekats = 2/3 of a cubit^3
⟨hieroglyph⟩	E1 cR	Khar (numerous hieroglyphs for both Sack and Khar)	At various points in Egyptian history the Khar and Sack were interchangeable
Unkown	?	cubic cubit	1 cubit^3 = 1 1/2 Khar = 30 Hekat
⟨hieroglyph⟩	E8 2-9	Multiples of Hekat from 2 to 9. Keys provide 2-9 in sequence.	Example: ⟨hieroglyph⟩ 4 Double Hekats

2.11.2 Jobs for the Boys

It is not surprising that scribes were given a privileged status; they didn't even pay taxes. So they had no incentive to simplify anything as their jobs were usually kept within the family and protected. All their work was shrouded in mystery, including the everyday arithmetic which they did for others. The systems they adopted for describing multiples and fractions of volumetric measure demonstrate this complexity.

Numeric values placed in front of the unit of measurement meant multiplied 100 times the value in front. Numbers from 1 to 9 placed after the measurement meant multiplied by multiples of 10.

Multiples of a unit of measure in the range of 2-9 were denoted by a number of dots from 2-9 respectively, placed after the unit of measure.

The hieroglyphs (𐦈) and (X) placed after the unit of measure represent 50 and 25 respectively, because ½ times 100 = 50 and ¼ times 100 = 25.

Examples of multiples and fractions of a

Hekat: 𓎈𓎈 ||| ▱ 𐦈 X || ⦾ = 4,398 Hekats

4000 + 300 Hekat + 50 + 25 + 20 + 3 = 4,398

𓎈𓎈𓎈 ||||| 🐟 𓏛 |||| Sack = 104,640 Hekats

6000(x 16) + 500(x 16) + 40(x 16) = 104,640

Corn of
Lower Egypt

⸺ ▱ ⊚ 𓎈 || 🦅 ▱ 𓎉 ～ ⦿ ||| 👁

    132   Double
  x 200   Hekat

(50+10+6 +1/8 +1/32+3R3) x 2
26,400 + 132 + (40R+10R + 3R3) x 2
26,532 Hekats + 106 2/3 Ro = 26,532 1/3 Hekats

There is a sound logic with this methodology of course. Unfortunately, there is very little consistency with any of the other systems they used for recording and manipulating fractions and multiples of units. The opportunities for creative accounting as they would call it today must have been enormous.

The following table provides the keyboard locations of two commonly used hieroglyphic ideograms associated with ancient Egyptian weights and measures.

Hieroglyph	Key	Description	Ideogram
◗◗◗	E8 1	Three grains of sand. Pellets of metal or mineral.	Sand
⌒⌒⌒ ooo	E7 A	Collar of beads. Means Gold and precious metal	Gold

2.12.0 Measuring Weight

2.12.1 The Deben

For the measurement of weight, the ancient Egyptians employed a unit called the Deben; it was equivalent to about 91 Grams.

2.12.2 Ancient Egyptian Units of Weight

Hieroglyph	Key	Description	Unit and Equivalent
	E8 Q	Cylinder seal attached to bead necklace, stroke, and brick.	Seal = 1/12 Deben 7.58 Grams
	E8 R	Plasterer's float, half loaf, and brick.	Kite = 1/10 Deben 9.1 Grams
	E8 S	Intestine, brick, and water	Deben = 10 Kites 91 Grams
	E8 T	Intestine, a grain of sand, and water.	

Various metal ring weights were used as measures. They were made mainly of copper, sometimes gold or silver, and occasionally lead.

They effectively provided a standard means of accurately weighing goods across the nation and wider a field. Metal and stone Ingots of measured weight were also used for weighing materials. Deben rings were occasionally used as units of currency.

The number of units and any fractions specified were always placed after the hieroglyph representing the unit for measuring weight.

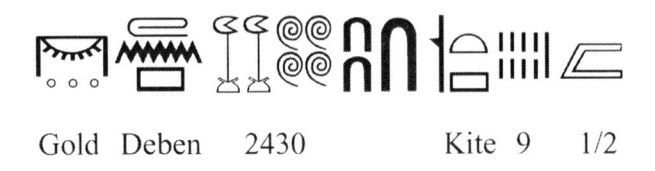

Gold   Deben   2430   Kite   9   1/2

2430 Deben and 9½ Kite of Gold

2.13.0 MEASURING TIME

2.13.1 PHARAOHS USED SEVERAL CALENDARS

The ancient Egyptians were very interested in astronomy. They knew the difference between stars and planets, and could identify Mercury, Venus, Mars, Jupiter, and Saturn. Through their knowledge of astronomy, they were able to create several calendars for various purposes.

The first calendar of the ancient Egyptians was based on the stars, the most important of which was Sirius (The Dog Star). They observed that Sirius disappeared below the horizon at the same time every year and reappeared just before sunrise, two days later. This always occurred as the level of the Nile began to rise for the annual flooding, the inundation. As this was such an important event, they made this the start of the new year in their calendar and called it 'Wepet-renpet' (𓋹) for New Year's Day.

The second calendar was based on the twelve lunar cycles. Unfortunately for the ancient Egyptians, they had to constantly adjust this calendar. The reason for this was that one lunar cycle lasted 29½ days, but their calendar worked on the basis of 30 days in a month.

Having said this, the calendar served its purpose for a long period of the ancient Egyptians history and was used for calculating the dates of festivals.

2.13.2 THE 365-DAY CALENDAR

Another calendar introduced very early on was based on there being 360 days in a calendar year, because they were already working with twelve, thirty-day months in a year.

Nevertheless, Egyptian astronomers quickly understood that a 365-day year was necessary because of their observations of Sirius and other cosmic bodies. So five days holiday were added to the existing 360-day calendar called epagomenal days.

The Egyptians being a very superstitious people, considered the five-supplementary days to be a dangerous period. The old year had died, and the New Year had not been born yet. They believed that the evil goddess sekhmet would send hordes of unwholesome and foreboding horrors, diseases, and general nastiness. Fortunately, this was mostly repelled with the appropriate rituals and celebrations. It seems strange how they did not seem to be bothered by these miasmas before they added the epagomenal days to their calendar; only afterwards. As they say, any excuse for a party!

The five-days holiday were used to celebrate the birthdays of the Gods Osiris, Isis, Set, Nephthys, and Horus which all came at the end of the year. This five day festival coincided quite nicely with the end of the harvest season, which was an ideal time for the ancient Egyptians to take their holidays. These festivals, as well as others, were recognized as public holidays and every tenth day was also a holiday.

When Julius Caesar visited Egypt, he was so impressed by the Egyptian Calendar that the Roman's adopted it. This calendar then developed into our Gregorian calendar which was introduced to us in the sixteenth century.

The ancient Egyptian year was further split into three seasons. Each season consisted of four months based on the state of the river Nile; inundation, winter, and the summer. The year began traditionally around mid-July when the inundation started.

By necessity, dates for such things as festivals, holidays, and ceremonies were based on a 365-day calendar. For everything else, which included business and taxation, there was a tendency to regard the year as only 360 days. For example, the daily income of a temple was stated as 1/360th of its annual income.

2.13.3 Ancient Egyptian Units of Time

Hieroglyph	Key	Meaning
	E8 [	Minute
	E8 Y	Hour = 60 Minutes
	E8 Z	Hour = 60 Minutes
	E8 V	Daytime = 12 Hours.
	E8 J	Night time = 12 Hours.
	E8 W	Day = 24 Hours; this format used in dates. Day number 1-30, written beneath sun.
Unknown	?	Week = 10 Days. 3 weeks = 1 month
	E8 U	Month = 30 days Month 8
	E8 A	Month; number 1-4 is written beneath the crescent moon. Month = 30 days
	E8 X	Season = 4 months = 120 Days

🌾🌾🌾⊙	E8 ^	Season (Inundation), annual flooding of the Nile, and providing fertile silt for agriculture.
🌾🌾🌾	E8 −	Season (Inundation), annual flooding of the Nile, and providing fertile silt for agriculture.
	E8]	Season (Winter); the time of growing; emergence of fields from water.
	E8 \	Season (Summer), of 'deficiency of water'.
	E5 T	Year=12 Months + 5 Days; used to count of years of 365 days. = Year 10

§ 2.13.3 Notes of Interest

One week consisted of ten days and there were three weeks in a month. Weeks were referred to as 'Decades' from the 36 constellations called 'The Decans'.

2.13.4 THE 24-HOUR DAY

The ancient Egyptians were the first to introduce the concept of twenty-four hours in a day. Night and day were both divided into twelve hours. Prior to 127 BC, the length of the hours varied depending on the season.

To tell the time and measure an hour, the ancient Egyptians used shadows cast by the sun and water clocks. These water clocks were conical vessels with hours marked off on the inside in a vertical column. Water was allowed to drip out of a hole at the bottom of the vessel at a carefully measured rate. As the level of water went down, different markings were revealed indicating how many hours had passed.

The devices for casting shadows of the sun, in their simplest form were just vertical sticks. Such devices for casting shadows were called gnomons, and were used to distinguish broad divisions in the daytime. Gnomons were eventually combined with scales to produce sundials, which allowed the Egyptians to tell time by measuring the length or direction of the shadow cast by the Sun. The Ancient Egyptians are credited with the invention of sundials.

As well as making small-scale sundials, some of which could be held in the hand and were portable, the ancient Egyptians built tall-stone obelisks. With these giant needles, everybody could tell the time by looking at the obelisk's shadow.

Although obelisk's were built as far back as 3,500 BC, perhaps the earliest portable sundial that has survived, often referred to as an Egyptian shadow clock, became popular around 1,500 BC. The shadow clocks were either T-shaped or L-shaped and were used to measure the morning hours as the sun swept overhead. Then, they were turned around to count down the afternoon hours. In 2 AD, the Alexandrian-scholar Claudius Ptolemaeus introduced the division of the hour into sixty minutes.

2.13.5 CALENDARS

The ancient Egyptians recorded their dates according to the regnal year of the reigning king, and not from some absolute point in time such as the supposed year of the birth of Christ.

So when a new king entered the throne, they started counting the years again from one. In order to translate an ancient date into a BC format, you must take into account whoever was on the throne at that moment; and all the others after that point and their duration in office.

Basically, the ancient Egyptians employed a standard format based upon the time of the king's reign. This would be expressed in the number of years and sometimes the season, months, and days as well. Added to this would be the name of the reigning king and possibly royal titles and epithets.

A royal epithet is a few additional descriptive words added to the name of a king, such as 'Living Enduringly', while a royal title denotes the king's rank, such as 'The King of Upper and Lower Egypt'.

§ 2.13.5 Notes of Interest

The East Bank of the River Nile was used primarily for the construction of the cult temples and settlements. The ancient Egyptians considered the East Bank to be the land of the living because the sun rose in the East; this is where it was reborn, bringing new life.

The West Bank of the Nile was where cemeteries and funeral temples were built and was referred to as the "Land of the Dead". The West was where the sun set starting its nocturnal journey into the afterlife.

2.13.6 General Date and Time Vocabulary

Hieroglyph	Key	Examples of Usage
	E4%	First. Used in first day, month, and season.
	E8:	Means New Year's Day, called Wepen-renpet.
	E8;	Means New Year's Day, called Wepen-renpet.
	E8b	Regnal Year = 12 Months + 5 Days Holiday; used in full date formats. (365 days)
	E8#	Means Time.
	E1M	In
	E8c	Majesty (Fullers club with stroke)
	E4- E1=	Given Life
	E1N	Of
	E3r	*under* the majesty of
	E2r E3{	Like Re
	E8i	Eternal

2.13.7 Examples of Date Structure

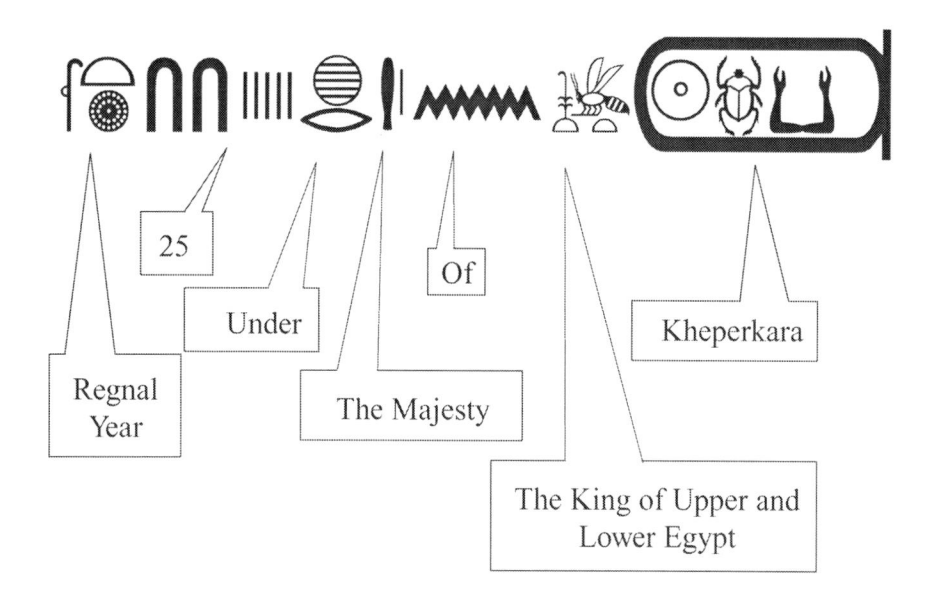

- Regnal Year
- 25
- Under
- The Majesty
- Of
- The King of Upper and Lower Egypt
- Kheperkara

We could add an epithet after the cartouche above,  'Given Life'.

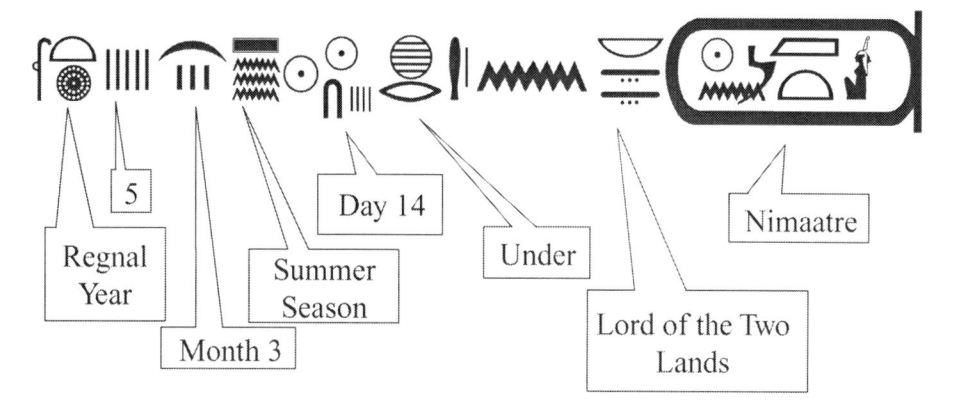

- Regnal Year
- 5
- Month 3
- Summer Season
- Day 14
- Under
- Lord of the Two Lands
- Nimaatre

We could add an epithet after the cartouche above,  'Like Re'.

Even though the ancient Egyptian calendar indicated months by numbers and seasons, each of the twelve months had their own individual names.

The months were usually named after a festival that took place in them or in the following month. These names were rarely used in hieroglyphic texts but were probably in common use when the language was spoken.

2.13.8 ORDINAL UNITS OF TIME

Hieroglyphs	Key	Meaning
	E2r E4%	First Day
	E2r|	First Day
	E2r E4B	Eighth Day (Standard ordinals used).
	E4(	Last Day of month (Day 30).
	E1\Qy E2r	Thirtieth day of the month (last day).
	E4% E1 N E8^	First month of the Season of Inundation.
	E4% E8\	First month of the Season of Summer.
	E9L	Last Year

It is easy to see how modern languages developed the use of simple squiggles, which were abbreviations for laborious complex hieroglyphs.

2.13.9 Translating Modern Dates

As our date system is based on Christ, 'The Anointed One', we must incorporate his name in the date format. This is similar to the way the ancient Egyptians would include the names of kings or deities into their dates. The following is an example of a modern date in the format described in section 2.13.7.

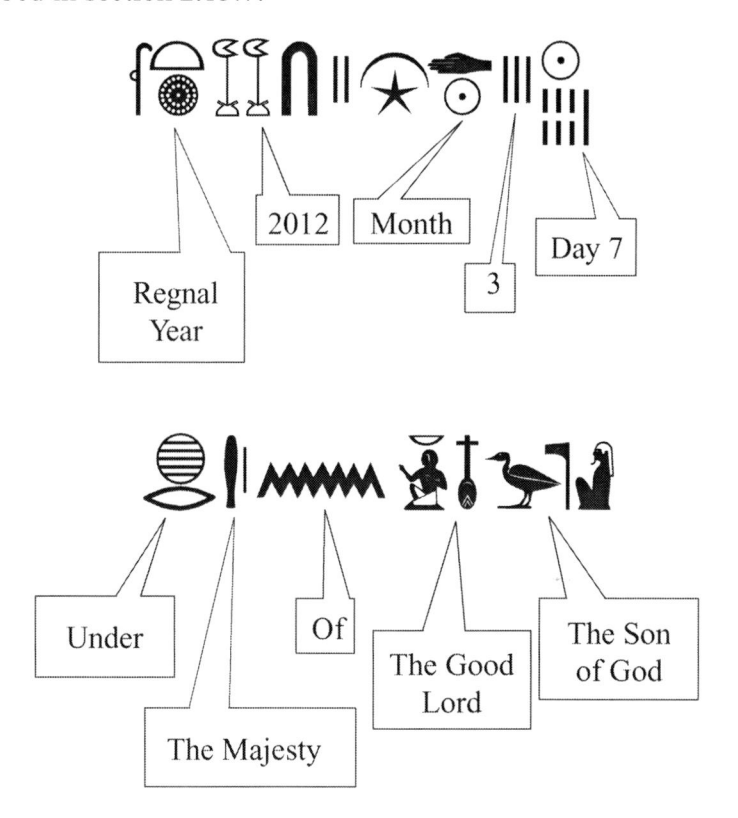

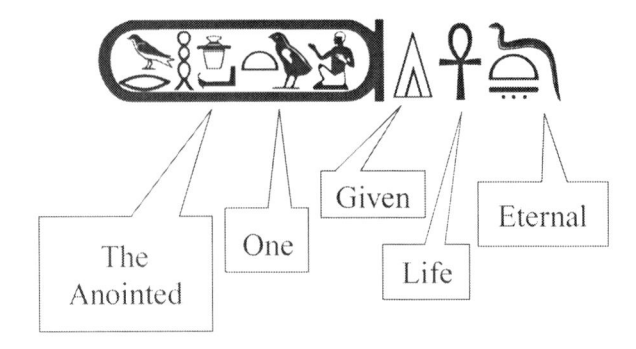

The whole of the above equates to 7 March 2012. Remember that the name Christ means 'The Anointed One'.

2.13.10 THE STELA BY ITY

The following example of a date was found on a stela erected by an official called Ity; it is similar to an example described earlier in section 2.13.7. The date below is based on the reign of Senusret (I). Senusret is the family name of the king, the name in the cartouche is the throne name which says king Kheperkara.

Archaeologists prefer to use the family name of a king rather than the throne name for identification purposes. Using the throne name alone can be confusing because this name is often retained by successive generations of kings as they inherit the throne.

Also, many experts disagree about the exact start date of when most of the king's came to the throne, and they even disagree about the duration of time that most kings spent in power.

So when an attempt is made to convert an ancient Egyptian date to a modern BC style date, there is a great possibility that the result may be inaccurate by more than a few years.

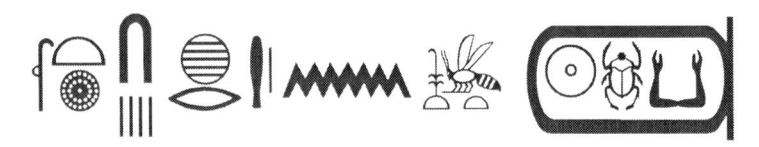

There is some disagreement as to when Senusret (I) came to power, but the general consensus of opinion is that he reigned from 1971 BC to 1926 BC.

Therefore, the date above represents 1957 BC which is fourteen years before 1971 BC.

2.13.11 Hours and Minutes

The ancient Egyptians gave each hour in the day and night a unique name. This naming was done for astronomical reasons and to mark religious activities.

Even though they divided an hour into sixty minutes, it is debatable how accurately they could measure a minute with just sun dials and water clocks.

Their methods for documenting hours and minutes were quite simple. The unit of time was followed by a number or word representing an ordinal number. When declaring a particular hour, it was important to state whether it belonged to the daytime or the night time.

§ 2.13.11 Notes of Interest

Every year for two months between July and October the Nile flooded, covering the land on both banks with about two feet of water. After the water receded, a black silt was left behind which was very fertile for crops. From this black silt, the ancient Egyptians named their country Kemet, which means "The Black Land".

2.13.12 Examples of the Time of Day

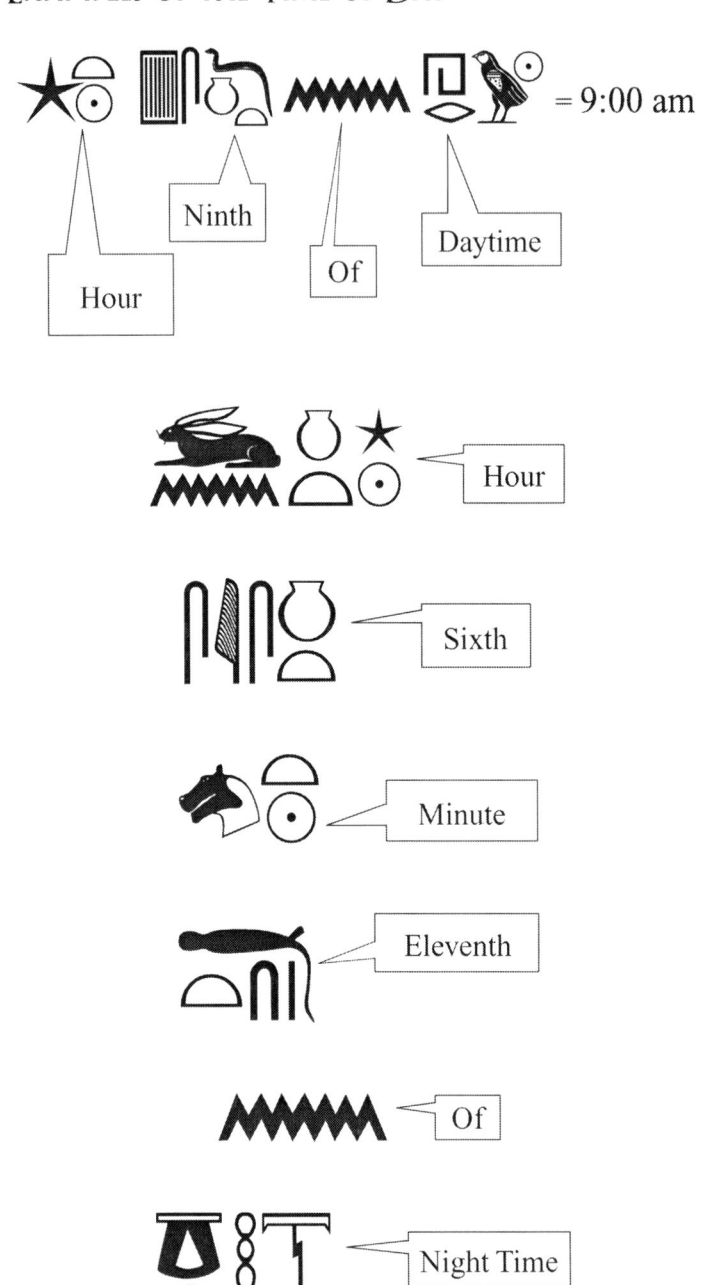

= 9:00 am

- Hour
- Ninth
- Of
- Daytime

- Hour
- Sixth
- Minute
- Eleventh
- Of
- Night Time

= 6:11 p.m.

2.13.13 USING TIME TO MEASURE DISTANCE

It is interesting to note that Egyptian surveyors used the time of someone marching in a straight line to measure distance. For example, one minute of marching was equivalent to 350 Cubits about 183.75 m. One hour of marching was equivalent to 21,000 Cubits, about 11.025 km. They used this system to measure large expanses of land after the Nile's waters had retreated.

2.14.0 MEASURING STRENGTH OF BREAD AND BEER

2.14.1 PEFSU (PESU)

The strength of beer and bread after they have been made is measured in Pefsu. Some ancient texts refer to Pefsu as Pesu.

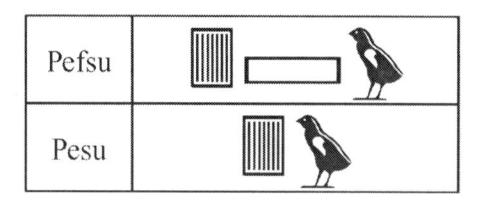

Pefsu	
Pesu	

A pefsu is not a measure of the quality of the barley, wheat, wedyet flour, emmer, besha, spelt-date, or grain that may have been used to make the beer or bread.

Of course, all these commodities could vary in quality and strength. Consequently, these factors will have an effect on the strength or quality of the beer or bread produced. This is why the type or quality of grain is sometimes mentioned before measuring or calculations take place. The pefsu of the beer or bread made was determined by the ancient Egyptians as follows:

> *If one hekat of grain were used to produce only one loaf or one des-jug of beer, then the pefsu of both the bread and the beer was said to be one. If one hekat produced two loaves or two des-jugs of beer, then their pefsu was said to be two.*

If one hekat produced three loaves or three des-jugs of beer, then their pefsu was three, and so on, so that the higher the pesu, the weaker the beer or bread, and possibly the smaller the loaf.

2.14.2 THE PEFSU FORMULA

The relationship between the amount of grain used and the pefsu of the beer or bread produced was thus:

$$\text{Pefsu} = \frac{\textit{Number of Loaves or Des-jugs of Beer}}{\text{Number of Hekats of Grain}}$$

Generally speaking, when the ancient Egyptians made beer and bread, they used more grain for their beer than for their bread. Alternatively, we could say that the same quantity of grain would produce more loaves than des-jugs of beer, which was therefore relatively stronger.

In pefsu, problems of the Rhind Mathematical Papyrus and the Moscow Mathematical Papyrus the pefsu value of the beers lie between 1 and 4, while for the loaves of bread the pefsu value varies from 5 to as much as 45.

2.15.0 MEASURING SLOPE

2.15.1 MODERN INCLINATION BY DEGREES

In modern geometry, we measure angles and the inclination of slopes in degrees, minutes, and seconds. The ancient Egyptians used a type of fraction similar to the way vehicle drivers were informed of how quickly a slope of a hill descended, such as 1 in 14. This means, for every fourteen feet along the road, the road would drop by one foot.

2.15.2 THE SEKED

The ancient Egyptians used a term called the Seked (Seqed, seqt or sqd) to describe the slope of an inclined surface based on their linear unit the Royal Cubit, which was equal to 7 Palms or 28 Digits.

The angle of a slope was therefore expressed as the number of Palms and Digits that had to be moved horizontally to give a vertical rise of 1 Royal Cubit.

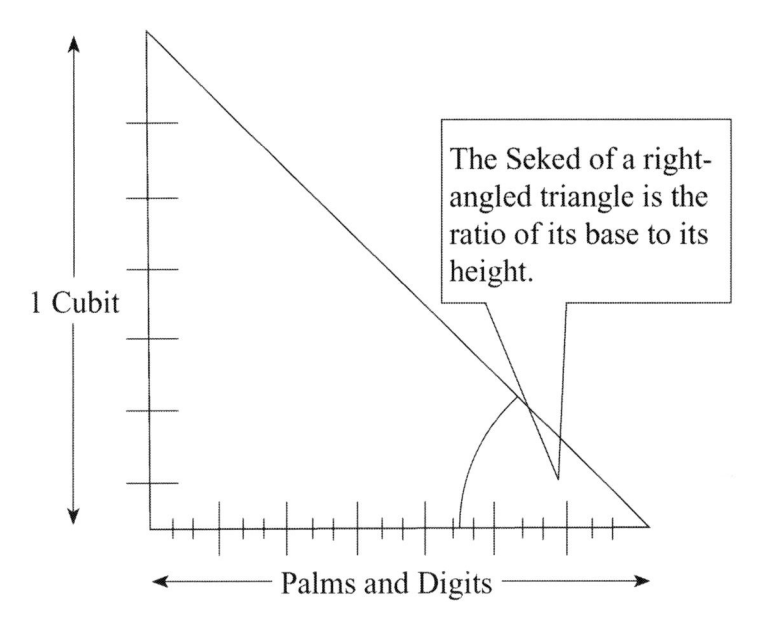

> The Seked of a right-angled triangle is the ratio of its base to its height.

1 Cubit

◄── Palms and Digits ──►

The Seked of a pyramid is the inclination of any one of the four-triangular faces to the horizontal plane of its base. The ancient Egyptian word 'Seked' is similar in meaning to our word 'gradient'.

> **§ 2.15.2 Notes of Interest**
>
> During the battle of Kadesh between the Egyptians and the Hittites, the Hittites used a common technique to break up the Egyptian army. Stallions pulled the Egyptian chariots, so the Hittites let loose onto the battlefield a mare in season. Fortunately for the Egyptians, they caught up with her in time and won the battle.

It is clear from the ancient Egyptian Rhind Mathematical Papyrus, they considered the Seked as a unit of length, not a ratio.

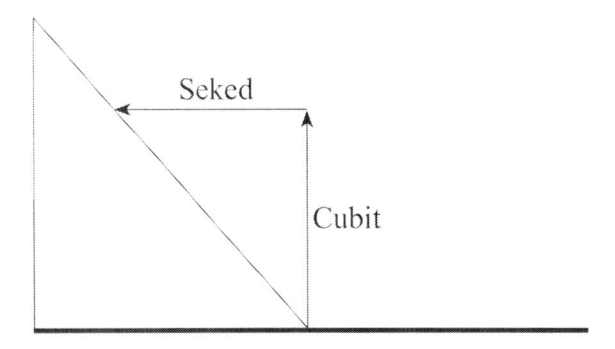

The Seked for a pyramid is calculated as one-half of the base divided by the height. It is the same as what we would call the cotangent today.

2.15.3 Angle of Slope for Different Sekeds

Seked			Angle
Palms	Digits	-	Degrees
4	0	-	60.25°
4	1	-	58.74°
4	2	-	57.26°
4	3	-	55.84°
5	0	-	54.46°
5	1	-	53.13°
5	2	-	51.84°
5	3	-	50.60°
6	0	-	49.40°
6	1	-	48.24°
6	2	-	47.12°
6	3	-	46.04°
7	0	-	45.00°
7	1	-	43.99°
7	2	-	43.02°

§ 2.15.3 Notes of Interest

Permanent paints were generally made from natural minerals. This is why the intense colours in tombs have not faded over the millennia. The paints were made by grinding raw material to a powder and mixing them with a binding agent such as vegetable gum. Many pigments were frit, made by roasting powdered ores and other minerals which fused creating a brightly coloured glass.

§ 2.15.3.1 Notes of Interest

The main substances used as pigments were:

Black—Carbon; from lamp black, charcoal, burnt bones or soot.

White—Chalk or gypsum which is calcium sulphate.

Blue—Malachite, quartz, natron, and chalk. The copper compounds in the malachite contribute to the blue colour.

Yellow—Yellow ochre—silica and hydrated iron oxides. Orpiment was also used, which consisted of arsenic sulphide that had been imported from Persia.

Green—Copper ore or powdered malachite.

Red—Oxides of iron or red ochre which is similar to yellow ochre.

2.15.4 COMMON SEKEDS FOR PYRAMIDS

From the measurement of the gradients of all the pyramids, it was discovered that the two commonest Sekeds were 5 Palms 1 Digit, and 5 Palms 2 Digits. These two Sekeds are based on simple ratios. The first is a height to base ratio of 4: 3 (28 Digits to 21 Digits) the hypotenuse of such a right-angle triangle is 5. This, of course, makes up the three sides of a Golden Triangle. The second is a height to base ratio of 11:14.

By adopting a Seked of 5 Palms 1 Digit for pyramid building, the ancient Egyptians made it considerably easier from a technical point of view in ensuring that the correct angle of slope was always maintained.

From wooden, metal, and stone rules that have been recovered, it is clear that the ancient Egyptians were quite capable of measuring to an accuracy of 1/16 of a digit.

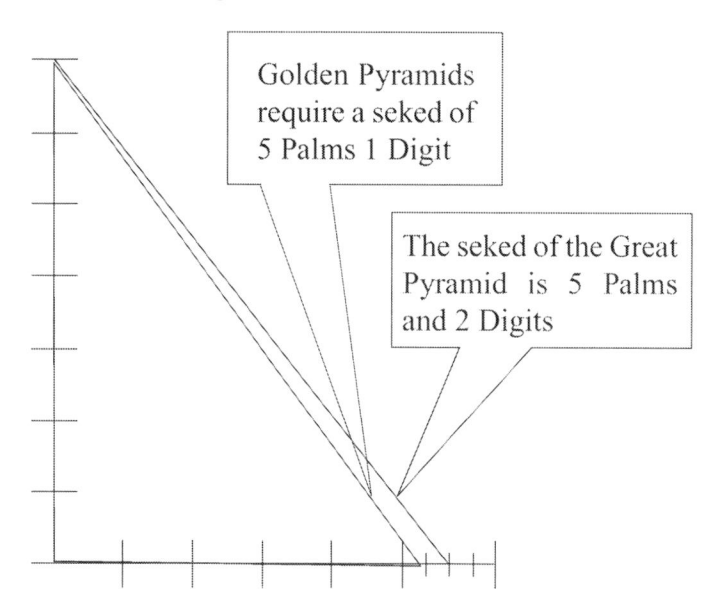

> Golden Pyramids require a seked of 5 Palms 1 Digit

> The seked of the Great Pyramid is 5 Palms and 2 Digits

The fact that a Seked of 5 Palms 1 Digit was so easy to work with begs the question as to why the Seked for the Great Pyramid was 5 palms and 2 digits. There appears to be two possible reasons for this. The first seems to lie with the fact that the architecture of this pyramid was based on π. As there is a mathematical relationship between π and the sacred ratio, incorporating π into the structure, provided a more sophisticated alternative for including the sacred ratio in the pyramid design. The second reason will be discussed in the following section.

2.15.5 THE CUBIT AS A PRIME NUMBER

The second reason for using this Seked of 5 palms 2 digits seems to lie with the division of the cubit into 7 palms, which is strange, since 7 is a prime number and has no divisors. Probably, this is why a short cubit was introduced of 6 palms, which could then be divided into halves and thirds.

There is, however, one practical reason why the ancient Egyptians might have chosen to divide their cubit into seven parts. This was when they needed to deal with circles or any problem that required the use of the simple ratio for π as 22/7.

Using the formula, {2 x π x R}, where (R) is the radius, a circle with a radius of say 7 Cubits has a circumference of 44 Cubits. In other words, a circle with a radius of 1 cubit has a circumference of 44 Palms. With this method, it is very easy to sub-divide the circumference into halves and quarters; there being 22 palms in a semi-circle; 11 Palms in a quadrant.

Without even doing any calculations involving pi, (π) it is easy to arrive at a length of the circumference of a circle if the radius is known to be a number of cubits long. For example, for circles with radii of 1, 2, 3 or 4 cubits, we get circumferences of 44, 88, 132 and 176 Palms respectively. Given a circle with radius of 1.5 cubits, we get a circumference of 66 Palms and so on.

2.15.6 THE RHIND PAPYRUS PROBLEM 56

In the ancient Egyptian Rhind Mathematical Papyrus problem 56 reads:

If a pyramid is 250 cubits high and the side of its base 360 cubits long, what is its Seked?

As you will discover later in sections 2.16.2 and 2.17.1, the ancient Egyptian Scribes relied heavily on the use of all sorts of mathematical tables. Unless they had seen a problem before or they were very good at mental arithmetic, they would always tabularise figures to assist them with the calculations. They also used existing reference tables to help them with multiplication and division of whole numbers and fractions.

2.15.6.1 THE SCRIBE'S SOLUTION

Take 1/2 of 360; it makes 180. Multiply 250 so as to get 180; it makes 1/2, 1/5, 1/50 of a cubit. A cubit is 7 palms. Multiply 7 by 1/2, 1/5, 1/50.

The scribe did not document which method he used to get the answer of 1/2, 1/5 and 1/50 Cubits; he may have used tables or mental arithmetic to perform the calculation. Whichever method he adopted to get the answer, he then converted it from cubits into palms. To do this, a sort of table was set up. The table in the papyrus is difficult to understand, the following is the anglicised version.

2.15.6.2 CONVERTING CUBITS TO PALMS

Cubits	Palms		
1/2	3	1/2	
1/5	1	1/3	1/15
1/50		1/10	1/25

Do not worry about table usage at this stage. Tables will be discussed in greater detail later. In this example, column one is multiplied by seven to produce the remaining columns.

The seked is 5 + 1/25 Palms, that is;
(3 + 1/2) + (1 + 1/3 + 1/15) + (1/10 + 1/25) = 5 + 1/25 Palms.

Don't you just hate it when you can't see how they got the answer! It has been assumed the reader is happier studying this question and answer in English as opposed to ancient Egyptian hieroglyphs. Basically, the question is asking the student to calculate the cotangent of the angle for the following pyramid.

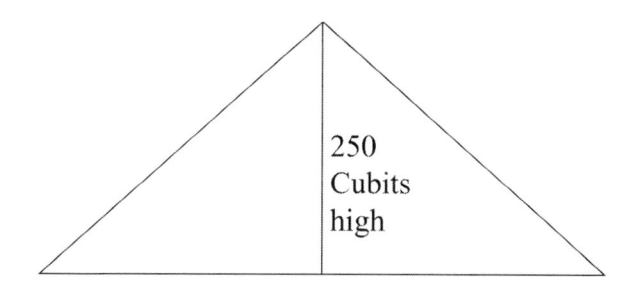

250 Cubits high

Half of the base of the pyramid gives us the base of our triangle as 180 Cubits.

250 Cubits
(The Rise)

180 Cubits (The Run)

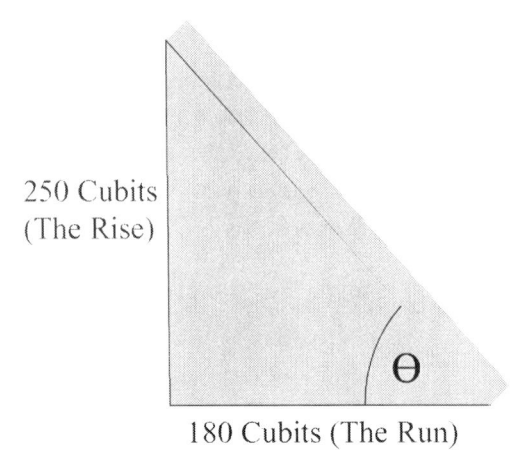

The seked is the base length over height, but expressed as a unit fraction. If we let X be the unknown value in the expression, then the phrase 'Multiply 250 so as to get 180' would look like: 250 multiplied by X = 180. This equates to X = 180/250 = 18/25 = 1/2 + 1/5 + 1/50. The Egyptian student did have access to tables of fractions, a sort of ready reckoner to help them with arithmetic. We can use a calculator, of course, which is fine for decimals, but not much help with fractions!

In the next step, the Egyptian student multiplies all these fractions by 7. The reason for this is that by convention, the units of the seked were expressed in Palms (7 Palms to a Cubit), fractions of a Palm in Digits (4 Digits to a Palm), and fractions of digits which were also necessary.

The table above, in effect shows the student's workings for converting the answer from Cubits to Palms. Each of the fractions on the left of the table starting with a 1/2 is multiplied by 7 to give the horizontal result. The row for the 1/2 provides (3 + 1/2).

The following two lines for a 1/5 and a 1/50 times 7 provide (1 + 1/3 + 1/15) and (1/10 + 1/25) respectively.

Finally to arrive at the seked, all the derivatives are totalled as follows:

(3 + 1/2 + 1 + 1/3 +1/15 + 1/10 + 1/25) = 5 1/25 Palms.

Hieroglyphs and Arithmetic of the Ancient Egyptian Scribes

To build a pyramid, you would need to maintain the angle of the pyramid and this would be achieved by maintaining the run-to-rise ratio. In the above example, you would move in 5 1/25 Palms and up one Cubit, then in a further 5 1/25 Palms, then up another cubit and continue this process as required.

2.16.0 Addition and Subtraction

2.16.1 The Importance of Text Direction

It has been said earlier, but it is important, so it is being said again, the ancient Egyptians could write text and numbers starting in either direction. They preferred reading and writing from right to left.

Like us, they processed numbers starting with the units, then the tens and then the hundreds and so forth. They processed numbers in the opposite direction to which the text was being read; we do the same today. We read words in a sentence in the opposite direction to the order we add or subtract the columns of digits. We always process numbers starting with the right hand units column first! Then we deal with the tens column, the hundreds, then the thousands, continuing this process until we have processed the numbers in the column that represent the highest values.

This means we are doing it properly if we keep the hieroglyphic numbers that represent the units, on the right of a number string; process these first, and then process the ever increasing larger numbers to the left in the order of their size.

It is assumed that the ancient Egyptian scribes would have remembered the answers to a lot of simple calculations 'off the top of their head's', the way that we do. It is unlikely that they would have needed to resort to brush and papyrus to add 8 and 11, even though you may know a few people today that would need a calculator for this.

§ 2.16.1 Notes of Interest

Ancient Egyptians built massive structures without the sophisticated mathematics engineers would use today. Yet the arithmetic expertise of the ancient Egyptians extended only to addition and subtraction, not even multiplication or division. Due to this limitation, they substituted clever tricks and found practical ways to arrive at the solutions they needed.

Surprisingly, no matter how complex a calculation may be that a modern day computer is processing, at the basic level it does it all by addition alone. A computer even uses addition to subtract numbers! This system is called complimentary mathematics.

2.16.2 Tables Used as Ready Reckoners

When a scribe has to find the answer to calculations that went beyond their powers of mental arithmetic, they had access to a number of tools. These included counting boards, an abacus of sorts; no doubt they even used pebbles in the sand, but they mainly relied upon reference tables of numbers, like ready reckoners. They used different tables to help them with all sorts of arithmetic, even those involving fractions. The following is an example of an addition and subtraction table:

1	9	10	1	8	9	1	7	8	1	6	7
2	9	11	2	8	10	2	7	9	2	6	8
3	9	12	3	8	11	3	7	10	3	6	9
4	9	13	4	8	12	4	7	11	4	6	10
5	9	14	5	8	13	5	7	12	5	6	11
6	9	15	6	8	14	6	7	13	6	6	12
7	9	16	7	8	15	7	7	14	7	6	13
8	9	17	8	8	16	8	7	15	8	6	14
9	9	18	9	8	17	9	7	16	9	6	15
1	5	6	1	4	5	1	3	4	1	2	3
2	5	7	2	4	6	2	3	5	2	2	4
3	5	8	3	4	7	3	3	6	3	2	5
4	5	9	4	4	8	4	3	7	4	2	6
5	5	10	5	4	9	5	3	8	5	2	7
6	5	11	6	4	10	6	3	9	6	2	8
7	5	12	7	4	11	7	3	10	7	2	9
8	5	13	8	4	12	8	3	11	8	2	10
9	5	14	9	4	13	9	3	12	9	2	11

§2.16.2 Notes of Interest

The ancient Egyptians were very fond of portraying scenes taken from everyday life or based upon stories, myths, or spells and the like.

It was quite common for inscriptions to be placed near or above a scene often telling you the name of someone, or provide a caption telling you what was going on. A little bit like the way we see a speech bubble used in modern comic strips, but without the text being deliberately ringed.

It is interesting to observe that carvings and painting of people facing each other have their text in different directions. The text for each person speaking has its direction such that the other facing person in the picture can read it.

2.16.3 Hieroglyphic Vocabulary for Arithmetic

Hieroglyphs	Key	Meaning
	E3r	Therefore
	E3g	Find

	E2$	Remainder or Balance
	E1 l	Unknown (**X**)
	E6{	Add
	E6}	Subtract
	E2%	Total
H	E5H E1 1	Added to
	E1M	Namely or Equals
	E1b	Times by 2
	E1r	Times by 2
	E1N	Of or Times
	E1F	Of It

Hieroglyphs	Key	Meaning
✕	E3\	Divide or Subtract
✕	E3/	Divide or Subtract
⬯	E1R	By, as in 4 by 6
(glyph)	E8k	Total
(glyph)	E8l	Multiply
(glyph)	E8m	Divide

2.16.4 Examples of Simple Arithmetic

Find   43 Plus 5 equals 48

Find   9 times 2 minus 10 equals 8

Hieroglyphs and Arithmetic of the Ancient Egyptian Scribes   173

§ 2.16.3 Notes of Interest

Bearing in mind the serious purpose of the majority of the artistic and scribal works, it may be surprising to learn that the ancient Egyptians occasionally did not miss the opportunity to have a little joke. For example, wall painters have been known to include themselves in their artwork and there is plenty of funny literary work in existence. Their style of humour was very rich and varied, as the following short comical tale confirms.

And there was a priest there called Nesiptah; and as Naneferkaptah went into the temple to pray, it happened that he went behind this priest, and was reading the inscriptions that were on the chapels of the gods. The priest mocked him by laughing. So Naneferkaptah said to him, 'Why are you laughing at me?' The priest replied, 'I was not laughing at you, or if I happened to do so, it was at your reading of the writings that are worthless.'

2.17.0 Multiplication

2.17.1 The Method of Doubling

The following method adopted by the scribes of ancient Egypt for multiplying two numbers together is rather cumbersome, but it is not that different to a similar method that was used in most parts of Europe in the late sixteenth century. The ancient Egyptians achieved the process of multiplication by a clever form of addition, called the Method of Doubling.

Let us consider the multiplication of 15 by 8. First the scribe would make two columns of numbers. Starting with a 1 in column 1, the multiplier column, he creates a sequential list of binary numbers in ascending order. Each number down the list is double the previous one. This is done until the final entry in the list is equal to or just less than the multiplier, in this case 15. No more entries to this column are added because the doubling of 8 gives us 16, which is greater than 15.

Then the scribe would place the second number, the multiplicand, in this case 8, at the head of the second column. This column is also made into a sequential list like the first, except, in this case, the 8 is doubled, then 16 doubled; the doubling stops when the multiplicand column has the same number of entries as the multiplier column. For this example, the columns would look like the following:

Doublings (15)	Sum (8)
1	8
2	16
4	32
8	64
(Total)	120

By adding all the numbers in the last column, we find that

15 multiplied by 8 = 120

This method works equally well for whichever number is used for the binary sequence as the multiplier in column one, or the multiplicand at the head of column two, for that matter.

When looking at this system, two things may come to mind. First, what happens if you are multiplying big numbers together? Second, what happens if the number sequence in the first column does not exactly add up to the multiplier? Instead of 15, what would we do if we wanted to multiply by, say, 18?

The answer to the first question is that you will probably need a very long list. The second question is better answered with another example.

To answer the second question, we will make the problem even more difficult; we will assume that the scribe has to multiply 18 by 7 but force him to use 18 as the multiplier instead of 7 for the first column. As we can use either number as the multiplier, we have deliberately chosen the more awkward option.

The scribe would then fill out his table like the one below:

Doublings	Sum
(18)	(7)
1	7
2	14
4	28
8	56
16	112
(Total)	(unknown)

Even after stopping the list at 16 because double 16 is greater than 18, he would notice that the multiplier column already adds up to more than 18. So the next step is to cross out entries which cause the column total to exceed 18.

 (18)	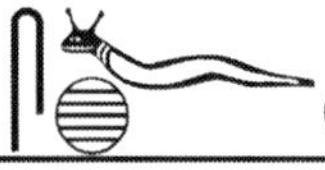 (7)
1	7̶
2	14
4	28
8̶	56
16	112
(Total) 	126

After totalling the multiplicand column, the scribe has his answer:

18 multiplied by 7 = 126

Multiplying by 10 was quite simple for the ancient Egyptians. It was just a case of changing all the hieroglyphs to the next base 10 highest unit.

2.17.2 MULTIPLYING BY TEN

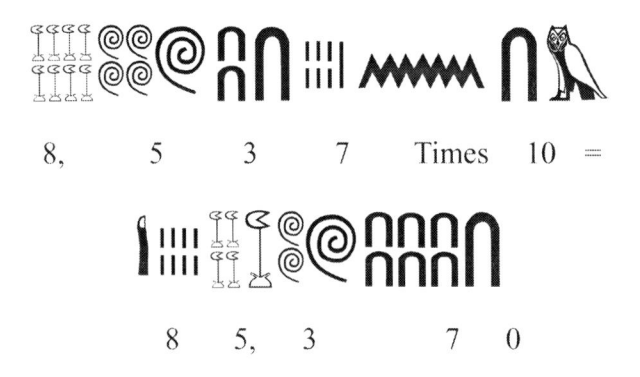

8, 5 3 7 Times 10 =

8 5, 3 7 0

2.18.0 DIVISION

2.18.1 MULTIPLICATION IN REVERSE

The processes for multiplication and division for the ancient Egyptians were very similar. Let us consider the problem of 287 divided by 9. Again the scribe would construct a table.

At the head of the dividend column on the right he would place 9, the divisor. Then he would make a sequential list down this column by doubling up each consecutive entry. He would stop appending to the list when the last value he entered equalled the dividend of 287 or if the next value to be entered exceeded the dividend if it were doubled.

In this case the last entry must be 144, because if it were doubled it would exceed 287.

(287)	(9)
1	9
2	18
4	36
8	72
16	144
Equals	(unknown)

The next step for him would be to work out which individual entries in the dividend column added up to exactly equal the original dividend, i.e. 287, or are just less than, and cross out the rest.

In our example, all the entries in the dividend column only total 279. This means that no entries can be rejected and all the values in the first column can be totalled to give the quotient.

$$1 + 2 + 4 + 8 + 16 = 31$$

The table is now complete:

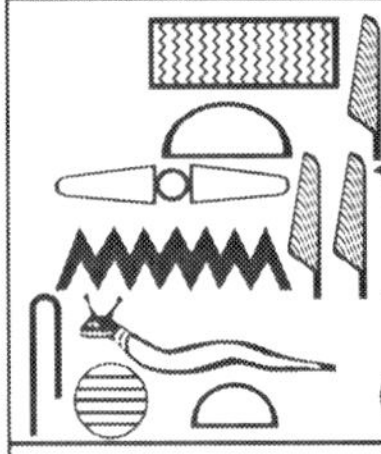 (287)	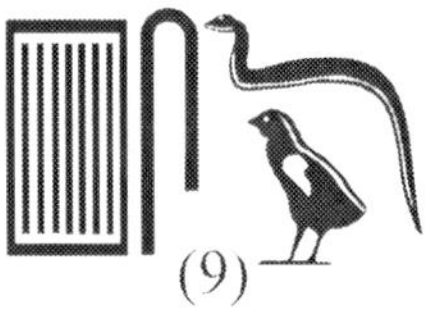 (9)
1	9
2	18
4	36
8	72
16	144
 Equals 31	279

It can be seen that 287 divided by 9 gives 31, with a remainder of (287 - 279) = 8

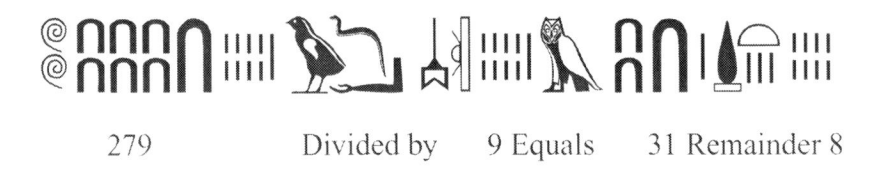

| 279 | Divided by | 9 Equals | 31 Remainder 8 |

The remainders, in such calculations did not pose too much of a problem. This is because the units of measure involved could usually be broken down into smaller units of measure. If the calculation above had been done in Cubits, then the remainder of 8 Cubits could have been converted into Palms. This would have provided a quotient after division by 9, of 6

Hieroglyphs and Arithmetic of the Ancient Egyptian Scribes 179

and 1/8, 1/12, 1/72 Palms. The level of accuracy required by the scribe would determine which fractions were unnecessary and ignore them. The smaller units after division might just happen to give an answer without remainder!

2.18.2 An Example—957 Divided by 11

It should be noted that 957 divided by 11 has no remainder. Again, the scribe would lay out a table of figures as shown below. Remember the last entry in the right-hand column must not exceed the original dividend of 957.

(957)	(11)
1	11
2	22
4	44
8	88
16	176
32	352
64	704
?	?

The scribe now has to find all the entries in the right hand column which add up to 957, or just less than. Then cross out the unwanted entries in the last column and also the corresponding entries in the first column.

After this procedure, each column is totalled and it can be seen that there is no remainder, 957 divided by 11 = 87 exactly.

(957)	(11)
1	11
2	22
4	44
8	~~88~~
16	176

32	~~352~~
64	704
87	957

The ancient Egyptians would have found great benefit in the use of computerised spreadsheets!

2.19.0 More about Aliquot Fractions

2.19.1 Reasoning that Remains a Secret

A scribe would never write 1/6 + 1/6 + 1/6 + 1/6 + 1/6 for 5/6 except in reference tables used as calculator assistants. Even though, the same fractions may have been repeated more than once within the process of a calculation, the same fractions would never occur in an answer to a problem.

The logic behind the scribe's reasoning for this is not clear and we will probably never know the answer to this. One possible reason is that as the ancient Egyptians developed new mathematical concepts, they did not update their notation to accommodate these new ideas. Consequently, this would have had a detrimental affect on their existing methodologies by making some procedures unnecessarily complicated.

To understand how the ancient Egyptians manipulated their formulas and processed their numbers and fractions, you need to try and understand their mindset.

2.19.2 Dividing a Loaf Problem

For example, if we had to divide four loaves between five people, we would say each person should receive 4/5th of a loaf; we would cut the four loaves and that would be an end to the matter.

In practical reality, we probably would not do this. This would mean that the first four people would each get a nice thick chunk and the last person would end up with four scraps. If they didn't like crusts, you would have just become public enemy number one in their eyes.

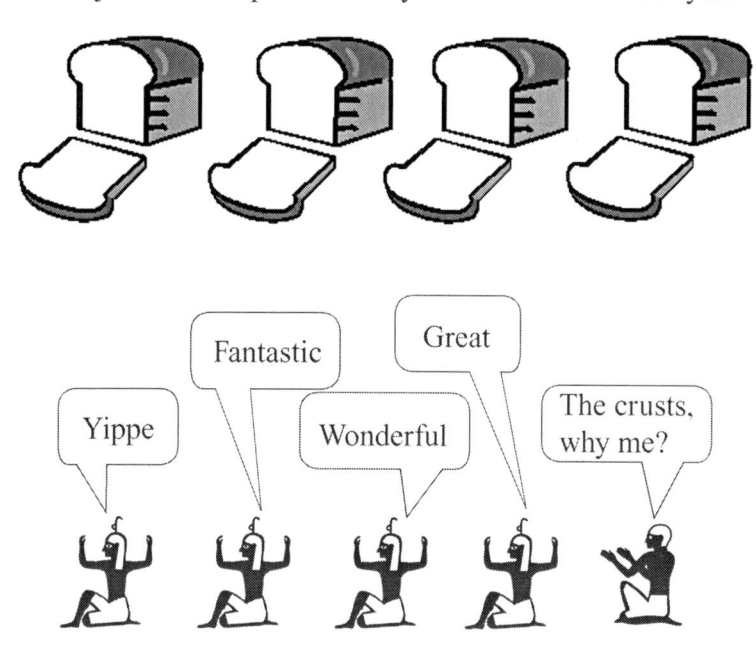

2.19.3 Work and Bread for All

Life for the ordinary people in ancient Egypt was quite fair compared to what people had to tolerate in other civilizations at the time. The pharaohs may have believed that it was their links with the gods that kept Egypt going, but in reality, it was the hard work of the general public.

Now you know why sliced bread was invented!

Ordinary people did the farming, mined the quarries, built the pyramids, and sailed the boats. Slavery was not very important in ancient Egypt, but it did exist. Most of the slaves were prisoners of war. They were soldiers that had been captured during the many wars that Egypt had fought with their neighbours in the Near East. Slaves were usually treated well and were allowed to own property. The ideas impressed on us by some film makers of thousands of slaves being whipped to death and crushed by heavy pyramid blocks is untrue.

The ancient Egyptians would have given each person three pieces of bread. Each of them would have been given a 1/2, 1/4 and a 1/20th of a loaf, which adds up to 4/5th. This way, not only does everyone get 4/5th of a loaf, but they all have the same-sized pieces.

Similarly, when we see an expression such as: (7/8) X, we think of 7X all divided by 8. If this represented a loaf, we would be back to sliced bread again. What the ancient Egyptians saw was, X—(1/8th)X, and this brings us back to unit fractions.

2.19.4 BREAKING DOWN FRACTIONS

Without getting involved in complex mathematical definitions, if we break down a single fraction into a number of equivalent unit fractions with different denominators, then these fractions are aliquot fractions.

Bearing in mind that the ancient Egyptians only used two fractions which were not unit fractions (2/3 and 3/4), aliquot fractions were very important to them. The aliquot fractions for 3/4 are 1/2 + 1/4, for 3/11 they are 1/6 + 1/11 + 1/66. Using trial and error to work out the series of some aliquot fractions could take a very long time. So how did the ancient Egyptians do it?

Again, they relied very heavily on pre-prepared tables, but they also had a system for calculating them which was discovered in the ancient Rhind Papyrus.

Multiplying anything by 1 remains unchanged. Therefore, any fraction multiplied by say, 4/4, 12/12, 24/24 or 56/56 will also remain unchanged, as these fractions also equal 1.

As it happens, the fraction 56/56 is very useful because 56 is a very divisible number. It can be divided by 28, 14, 8, 7, 4, 2 and 1. Let us consider two problems and their solutions from the Rhind Papyrus, which were actually both part of the same problem.

The first part required the conversion of 2/97 to aliquot fractions, to help break this fraction down 56/56 was used.

$2/97 \times 56/56 = 112 / (97 \times 56) = (97 + 8 + 7) / (97 \times 56)$

$2/97 = 97/ (97 \times 56) + 8/ (97 \times 56) + 7/ (97 \times 56)$

$2/97 = 1/56 + 1/ (97 \times 7) + 1/ (97 \times 8)$

$2/97 = 1/56 + 1/679 + 1/776$

The second part required the conversion of 26/97 to aliquot fractions, to help break this fraction down 4/4 was used.

$26/97 \times 4/4 = 104/ (4 \times 97) = (97 + 4 + 2 + 1)/ (4 \times 97)$

$26/97 = 97/(4 \times 97) + 4/(4 \times 97) + 2/(4 \times 97) + 1/(4 \times 97)$

$26/97 = 1/4 + 1/97 + 1/(2 \times 97) + 1/(4 \times 97)$

$26/97 = 1/4 + 1/97 + 1/194 + 1/388$

The initial problem required the scribe to convert 28/97 into a single aliquot series. In his wisdom he decided to split the original fraction into 26/97 and 2/97 then work on each.
Thus providing as a final solution:

$28/97 = 1/4 + 1/56 + 1/97 + 1/194 + 1/388 + 1/679 + 1/776$

Was this terrifying or what? Answers on a scroll please, care of Aahmes, Chief Scribe, Amun Temple, Karnak, Upper Egypt.

2.20.0 CALCULATING AREAS OF GEOMETRIC SHAPES

2.20.1 AREA OF A SQUARE OR RECTANGLE

As we have seen earlier, the scribes could accurately calculate different areas of land. To measure the areas of rectangles or squares, they did it the same way as we would today, by using the formula $\{A = B \times H\}$, where (A) is the area, (B) is the breadth and (H) is the height. Let us consider a simple problem from the Rhind Papyrus; a field of 10 Rods by 2 Rods. Remember that a Rod (Khet) equals 100 Cubits in length. Therefore we have an area of 1000 by 200 Cubits.

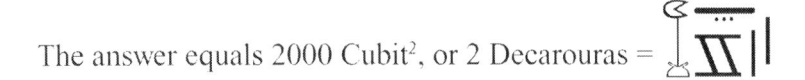

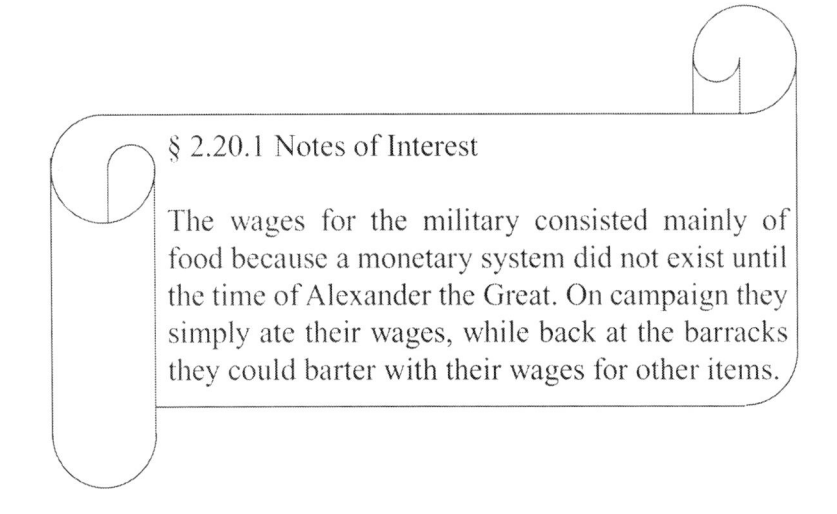

Find   a field   of   10 Rods by 2 Rods =2000 Cubits²

The answer equals 2000 Cubit², or 2 Decarouras =

§ 2.20.1 Notes of Interest

The wages for the military consisted mainly of food because a monetary system did not exist until the time of Alexander the Great. On campaign they simply ate their wages, while back at the barracks they could barter with their wages for other items.

2.20.2 Area of a Triangle

The ancient Egyptians used the same formula as we do for calculating the area of a triangle and that was {A = 1/2 B x H}. Where (A) is the area, (B) is the base and (H) is the height. This formula works equally well for all triangles even if they are not right-angled triangles.

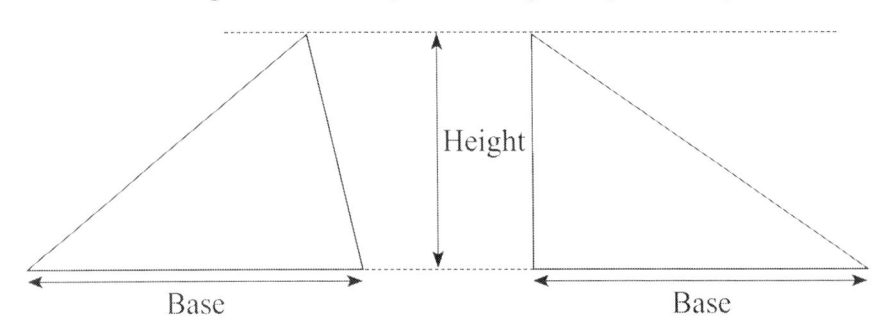

For a triangle of base ⟦hieroglyph⟧ (1 Foot = 4 Palms) and length of slope ⟦hieroglyph⟧ (1 Remen = 5 Palms), what is its area? As this is a sacred triangle, the height must be equal to:

⟦hieroglyph⟧ (1 Span = 3 Palms).

Area = 1/2 x 4 x 3 = 6 Square Palms

2.20.3 AREA OF A CIRCLE

The formula used by today's mathematicians for calculating the area (A) of a circle is $\{A = \pi R^2\}$ or $\{A = \pi (D/2)^2\}$, which translate into the same formulas when (R) is the radius and (D) is the diameter of a circle.

One of the formulas that the ancient Egyptians used for calculating the area (A) of a circle was $\{A = (8D/9)^2\}$, where (D) is the diameter of the circle. From this formula, it can be derived that the Egyptian scribes were using a ratio of 256/81 which is very close to 22/7, the approximation that we use for (pi) π today.

2.20.3.1 THE RHIND PAPYRUS PROBLEM 50

In the ancient Rhind Mathematical Papyrus, there is an example of a calculation for the area of a circle with a diameter of 9 Khets (⟦hieroglyph⟧). Using the formula $\{A = (8D/9)^2\}$, we will now show how the scribe produced his answer.

$$(D—(1/9) D) \times (D—(1/9) D) = A$$

Substituting 9 for the diameter we have:

$$(9—(1)) \times (9—(1)) = A$$

$$(8) \times (8) = A$$

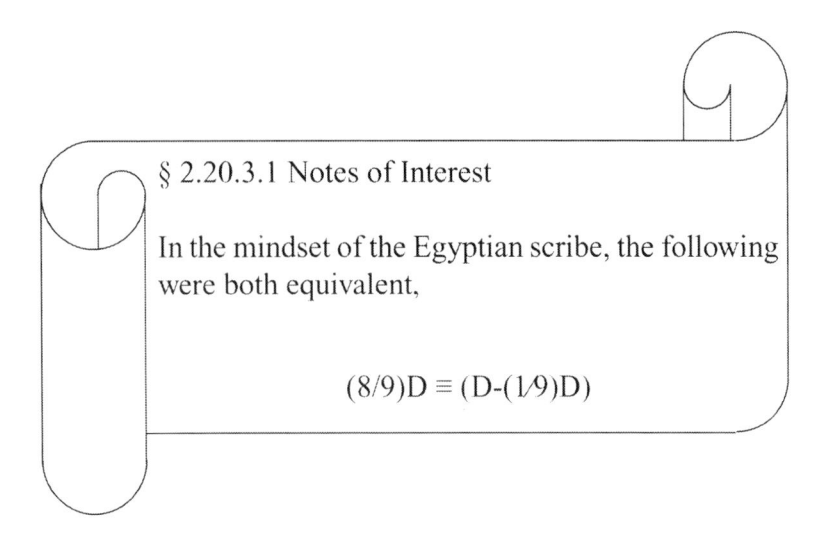

> § 2.20.3.1 Notes of Interest
>
> In the mindset of the Egyptian scribe, the following were both equivalent,
>
> $$(8/9)D \equiv (D-(1/9)D)$$

Similar to table usage demonstrated earlier, the scribe sets up a table to multiply 8 by 8:

Multiplier (8)	Multiplicand (8)
1	8
2	16
4	32
8	64

Starting at 1 in the first column, the multiplier column, each number is doubled repeatedly producing a binary sequence down the column. The sequence is stopped when the value doubled equals the multiplier or the next doubled number exceeds the multiplier. The second column is doubled up like the first, except it starts with the multiplicand and finishes level where the column ends in the multiplier column.

Multiplier (8)	Multiplicand (8)
1	8
2	~~16~~
4	~~32~~
8	64

Items in the multiplier column are retained that add up to the multiplier, the rest are crossed out including the corresponding items in the multiplicand column.

Thus the area equals 64 Square Khets or 64 Setats (𓊧𓏪𓏤𓏤𓏤𓏤).

2.20.4 AREA OF A HEMISPHERE

Problem 10 from the Moscow Mathematical Papyrus asks for a calculation which we must assume is of the surface area of a hemisphere.

The text of problem 10 approximates to the following:

> *Example of calculating a basket. You are given a basket with a mouth of 4 ½. What is its surface area? Take 1/9 of 9 since the basket is shaped like half an egg-shell; you get 1. Calculate the remainder, which is 8. Calculate 1/9 of 8 and you get 2/3 + 1/6 + 1/18. Find the remainder of this 8 after subtracting 2/3 + 1/6 + 1/18 and you get 7 + 1/9. Multiply 7 + 1/9 by 4 + ½ and you get 32. Behold this is its area, you have found it correctly.*

The solution amounts to the following expression:

$$Area = 2 \times \left(\frac{8}{9}\right) \times (diameter)^2 = 2 \times \frac{256}{81} (radius)^2$$

Modern mathematicians would use the formula of 2 pi r² to calculate the surface area of a hemisphere. If we substitute 22/7 as an approximation for pi and take 4 ½ as the diameter, we get a result of 31.82. The scribe's answer of 32 is very close to our answer of 31.82.

2.21.0 CALCULATING VOLUMES

2.21.1 JARS USED FOR VOLUME

The ancient Egyptians were a very practical-minded race. They obviously visualized the volume of something more easily if it were seen as a volume of sand or a liquid poured into measuring jars. This probably explains why specific hieroglyphs or other symbols have not yet been found that represent the Cubic Cubit. Before any answer in a calculation appears in the form of Cubic Cubits, the result is usually converted to a unit such as the Khar.

The hieroglyphs for Khar are

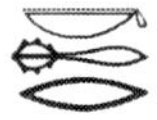

2.21.2 VOLUME OF A BLOCK

The ancient scribes used the same formula as modern day mathematicians to calculate the volume of a cuboid. That is {V = L x W x H} where (V) is the volume, (L) is the length, (W) is the width and (H) is the height.

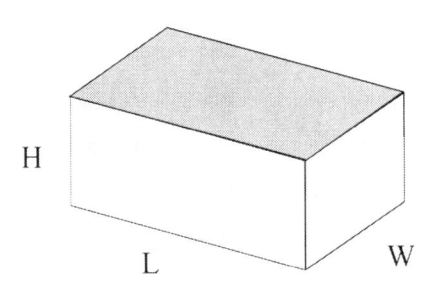

§ 2.21.2 Notes of Interest

Maat or Ma'at was the ancient Egyptian concept of truth, balance, order, law, morality, and justice. Maat was personified as the goddess Maat. She regulated the stars, seasons, and the actions of both mortals and deities; at the moment of creation, she set the order in the universe. It was believed that if Maat didn't exist, the universe would become chaos, once again!

Her name in ancient Egyptian literally meant 'truth'. The Goddess Maat was harmony; she was what was right and what things should be.

The primary duty of the pharaoh was to uphold Maat and retain this order by maintaining the law and administering justice. To reflect this, many pharaohs took the title 'Beloved of Maat', emphasizing their focus on justice and truth.

2.21.3 VOLUME OF A CYLINDER

In the ancient Rhind Mathematical Papyrus there is a problem which involves the volume of a cylindrical grain store, which has a height (H) of 6 Cubits and a diameter (D) of 8 Cubits. The method that the scribe chose to solve the problem is exactly the same as we would have used today, that is, {V = A x H}. (V) is the volume of the cylinder, (A) is the area of the circular base and (H) is the height of the cylinder.

When distributing grain, the scribes preferred to use their jar measures instead of working with Cubic Cubits. The main reason behind this was one of practical convenience. Therefore, when the volume of grain was in Cubic Cubits, the scribes multiplied this volume by 1½; this was the conversion factor to units of Khar, a jar measure.

Coming back to the main problem, the scribe performed his calculation as follows:

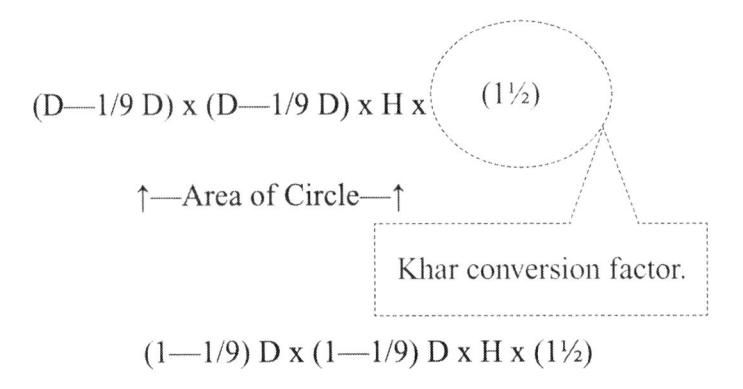

(D—1/9 D) x (D—1/9 D) x H x (1½)

↑—Area of Circle—↑

Khar conversion factor.

(1—1/9) D x (1—1/9) D x H x (1½)

Due to the fact that (1—1/9) was such a commonly used fraction i.e. 8/9, the scribe would probably have been able to transcribe it into its aliquot fractions quite easily. If not, he would have resorted to his tables. This would have provided the following:

(2/3+1/6+1/18) D x (2/3+ 1/6+1/18) D x H x (1½)

Remember, 2/3 was the only non-unitary proper fraction available besides 3/4.

For the majority of their calculations, the scribes appeared to be quite clever sometimes bordering on the genius, at manipulating their formulas. They added and removed factors in order to simplify the arithmetic, but at the same time keeping the equations balanced. We apply the same rule today, 'what you do to one side, you must do to the other.'

This meant that the scribe could take the calculation down a number of different routes, depending upon the nature of the numbers and fractions involved. Some of these approaches to a solution he used certainly appear obscure to us, but after a bit of 'Egyptian magic' the scribe is left with:

$$(2/3+1/6+1/18) \text{ D} \times (1½) \times (2/3+1/6+1/18) \text{ D} \times (1½) \text{ H} \div 1½$$

These extra 1½ values cancel out.

Now comes the tricky part, the scribe multiplies (2/3+1/6+1/18) by (1½).

The scribe would probably have completed the following table in his head, but he could have used his reference tables if he needed to.

1	2/3	1/6	1/18
½	1/3	1/12	1/36
Total =1	1	1/4	1/12

$$(1 + ⅓) \times \text{D} \times (1 + ⅓) \times \text{D} \times \text{H} \div (1½)$$

Division by 1½ was very common; therefore the scribe would have had no difficulty in recognising this as a multiplication by ⅔.

Substituting our dimensions into the equation, we get:

$$(1 + ⅓) \times 8 \times (1 + ⅓) \times 8 \times 6 \times (⅔)$$

$$(8 + 8 \times ⅓) \times (8 + 8 \times ⅓) \times 6 \times (⅔)$$

$$(10+⅔) \times (10+⅔) \times 4 = (40+2⅔) \times (10+⅔)$$

$$= (42+⅔) \times (10+⅔)$$

Multiplying 42 by 10 would have been very easy for the scribe. All they had to do was substitute all the hieroglyphs in the number by their next highest ranking hieroglyph.

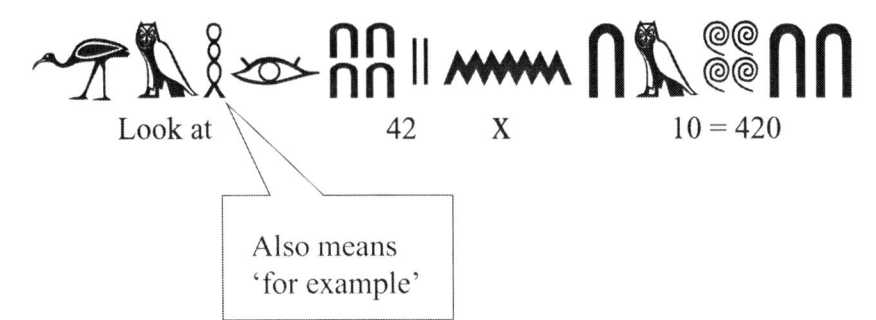

Look at   42   X   10 = 420

Also means 'for example'

§ 2.21.3 Notes of Interest

The way in which the ancient Egyptians recorded the dates of events can be very confusing to us. This is because their dates were based upon the time that the current king reigned, they worked in regnal years. For example, they might say that they were at war with someone from year 3 of Ramses II to year 3 of Merenptah.

Manetho, an ancient Egyptian historian and priest from the third century BC, devised the 'Dynastic System' of dating that is still in use today after a few corrections. He divided the kings of Egypt into 31 dynasties, subdivided into three 'Main Kingdoms' with turbulent 'Intermediate' periods between them.

Of course, the product of 42 and 10 could be worked out by the traditional table method:

Multi-plier (42)	Multi-plicand (10)
1	~~10~~
2 ✓	20 ✓
4	~~40~~
8 ✓	80 ✓
16	~~160~~
32 ✓	320 ✓
42	420

As the conversion factor was applied earlier, the answer will be in Khars:

	(42)	(2/3)	
(10)	420	6 2/3	
(2/3)	28	1/3	1/9

Multiplier (10)	Multiplicand (2/3)
1	~~2/3~~
2 ✓	1 1/3 ✓
-4-	~~2 2/3~~
8 ✓	5 1/3 ✓
10	6 2/3

Multiplier (42)	Multiplicand (2/3)
1	~~2/3~~
2 ✓	1 1/3 ✓
-4-	~~2 2/3~~
8 ✓	5 1/3 ✓
16	~~10 2/3~~
32 ✓	21 1/3 ✓
42	28

The scribe would probably have worked out in his head that the product of 10 and ⅔ was 6⅔ and the product of 42 and ⅔ was 28.

Multiplying the fraction ⅔ by ⅔ to produce 1/3 and 1/9 would probably have already been known to the scribe, as this calculation crops up frequently in mathematical papyri. As with this calculation and all preceding calculations, reference tables could always be relied upon. For the novice or student scribe, reference tables were probably a necessity.

$$(42 + \tfrac{2}{3})(10 + \tfrac{2}{3}) = 420 + 28 + 6 + (\tfrac{2}{3}) + (\tfrac{1}{3}) + (1/9)$$

| = | 455 | 1/9 Khars |

2.21.4 Volume of a Pyramid

The ancient Egyptians built square-based pyramids which took a lifetime to construct. As the pyramids were built in horizontal layers, the architects would have needed to find the volume of incomplete pyramids more frequently than finished ones.

A frustum of a pyramid is an incomplete pyramid or rather a pyramid with the top sliced off. In fact, you can have a frustum of lots of different solids such as cones and those which have exotic polygons for bases.

There is no doubt that the Egyptian scribes and architects were highly skilled at calculating the volume of massive pyramids. They used one of the same formulas that we use today. This formula for the volume of a square-based pyramid is basically the area of the base times the height, times ⅓. This is basically the volume of a cuboid, times 1/3. The formula for this is as follows $\{V = \tfrac{1}{3} \times H \times W^2\}$, where (V) is the volume, (H) is the height of the pyramid and (W^2) is the width of the base squared.

2.21.5 Volume of a Frustum

Keeping check of the volume of stone that had gone into each stage of the building of a pyramid must have been a frequent requirement. Each time a successive layer of stone was added to the last, there was a potential need to perform another volume of a frustum calculation.

Hieroglyphs and Arithmetic of the Ancient Egyptian Scribes   195

We will now look at a problem and solution taken from the Ancient Moscow Mathematical Papyrus about a frustum. This will give us a better understanding of the mindset of the scribe rather than concentrate on an ordinary pyramid.

One way in which we would calculate the volume of a frustum today is by calculating the volume of the complete pyramid first. Then subtract from this volume, the volume of the smaller missing pyramid.

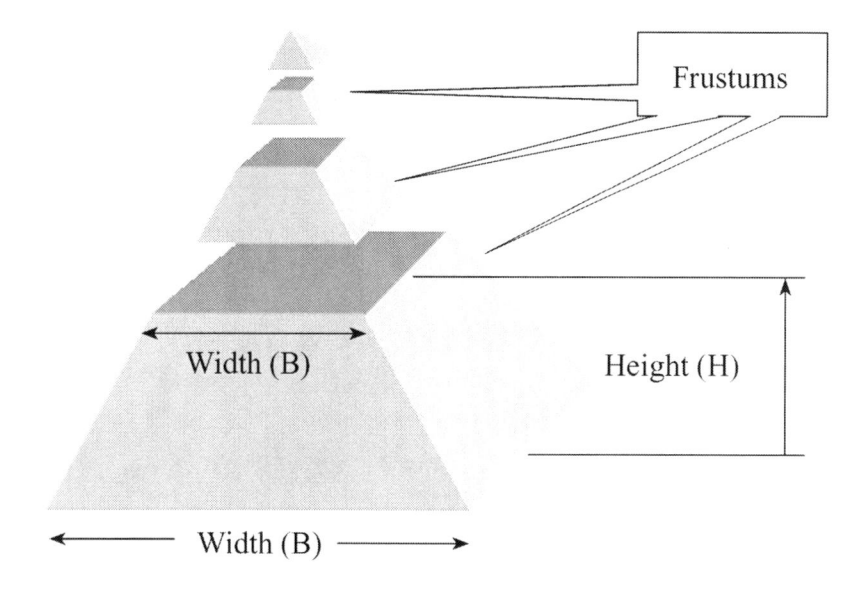

In the ancient Moscow Mathematical Papyrus, the scribe uses an alternative formula which we also use today:

$$\{V = 1/3\ H\ (A^2 + AB + B^2)\}$$

Where (V) is the volume of the frustum, (H) is the height of the frustum, (A) is the width of the base and (B) is the width of the top of the frustum.

Where does the ⅓ come from you may ask? It doesn't matter whether you are dealing with pyramids or cones; their volume is either ⅓ of the cuboid shape for a pyramid with the same base area as the cuboid, or ⅓ of the cylinder shape for a cone with the same base area as the cylinder.

> § 2.21.5 Notes of Interest
>
> The first ancient Egyptian pyramid was built at Saqqara in about 2650 BC. It was a stepped pyramid without continuous smooth sides. In theory, it was a series of separate frustums of decreasing size placed on top of each other. It has been estimated that the manual labour was provided by about 100,000 unskilled workers. These people, who were not slaves, had to offer their services each year when the flooding of the Nile prevented them from working in the fields.

2.21.5.1 How was the Frustum Formula Derived?

How the scribes arrived at this formula is not known. They may have found the formula by physically measuring existing pyramids and manipulating the numbers. They may have created models of hollow pyramids and measured the volume of sand they could contain. It is even possible that they were cleverer than we thought and they derived the formula using a brush and papyrus. They certainly had plenty of time to ponder on such things and get it right! For sufferers of insomnia, a modern derivation can be studied later.

2.21.5.2 The Moscow Papyrus Frustum Problem

The problem in the papyrus describes the frustum as 6 Cubits high with a base of 4 Cubits wide and a top of 2 Cubits wide. This would make a small complete pyramid of only 12 Cubits in height, but the figures are easy for the scribe without the need for tables.

Nevertheless, it is the principle that is important as follows:

Volume of Frustum = 1/3 x 6((4 x 4)+(4 x 2)+(2 x 2))

Volume of Frustum = 2 ((16) + (8) + (4))

= 56 Cubic Cubits

Well, that wasn't too painful. Would you like to now see how the formula is derived? If you skip this next part, no one would blame you.

2.21.5.3 Modern Derivation of Frustum Formula

First, a little bit about similar triangles. For the triangle below:

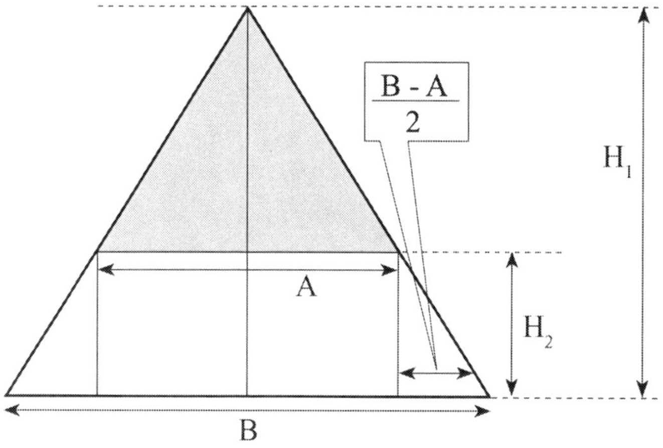
B - A
2
H_1
A
H_2
B

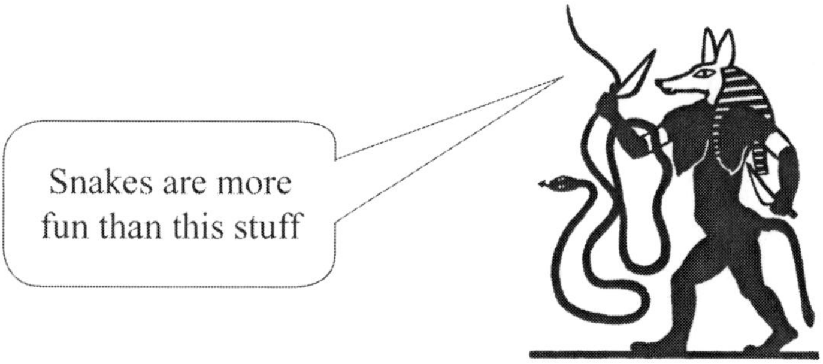
Snakes are more fun than this stuff

$$\frac{(H_1)}{(B)} = \frac{(H_1 - H_2)}{(A)} = \frac{(H_2)}{(B - A)}$$

$$(H_1)(A) = (H_1)(B) - (H_2)(B)$$

$$H_2 B = H_1(B - A)$$

$$\frac{H_2}{(B - A)} = \frac{(H_1)}{B}$$

Do you like my new hat?

$$\frac{H_1}{B} = \frac{H_1 - H_2}{A}$$

$$\therefore H_1 = \frac{H_2 B}{B - A}$$

$$\therefore H_1 - H_2 = \frac{H_2 A}{B - A}$$

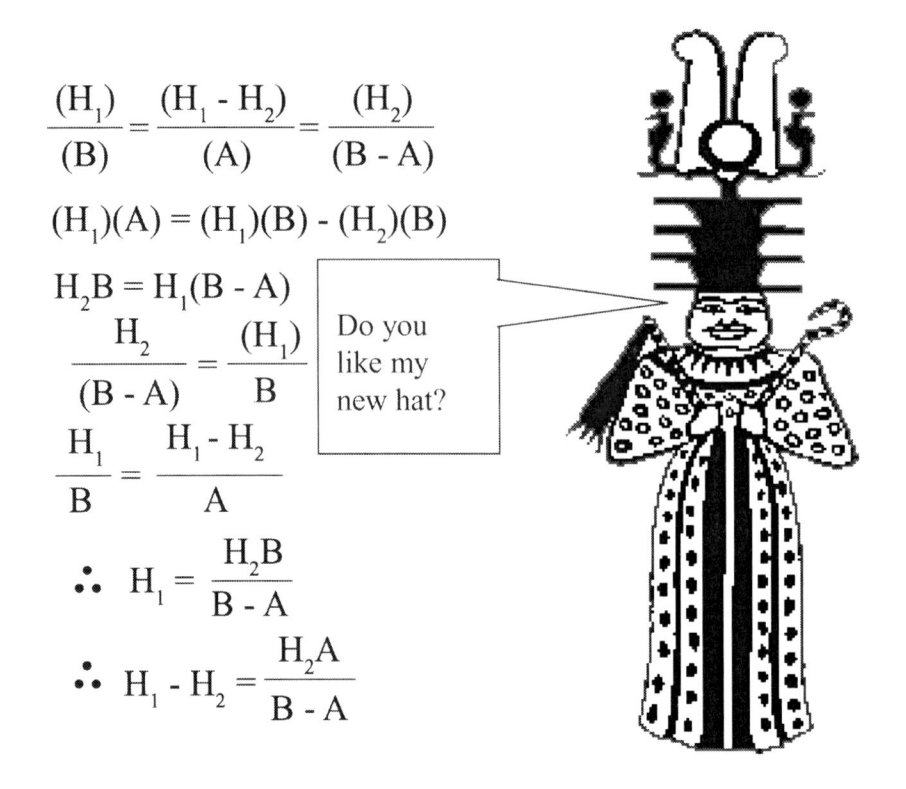

Volume of the Frustum above:

$$= \frac{1}{3} B^2 \times (H_1) - \frac{1}{3} A^2 \times (H_1 - H_2)$$

After some substitution, using: $H_1 = \dfrac{H_2 B}{B - A}$ and $H_1 - H_2 = \dfrac{H_2 A}{B - A}$

Volume of Frustum (V_F)

$$= \left(\frac{1}{3} B^2 \times \frac{(H_2 B)}{(B - A)}\right) - \left(\frac{1}{3} A^2 \times \frac{H_2 A}{B - A}\right)$$

Time for a sleep

$$V_F = \frac{1}{3} H_2 \left(\frac{(B^2 B)}{(B-A)} \right) - \left(\frac{(A^2 A)}{(B-A)} \right)$$

$$V_F = \frac{1}{3} H_2 \left(\frac{(B^3)}{(B-A)} \right) - \left(\frac{(A^3)}{(B-A)} \right) = \frac{1}{3} H_2 \left(\frac{(B^3 - A^3)}{(B-A)} \right)$$

$(B^3 - A^3)$ Factorizes as:

$$(B^3 - A^3) = (B-A)(A^2 + AB + B^2)$$

Therefore the formula for the volume of a frustum is:

$$V_F = \frac{1}{3} H_2 \left(\frac{(B-A)(A^2 + AB + B^2)}{(B-A)} \right)$$

$$V_F = \frac{1}{3} H_2 (A^2 + AB + B^2)$$

§ 2.21.5.3 Notes of Interest

King Akhenaten (1350–1333 BC) decided to change the religion of ancient Egypt from the worship of hundreds of gods to just two. The supreme god was the Aten or sun disc, only Akhenaten and the royal family were allowed to worship the sun god. Guess, who was the other god? Akhenaten of course, he raised himself to the full rank and status of a proper god, more divine than any other king. Everyone else except for the royal family had to worship "Old Arky". He was born under the name of Amenhotep and only later changed it to Akhenaten, meaning "Spirit of the Aten", in devotion to the sun god. From the evidence we have, it is strongly agreed that Tutankhamun was his son. Tutankhamun during his rule restored all the changes his father made!

2.22.0 Algebraic Mathematics

2.22.1 Algebra Origins

In its simplest terms, algebra is about finding an unknown quantity or putting real-life problems into equations and then solving them. Algebra allows the finding of unknown numbers from information that is supplied.

It is a system whereby letters are used to represent variables. These

variables such as X and Y are substitutes for numbers which represent unknown quantities at that instance. The unknowns become tangible when the equation is solved; if the equation can be solved. As a *defacto*

standard, X is nearly always used to represent the unknown quantity but any letter can be used. The numbers in equations are the constants.

An algebraic equation can be thought of as a set of weighing scales; to maintain equal balance. What is done on one side of the scale with a number or variable must also be done to the other side.

§ 2.22.1 Notes of Interest

The word 'algebra' comes from the book title 'aljebr w' almuqabala', written by the ninth-century Arabian mathematician Al Khowarizmi. The word al-jebr meant transposing a quantity from one side of an equation to another or bringing together broken parts. Muqabala meant simplification of the resulting expression.

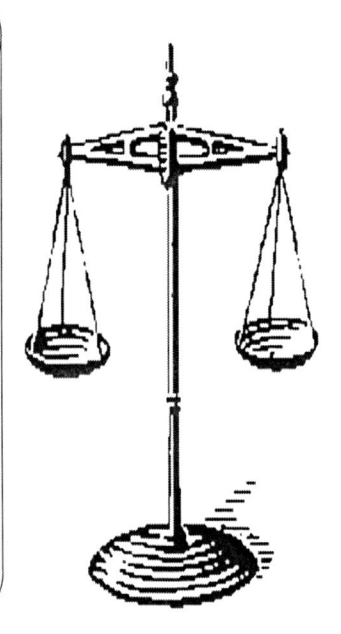

Algebra even in ancient times involved the application of a series of techniques, including reductions, simplifications, transpositions, which manipulated mathematical expressions. The reason algebra became so powerful was because the resulting expressions applied to a large number of cases. Arithmetic, on the other hand, dealt with and applied to one case at a time.

2.22.2 DEGREE OF AN EQUATION

Algebraic equations are categorized by their complexity. The higher the degree of an equation, the greater is its complexity. For a particular variable in an equation, the degree is determined by the numerical size of the exponent, or the highest power to which that variable is raised. A variable not raised to any power is recognized as having an exponent of value 1, as seen opposite... $x = x^1$

2.22.3 FIRST-DEGREE EQUATIONS

A first-degree equation is often a linear equation. The highest exponent of a linear equation is 1. The following are typical linear equations, since X is raised only to the first power:

$$10x - 4 = 2x \qquad 8 + 3x + 5x = 44$$
$$3x + 7 = 32 \qquad 7x + 3x = 19x - 12$$

They are also quite easy to solve.

2.22.4 SECOND-DEGREE EQUATIONS

Second-degree equations contain at least one variable with an exponent of 2 but not higher. Examples of second degree equations are: $y = 2x2 - 3x + 2$

$$5x^2 - 2x + 1 = 0 \qquad 56x^2 - 9 = 3$$
$$7x^2 + 6 - 3x^2 + 13 - 4x = 25$$

2.22.5 THIRD-DEGREE EQUATIONS AND HIGHER

Third-degree equations may look like the following:

$$2x^3 + x = 78 \qquad 4x^3 - 7x^2 = 0$$
$$12x^3 = 144 \qquad y = x^3 - x^2 + x - 4$$

A tenth-degree equation would contain one or more variables where their highest exponent was 10 such as:

$$6x^{10} - 3x^6 = 598$$

If the highest exponent were 50, we would have a fiftieth-degree equation, and so on.

2.22.6 EXCEPTIONS TO THE DEGREE RULE

There is one exception to this degree rule and this is when an equation contains different variables which are multiplied together. When more than one variable appears in an equation such as in the example opposite, it is necessary to add the exponents of the variables within a term to find out the degree of the equation.

$$xy = 5$$

The sum of the exponents for $x^1y^1 = 5$ are 2, therefore this equation is a second-degree equation.

This equation $3y + 9x = 21$ is only a first-degree equation because the variables are not multiplied together.

2.22.7 A PRACTICAL EXAMPLE OF DEGREE RULE

An example of a simple problem would be a man carrying a quantity of apples. If he dropped 7 and was left holding 2, how many did he start with?

This teaser is an example of a first-degree algebraic equation. In algebraic terms, it would look like the following:

$$x - 7 = 2$$

The X replaces the unknown that we are trying to find out. We know that 7 apples were dropped and we know that the man was left with 2 apples.

The goal in algebra is to find out the unknown. As the unknown is X, then we try to isolate X and end up with X on its own being equal to something by manipulating the variables and numbers.

As mentioned earlier, using the equals sign, when applying the rules of algebra, is like treating the equals sign as a set of balancing scales. Any processes we apply to one side of the equation, one side of the equals sign, to isolate X, we must apply to the other side of the equals sign.

To isolate X in the equation, we need to add 7 to the left side of the equals sign and add 7 to the right side of the equals sign. The whole computation is as follows:

$$x - 7 = 2 \qquad x - 7 + 7 = 2 + 7$$

Therefore $X = 9$

Suppose, I wanted to solve for X in the following second-degree equation:

$$x^2 - 4 = 0$$

By adding 4 to each side of the equation above, we quickly obtain a much clearer expression, one that can be solved quite easily:

$$x^2 - 4 + 4 = 0 + 4$$
$$x^2 = 4 \ x(times)x = 4$$

We all know that 2 times 2 equals 4.

> § 2.22.7 Notes of Interest
>
> The ancient Egyptians were polytheists, which means they worshiped not a single god but a vast array from which they could pick and choose. Surprisingly, common people took almost no part in religious rituals which was the sacred responsibility of the priestly class.

2.22.8 Types of Ancient Egyptian Mathematical Problems

Throughout all the ancient mathematical papyri, there are five distinctive types of problem:

- Aha problems which deal directly with unknown quantities.
- Ship's Part Problems include such calculations as working out the length of a ships rudder and the length of masts.
- Pefsu problems relate to the strength of bread and beer made from a hekat of grain.
- Baku Problems calculate the output of workers based on materials used or moved.
- Geometry problems include finding angles, distances and lengths, areas of polygons, areas of circles, and curved surfaces. These problems also include more complex calculations involving the volumes of three-dimensional structures.

All of the following problems used as examples below are accompanied by the scribes own suggested methods of approach and there solutions. It must be remembered that the amount of information that would be provided to the student who has to tackle a given problem would be entirely at the discretion of the scribe.

Except for geometry-type problems, which have already been dealt with, the remaining categories of problem listed above will be explained in greater detail later. All of the problems can be expressed in some sort of algebraic terms, from the very basic to various levels of complexity.

The problems in the Moscow Papyrus follow no particular order, and the solutions of the problems provide much less detail than those in the Rhind Mathematical Papyrus. Both these papyri provide a valuable source for a wide range of mathematical problems. A third ancient Egyptian text, the Berlin Papyrus, dating from 1800 BC was discovered at Saqqara in the early 19th century. The Berlin papyrus although containing less mathematical content than the Rhind and Moscow papyri, was the first Egyptian mathematical text to be studied in the modern era.

The Moscow Papyrus was not only a primary source of ancient Egyptian mathematical knowledge, but also a source of medical knowledge.

The papyrus included some important mathematical information, such as solutions to two second-degree algebraic equations and two problems that solve simultaneous equations.

§ 2.22.8 Notes of Interest

We have good evidence of how the ancient Egyptians decorated the walls in temples, tombs, and the like. First the stone wall was rubbed smooth with blocks of sandstone. If the wall was cracked or pitted, it was made flat with a coating of straw and mud. A final coat of gesso was added, a mixture of gypsum, and glue; this provided a smooth surface that held the paint well.

Strings coated with red ochre were then stretched and snapped against the wall, like a modern day chalk line; allowing an accurate grid to be drawn. This grid ensured that the figures could be created in the exact proportions in adherence to Egyptian principles of art.

Then a team of master draftsmen drew the outlines of figures and scenes in red. If the walls were to be raised in bas relief, carvers next cut away the background, so that the figures stood out away from the surface. Fine details were then cut into the figure outlines by another team of craftsmen.

Painters did their job next by filling in the figures with solid colours, and master painters went over the work and corrected any mistakes with black outlines. In many cases, a final protective coating of beeswax or resin was applied to the artwork like a varnish to seal the work surface.

2.22.9 Aha Problems

There are a group of ancient Egyptian mathematical problems called the 'aha problems', that are the precursor to algebra. 'Aha' in ancient Egyptian means 'something' or 'a quantity'. Whenever a problem called for an unknown, the ancient Egyptians would simply call it 'aha'.

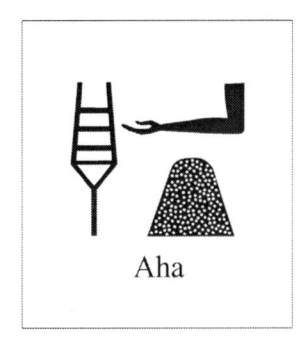

These hieroglyphs to the left, say 'Aha', meaning 'something'. In modern day terms, we would call this the unknown quantity or variable, probably denoted by the letter X.

Aha problems involve finding unknown quantities when the sum of the quantity and its parts are given. The Rhind and the Moscow Mathematical Papyri both contain a selection of Aha problems.

The problems were not expressed in modern algebraic notation as we would recognize today but instead written in longhand, in the format of a word problem. As you can imagine, translating ancient Egyptian mathematical text is difficult enough without the added complexity of unravelling what may seem like ancient riddles. Some Egyptologists today, still cannot agree with each other on the translation of some problems, particularly where parts of a papyrus are missing or damaged.

For example, one of the simpler aha problems, problem 19, taken from the Moscow Mathematical papyrus asks the student scribe to calculate a quantity taken 1 and ½ times and added to 4 to make 10. In modern algebraic notation, this would read as:

$$x + \frac{x}{2} + 4 = 10$$

2.22.10 The Hundred Loaf Problem

Problem 40 from the Rhind Mathematical papyrus is a lot more complex. The problem is basically about finding the difference between the terms in an arithmetic progression; this means finding the difference between each number in a series of numbers. Unfortunately for the student, as if the mathematics is not hard enough, the problem seems to be set within some sort of riddle. This format is typical of many problems set for the student. Allowing for a little poetic licence on translation to make the problem readable, the scribe writes:

> *Divide 100 loaves among 5 men in such a way that the shares received will be in arithmetical progression, and that 1/7 of the sum of the largest three shares, is equal to the sum of the smallest two. What is the common excess or difference of the shares?*

This problem begins with two unknowns; the *smallest-share* X and the *difference* Y. As these variables are not raised to any powers higher than 1 and they are not both part of the same term, i.e. XY or multiplied together, this problem is still a linear or first-degree set of equations. In modern day algebra, we would class this problem as one of simultaneous equations, because two equations are needed to find the unknowns.

We can write the shares received by the five men as:

Man N° 1: *smallest—share* (X)
Man N° 2: *smallest—share + difference* (X + Y)
Man N° 3: *smallest—share + 2 differences* (X + 2Y)
Man N° 4: *smallest—share + 3 differences* (X + 3Y)
Man N° 5: *smallest—share + 4 differences* (X + 4Y)

After adding what each man receives, this provides us with our first linear equation for the pair of simultaneous equations:

5 times (*smallest—share*) + 10 times (*difference*) = 100

$$5x + 10y = 10$$

The sum of the three-largest shares is the share for Man N° 3, Man N° 4, and Man N° 5. This equals 3 *smallest—shares* + 9 *differences*:

Sum of 3 largest shares $= 3x + 9y = 10$

The sum of the two smallest shares is the share for Man Nº 1 plus Man Nº 2. This equals 2 *smallest—shares* + 1 *difference*:

Sum of the 2 smallest shares $= 2x + y$

The second condition specifies that the seventh part of the first expression is equal to the second expression, yielding:

$$\frac{1}{7}(3x + 9y) = 14x + 7y$$

We can now simplify the equation by multiplying both sides of the equation by 7 to produce:

$$(3x + 9y) = 14x + 7y$$
$$9y - 7y = 14x - 3x \qquad 2y = 11x$$

2 *differences* = 11 *smallest—shares*

Using traditional algebra, we would normally apply the standard methodology for solving simultaneous equations or substitute *2y = 11x* back into the equation *5x + 10y = 100* to remove one of the variables; either way we end up with numeric values for X and Y.

The problem is that the ancient Egyptians did not know how to solve these equations directly, but they still managed to get the correct answers. How was this possible?

Whenever an Egyptian scribe reached this point in a mathematical problem, he solved it by using a clever-guessing technique. This may seem a bit impractical or far fetched, but this method not only came close to being correct, it arrived at the right answer.

The Egyptian scribe would make a guess at the correct answer. This guess would probably be wrong, but he would use this erroneous answer, basically by trial and error to navigate towards the right answer. This process is known as 'False Position'.

2.22.11 False Position

All of the aha and most other types of mathematical problems described by ancient Egyptian scribes can be expressed in modern algebraic form. Although, the methodologies the ancient Egyptian Scribes adopted for solving these brain teasers may seem to us as a problem in themselves.

Throughout the mathematical papyri and leather scrolls etc, the scribes had a wide choice of techniques available to them for manipulating numbers and variables. To help them solve mathematical problems, they could use duplication, halving, taking ⅔ and ⅓ of numbers, taking 10 times or 1/10th of numbers. Any or all of these techniques could be incorporated as part of an obscure-generic system called 'false position'.

False position is a rhetorical method for solving certain algebra problems.

The ancient Egyptians did not have the benefit of being able to represent quantities with variables exactly the same way as modern mathematicians do today, because they did not have symbolic notation. This is why they invented the technique called 'false position', as they say, 'Necessity is the mother of invention'.

False position begins by selecting a convenient answer or making an educated guess, one that makes the calculations of the problem simpler. It does not have to be the correct answer. After calculating the result from the convenient answer, a false position problem is solved by using the result to determine how to adjust the convenient answer to make it correct.

2.22.12 False Position Method of Computation

To try and explain the false position method of computation, let us consider the following example; a quantity and its 1/5th added together give 23. What is the quantity?

The solution using algebra would be quite simple; we would just need to evaluate in stages. Remember, what we do to one side of the equation we must do to the other, such as multiplying both sides by 5:

$$x + \frac{x}{5} = 23 \qquad (5)x + (5)\frac{x}{5} = (5)23$$
$$6x = 115 \qquad\qquad x = 19\frac{1}{6}$$

Using the method of false position to solve the equation looks a little bit more complex. We will demonstrate the solution in steps as follows:

Step 1: Suppose we guess at the quantity being 5. (5 is a good choice because we can work out a 1/5th of 5 in our heads).

Step 2: A 1/5th of 5 being 1, added to 5 gives 6.

$$5 + \frac{5}{5} = 6$$

Step 3: Now we have to do find out what to do to 6 that will change it to 23 and that would be, multiply by 23/6.

$$6 \times \frac{23}{6} = 23$$

Step 4: We then do the same to our original guess. Multiply 5 by 23/6 giving 115/6.

$$5 \times \frac{23}{6} = \frac{115}{6}$$

Step 5: The computation of 115/6 gives a result of 19 and 1/6th.

$$\frac{115}{6} = 19\frac{1}{6}$$

The ancient Egyptian Scribes certainly had no concept of any conventional modern techniques for solving equations, but they still managed to come up with the correct answers.

> § 2.22.12 Notes of Interest
>
> In these modern times, people that practice religion are expected to attend a church, temple, or mosque for participation in joint prayer, recitation of common beliefs, and practice of rituals. The lives of the ancient Egyptians were so filled with gods that they felt no need to set aside special times for praying together.
>
> Only on rare festival days might groups congregate outside a temple to witness a performance of holy rites. In the main, the business of religion for the commoners was conducted entirely by proxy. Only the priests were permitted inside temples, only they alone were allowed to perform rituals. Basically, just being a believer required no action whatsoever.

2.22.13 A Simple False Position Example

Problem 26 from the ancient Rhind mathematical papyrus is one of many good examples of the use of false position. The scribe states:

> *Find a quantity such that when it is added to a quarter of itself the result is 15.*

In algebraic terms this would look like: $x + \dfrac{x}{4} = 15$

It is a first-degree linear equation, so it is very easy to solve using algebra. We simply multiply both sides of the equation by 4 and juggle the numbers about until we isolate the X, or should we say (🝔).

For example; we start by multiplying both sides of the equation by 4 as follows:

$$x + \frac{x}{4} = 15 \qquad\qquad 4x + x = 60$$

$$5x = 60 \qquad\qquad \therefore x = 12$$

§ 2.22.13.1 Notes of Interest

$\therefore$ Means 'therefore'.

$\because$ Means 'because'.

$\approx$ Means 'approximately equal to' or 'similar to'.

$\neq$ Means 'not equal to'.

To use the method of false position, the scribe started by selecting a convenient answer.

His guess for the answer was to let X=4.

He probably chose 4 because he could see it would simplify his calculations.

$$4 + \frac{4}{4} \approx 15 \qquad\qquad 5 \approx 15$$

Next, he used the incorrect result to determine how to adjust his guess to home-in on the correct answer. He needed to do something to his first result of 5, to correct it to 15. By calculation, he realized the factor to multiply 5 by to get 15 was 3.

Therefore, by multiplying his original guess of 4, by the same factor of 3, he got the correct answer of X = 12.

$$12 + \frac{12}{4} = 15$$

> § 2.22.13.2 Notes of Interest
>
> Even though, the ancient Egyptians called hieroglyphs 'god's words', because they believed that the gods had invented writing and that it was sacred, they still managed to use swear words. From the walls of the tomb of the official Ti at Saqqara, around 2500 BC, a scene shows some boatmen fighting. One man in his boat is swinging a barge pole at the crew in the boat opposite. At the same time, he is saying, or more likely shouting with rage,
>
> 'Come here, you'
>
> No doubt you can work out a more accurate translation yourself! I will give you a clue, the word in hieroglyphs means copulate. The quail chick makes the term plural.

2.22.14 THE HUNDRED LOAF PROBLEM CONTINUED

To recap; the ancient Egyptian scribe was basically faced with two equations: $5x + 10y = 100$ $2y = 11x$

Where Y represents *differences* and X represents *smallest—share*

$$2 \text{ } differences = 11 \text{ } smallest\text{—}shares$$

Using the system of false position for the above problem, the scribe, Aahmes, needed to make a sensible guess to make life easy, although a ridiculous guess would still work. Bad guesses just make life more difficult.

In the text, Aahmes decided to try a convenient value of 11 for the *difference* Y. After inserting this guess into the equation, he noted that the *smallest—share* (X) was now equal to 2.

$$2y = 11x \quad 2(times)11 = 11x \quad \frac{22}{11} = x = 2$$

Plugging these values Y=11 and X=2 into the alternative equation, he was left with an incorrect answer of 120.

$$5x + 10y = 100$$
$$5(times)2 + 10(times)11 \approx 120$$

Aahmes realized this was an incorrect answer, 120 does not equal 100, so he proceeded to fine tune his first guess. His first answer may be wrong, but it was not too far out for a guess.

To reach the correct answer, Aahmes, the scribe, instructs his students as follows; *as many times as 120 must be multiplied to give 100, then so many times must 11 be multiplied to give the true difference in shares.*

What this means is, whatever you have to multiply 120 by to get a 100, multiply 11 by the same amount to get your answer.

If we multiply 120 by 100/120, we would get a 100. If we multiply 11 by 100/120, we get our answer:

$$(difference) = 11\left[\frac{100}{120}\right] = \frac{55}{6} = 9\frac{1}{6}$$

Substituting back into the equation 2Y = 11X to find the smallest share X, we get:

$$\frac{2}{11}y = x \qquad \left(\frac{2}{11}\right)\left(\frac{55}{6}\right) = x \qquad \frac{5}{3} = x$$

The fraction ⅔ was one of the few non-unit fractions the ancient Egyptians allowed themselves the benefit of. Therefore, they would have been quite happy with 1⅔ as the *smallest—share* for the correct answer.

If we double-check, we can confirm that our final answers are correct by inserting them into the following equation:

$$5x + 10y = 100 \qquad 5\left(\frac{5}{3}\right) + 10\left(\frac{55}{6}\right) = 100$$

I think all would agree that this was heavy going. Don't forget that it would have been even more difficult for the scribe, except for the fractions ⅔ and ¾ he could only work with unit fractions in particular, aliquot fractions. Below, we can see the unit fractions that would have had to be used instead of 2/11:

$$\frac{2}{11} = \frac{1}{11} + \frac{1}{22} + \frac{1}{33} + \frac{1}{66}$$

2.22.15 RHIND MATHEMATICAL PAPYRUS PROBLEM 24

The question states; *A quantity with ⅐ of it added to it becomes 19, what is the quantity?*

In algebraic terms this would look like the following:

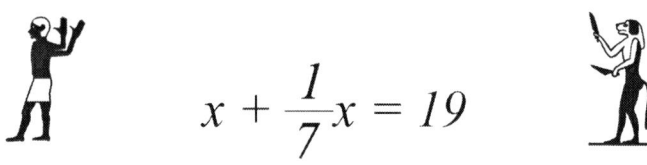

$$x + \frac{1}{7}x = 19$$

The Scribe assumes $X = 7$; $(7) + \frac{1}{7}(7) = 8$ and states that,

> *As many times as 8 must be multiplied to give 19, so many times 7 must be multiplied to give the required number.*

In the same way that many of us can recall our multiplication tables from memory, the ancient Egyptian Scribes would have remembered the results of many arithmetic calculations. The scribe would be able to recall from memory common multiplications and divisions of fractions and whole numbers. Anything that could not be remembered would be looked up in pre-prepared reference tables.

The following table prepared by the scribe show his workings to find what must be multiplied by 8 to produce 19.

Times by 8	Product	→	Times by 8	Product
2	16	→	2	16
1	8			
½	4			
¼	2	→	¼	2
⅛	1	→	⅛	1
			Total	19

The scribe tries to be very helpful by saying;

> *From these workings, it can now be seen that 2 + ¼ + ⅛ multiplied by 8 gives us 19. Therefore, 2 + ¼ + ⅛ multiplied by 7 will give us the value for X.*

The workings of the scribe in the following table provide this answer X.

1	Times (2 + ¼ + ⅛) =	2 + ¼ + ⅛
2	Times (2 + ¼ + ⅛) =	4 + ½ + ¼

218   DONALD FRAZER

| 4 | Times (2 + ¼ + ⅛) = | 8 + 1 + ½ |

| 7 | Times (2 + ¼ + ⅛) = | 16 + ½ + ⅛ |

Therefore X = 16 + ½ + ⅛.

The scribe finishes the problem with a proof; *Do it as follows; the quantity is 16 + ½ + ⅛ and its ¹/₇ is 2 + ¼ + ⅛. Hence the total is 19 as originally specified.*

2.22.16 RHIND MATHEMATICAL PAPYRUS PROBLEM 25

The question states; *A quantity with ½ of it added to it becomes 16. What is the quantity?*

In algebraic terms this would look like the following:

$$x + \frac{1}{2}x = 16$$

The scribe assumes $X = 2$. After substitution we find we have an incorrect result of 3.

$$(2) + \frac{(2)}{2} = 3 \neq 6$$

Remember, this means 'not equal to'

The scribe states, *as many times as 3 must be multiplied to give 16, so many times 2 must be multiplied to give the required number.*

The following table prepared by the scribe shows his workings to find what must be multiplied by 3 to produce 16.

Times by 3	Product	→	Times by 3	Product
4	12	→	4	12
2	6			
1	3	→	1	3
⅔	2			
⅓	1	→	⅓	1
			Total	16

From these workings, it can now be seen that 4 + 1 + ⅓ multiplied by 3 gives us 16. Therefore, 4 + 1 + ⅓ multiplied by 2 will give us the value for X.

The workings of the scribe in the following table provide this answer X.

1	Times (4 + 1 + ⅓) =	4 + 1 + ⅓
2	Times (4 + 1 + ⅓) =	8 + 2 + ⅔

2	Times (4 + 1 + ⅓) =	8 + 2 + ⅔

Therefore X=10 + ⅔

The scribe finishes the problem with a proof; *Do it as follows; the quantity is 10 + ⅔ and its ½ is 5 + ⅓. Hence the total is 16 as originally specified.*

2.22.17 RHIND MATHEMATICAL PAPYRUS PROBLEM 26

The question states; *A quantity with ¼ of it added to it becomes 15. That is, multiply 4, making ¼, namely 1, so that the total is 5 proceeding in the usual manner.*

In algebraic terms this would look like the following:

$$x + \frac{1}{4}x = 15$$

The original question and workings are worded slightly different to the others. This is probably due to the fact that the scribe has tried to make the problem look more difficult than it really is, although the scribe does give the student a clue that he should make his guess for X equal to 4.

After substitution, we find we have an incorrect result of 5.

$$(4) + \frac{(4)}{4} = 5 \neq 15$$

The scribe states, *as many times as 5 must be multiplied to give 15, so many times 4 must be multiplied to give the required number.*

The following table prepared by the scribe show his workings to find what must be multiplied by 5 to produce 15.

Times by 5	Product	→	Times by 5	Product
1	5	→	1	5
2	10	→	2	10
		→	Total	15

From these workings, it can now be seen that 3 multiplied by 5 gives us 15. Therefore, 3 multiplied by 4 will give us the value for X as shown by the scribe's workings as follows:

Hieroglyphs and Arithmetic of the Ancient Egyptian Scribes

1	Times (3) =	3
2	Times (3) =	6
4	Times (3) =	12

| 4 | Times (3) = | 12 |

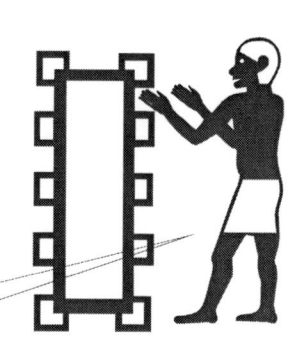

> I never have any luck with flat-pack furniture; I think these drawers are wrong.

Therefore X=12.

The scribe finishes the problem with a proof; *hence, the quantity is 12 and its ¼ is 3 and the total is 15. This is correct since the sum agrees with what was originally specified.*

2.22.18 RHIND MATHEMATICAL PAPYRUS PROBLEM 27

A quantity with $\frac{1}{5}$ of it added to it becomes 21. What is the quantity?

In algebraic terms, this would look like the following:

$$x + \frac{1}{5} = 21$$

The scribe assumes $X = 5$. After substitution, we find we have an incorrect result of 6.

$$5 + \frac{(5)}{5} = 6 \neq 21$$

The scribe states, *as many times as 6 must be multiplied to give 21, so many times 5 must be multiplied to give the required number.*

The following table prepared by the scribe show his workings to find what must be multiplied by 6 to produce 21.

Times by 6	Product	→	Times by 6	Product
2	12	→	2	12
1	6	→	1	6
½	3	→	½	3
			Total	21

From these workings, it can now be seen that 2 + 1 + ½ multiplied by 6 gives us 21. Therefore, 2 + 1 + ½ multiplied by 5 will give us the value for X.

The workings of the scribe in the following table provide this answer X.

1	Times (2 + 1 + ½) =	2 + 1 + ½	→	2 + 1 + ½
2	Times (2 + 1 + ½) =	4 + 2 + 1		
4	Times (2 + 1 + ½) =	8 + 4 + 2	→	8 + 4 + 2

5	Times (2 + 1 + ½) =			17 ½

Therefore X=17½

The scribe finishes the problem with a proof; *The quantity is 17 + ½ and 1/5 of it is 3 + ½ and the total is 21. This is correct since the sum agrees with what was originally specified.*

We can check this out for ourselves as follows:

$$(17 + \frac{1}{2}) + \frac{1}{5}(17 + \frac{1}{2}) = (\frac{35}{2}) + \frac{1}{5}(\frac{35}{2}) = 21$$

$$\frac{35}{2} + \frac{7}{2} = \frac{42}{2} = 21$$

2.22.19 RHIND MATHEMATICAL PAPYRUS PROBLEM 28

This problem looks like a monster at first glance, but it turns out to be quite easy with the help of the scribe's notes. The problem's solution provided by the scribe is given rhetorically. Also, this problem is unlike the preceding problems because the scribe did not provide us with the assistance of the tabular multiplications. We can only presume that the procedures for solving the problem were the same; however, the scribe does give the student some clues of how to solve it.

The problem is stated as follows, *If a quantity and ⅔ of it are added together, and from the sum is subtracted ⅓ of the sum, 10 remains. What is the quantity? Make 1/10 of 10 and this becomes 1. Subtract 1 from 10 and the remainder is 9, which is the desired quantity. ⅔ of 9 is 6, which added to 9, makes 15. ⅓ of 15 is 5, and ⅓ of 15 taken away from 15 leaves 10. Do it in this way.*

In algebraic terms, this would look like the following:

$$(x + \tfrac{2}{3}x) - \tfrac{1}{3}(x + \tfrac{2}{3}x) = 10$$

The scribe tells the student to assume X=9. It is quite possible that the scribe that authored the problem first solved it by breaking the problem down as follows:-

$$\boxed{A} \quad y = (x + \tfrac{2}{3}x) \qquad \boxed{B} \quad y - \tfrac{1}{3}y = 10$$

This table finds a value for Y using 9 as a guess for X

1	Times (9) =	9
⅔	Times (9) =	6
	Y = Total =	15

$$\boxed{A} \quad y = (9 + \tfrac{2}{3} \cdot 9)$$

224   DONALD FRAZER

This table evaluates the equation using 15 as a value for Y.

1	Times (15) =	15
⅓	Times (15) =	5
	remainder =	10

$$\boxed{B} \quad 15 - \frac{15}{3} = 10$$

As a sort of proof, the scribe goes on to say; *as many times as 10 must be multiplied to give 10, that is, once, so many times 9 must be multiplied to give the required number, and therefore the required unknown is 9.*

As they say, you can't get it wrong all of the time. A guess of 9 for the value of X was the correct answer in the first place!

2.22.20 RHIND MATHEMATICAL PAPYRUS PROBLEM 29

> *A quantity and its ⅔ are added together, and ⅓ of the sum is added; then ⅓ of this sum is taken and the result is 10. What is the quantity?*

In algebraic terms, this would look like the following:

$$\frac{1}{3}\left[(x + \frac{2}{3}x) + \frac{1}{3}(x + \frac{2}{3}x)\right] = 10$$

Using 27 as a guess for the value of X, the scribe evaluated the whole equation in one table as follows.

1	Times (27) =	27
⅔	Times (27) =	18
	Sub-total =	45
⅓	Of Sub-total =	15
	Total =	60
⅔	Of Total	40
½	Of Above	20

HIEROGLYPHS AND ARITHMETIC OF THE ANCIENT EGYPTIAN SCRIBES   225

A ½ of ⅔ of something is the same as taking ⅓ of something. Why the scribe decides to take this route is a mystery, he could just as well have finished the equation by taking ⅓. There were reference tables available for calculating ⅓ of numbers as well as ⅔ and ½. Maybe, he was trying to demonstrate the equivalence of some different fractions to his students.

Anyway, after a guess of 27 for X we have a value of 20 instead of 10 for the equation; we still need to find the correct value of X.

At this stage in the calculations, we would expect the scribe to say; *as many times as 20 must be multiplied to give 10, so many times 27 must be multiplied to give the required number.* As in previous problems, this is how we would expect the solution to this problem to be found.

It does not take too much brain power to realize that we must multiply 20 by ½ to get 10. Therefore after multiplying 27 by ½ we get 13 ½ as the true value for X. We can prove this is right by substituting 13 ½ (27/2) into the original equation as follows.

$$\frac{1}{3}\left[\left(\left(\frac{27}{2}\right)+\frac{2}{3}\left(\frac{27}{2}\right)\right)+\frac{1}{3}\left(\left(\frac{27}{2}\right)+\frac{2}{3}\left(\frac{27}{2}\right)\right)\right]=10$$

$$\frac{1}{3}\left[\left(\frac{45}{2}\right)+\frac{1}{3}\left(\frac{45}{2}\right)\right]=\left[\left(\frac{15}{2}\right)+\frac{1}{3}\left(\frac{15}{2}\right)\right]=\frac{20}{2}=10$$

Instead of simply dividing 27 by 2 to get X, for some unimaginable reason, the scribe decided to take the students down another path of complexity. Don't forget, these ancient Egyptians are working with hieroglyphs and without a zero.

To our surprise at this stage, the scribe says, 'As many times as 20 must be multiplied to give 27, so many times 10 must be multiplied to give the required number'.

You still get the correct answer for X in the end, but is this weird or what? The scribe uses the following table to find the amount that must be multiplied by 20 to give us 27.

Times by 20	Product	→	Times by 20	Product
1	20	→	1	20
½	10			
¼	5	→	¼	5
1/10	2	→	1/10	2
			Total	27

Therefore, we must multiply 10 by 1 + ¼ + 1/10 to find the correct value for X, again we get 13 ½.

§ 2.22.20 Notes of Interest

Ancient Egyptian carpenters made wood glue by boiling down the bones and cartilage of animals. They even made plywood composed of six very thin sheets of imported Syrian cypress wood. The sheets were laid on top of each other with the wood grain of each sheet running alternate directions for strength. This is how we construct plywood today.

Cheap wood or plywood was often coated with a very thin veneer of quality wood. This allowed the finished products such as funerary items, furniture, and coffins to be masqueraded as though they were made of very expensive high quality wood.

I feel a little bit crabby

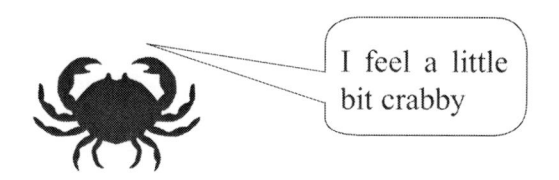

2.22.21 Solving Equations by the Method of Division

Problems 24 to 27 taken from the Rhind Papyrus relied upon the method of false position for their solution, Problems 30 to 34 demonstrate a method of solving first degree algebraic-type equations by division. The method of division is sometimes called 'Division by Fractional Expressions'.

When the scribe uses the method of division to produce the entries for a table of workings, he may still have relied upon a sort of false position method afterwards. The method of false position would only be used if his table of workings had only produced an approximate answer.

2.22.22 Division by Fractional Expressions

This is a process of repeatedly multiplying the numeric terms in an equation by multiples of twos or fractions or a combination of these. This process is continued until a solution or an approximation for the unknown quantity is found.

To better understand this method, let us look at an example of solving the following equation by the process of division:

$$x + \frac{1}{2}x + \frac{1}{4}x + \frac{1}{6}x = 31$$

This problem works with such simple fractions that a scribe would

immediately know the correct value of X as soon as he saw the approximate equation value of 30 2/3 in the table below. We will progress with the full method as if we did not know the answer.

Step1; in the equation identify the numeric terms $1 + \frac{1}{2} + \frac{1}{4} + \frac{1}{6}$

Step 2; setup a multiplication table:

X	Equation value	
1	1 + ½ + ¼ + 1/6	✗
2	3 + ½ + ⅓	✗
4	4 + 2 + 1 + ⅔	✗
16	30 + ⅔	✓
32	61 + ⅓	✗

The closest we can get to the correct value for X with this table is 16. When X is 16, the equation evaluates to 30 2/3 which is just short of 31. In the table above, more than one value in the X column may need to be added together to provide the exact or closest approximation for X.

In this example, only one row provides the closest answer. We could proceed with different fractions in the table to try and get the required result of 31, but we might be unlucky in our choices and take forever to get the right answer.

Step 3; take the product of all the equation's denominators

$$1*2*4*6=48.$$

Step 4; apply all the fractions that are part of the solution from the table above to the product of the denominators. Remember if more than one row was used to create the approximate value of X, then any proper fractions in these rows must be used. So far in our example, we have ⅔ of 48 = 32.

Step5; take the difference between the denominator product and the value found in Step4 expressed as a fraction 48-32=16. 16 is ⅓ of 48.

Step 6; we apply the numbers of the equation $1 + \frac{1}{2} + \frac{1}{4} + \frac{1}{6}$ to the product of the denominators (48) which provides us with 48+24+12+8 = 92. This gives us a ratio between the shortfall in the value of the equation and the shortfall in the value of X.

HIEROGLYPHS AND ARITHMETIC OF THE ANCIENT EGYPTIAN SCRIBES 229

Remember, we know that the equation approximate value is 30 ⅔ and the true value is 31. The difference of ⅓ needs to be generated in the table below.

Shortfall in value of X		Shortfall in value of equation
48	:	92
1/92	:	1/48
Multiply both sides of the ratio by 12 to get ⅓		
4/23	:	⅓

A ratio between two values is maintained even if you take the reciprocal of both sides. Once we have a ratio between the shortfalls of the value of X and the equation, we simply adjust our equation shortfall to equal the calculated shortfall. After making the same adjustment to the X side of the table, we have our answer.

Step 7; add the true shortfall for the value X to the approximate value of X, which is 16 + 4/23.

Of course, the ancient Egyptians, besides their use of ⅔ and ¾, could only use unit fractions. Therefore their answer for this problem would have been:

$$16 + \frac{1}{7} + \frac{1}{33} + \frac{1}{1329} + \frac{1}{2353659}$$

It is quite possible that a fraction like the last one in the answer above would be ignored by the ancient Egyptians, because it is tiny in relation to the rest of the answer.

2.22.23 RHIND MATHEMATICAL PAPYRUS PROBLEM 30

If a scribe says to you, 'What is the quantity of which ⅔ and 1/10 of the quantity will make 10? Let him hear the following; multiply ⅔ and 1/10 by amounts in order to get 10'.

In algebraic terms, this would look like the following:

$$\frac{2}{3}x + \frac{1}{10}x = 10$$

Times ⅔+1/10	Product	→	Times ⅔+1/10	Product
1	⅔+ 1/10	→	1	⅔+ 1/10
2	1+ ⅓+⅕			
4	3+1/15	→	4	3+1/15
8	6+1/10+1/30	→	8	6+1/10+1/30
	Totals =		13	9 + 29/30

The table entry that follows was not included by the scribe because 12 + ⅕ + 1/15 is larger than the required value of 10 for the equation.

Times +1/10	Product	→	Times ⅔+1/10	Product
16	12+1/5+1/15			

So we are now left with a result of 13 for X, unfortunately this only provides a value for the whole equation of 9 + 29/30. We are short by

a factor of 1/30 from the required amount of 10. The true value for X must be greater than 13 and less than 16.

At this stage, the scribe makes a statement; *the making of 1/30 you must times 1/23 for finding of ⅔ + 1/10. The total is the desired quantity so stated; it is 13 1/23.*

How the scribe derives the 1/23 as an additional factor to 13 for providing the true value of X is not known. When this value of 13 1/23 is substituted for X in the original equation, we get the required value of 10.

The scribe even provided the table below as proof:

Times 13+1/23	Product	→	Times 13+1/23	Product
1	13 + 1/23			
2/3	8 + 2/3 +1/46 + 1/138	→	2/3	8 + 2/3 +1/46 + 1/138
1/10	1 +1/5+ 1/10+1/230	→	1/10	1 +1/5+ 1/10+1/230
			Total =	10

Finding this true value for X by modern algebraic means is very simple. We can only speculate that the information of how the ancient Egyptian scribe derived it has been lost to antiquity. It can only be assumed that another table of workings was setup containing a series of fractions as guesses. This series was probably a list of the most likely fractions, such as 1/20 down to 1/30. Each multiplication would have been computed until the correct answer came to light.

> As I am Bes, the god of parties and fun, I can always get a good tune out of my air-harp

§ 2.22.23 Notes of Interest

The afterlife was believed to be a tangible spiritual realm, a concrete real destination mirroring life in this world. Attaining eternal life did not require a person to perform any acts of good, but simply to avoid doing any wrong.

2.22.24 RHIND MATHEMATICAL PAPYRUS PROBLEM 31

If a scribe says to you, 'A quantity, ⅔ of it, ½ of it, and ⅐ of it added together become 33. What is the quantity'?

In algebraic terms, this would look like the following:

$$x + \frac{2}{3}x + \frac{1}{2}x + \frac{1}{7}x = 33$$

For the solution to this problem, the scribe begins by setting out a table which substitutes different values for X into the equation. As with preceding problems, the hope is that one or a total of a number of rows offer the solution to the problem. Remember we are trying to find one or more rows that will total 33.

Ignore	1	1 + ⅔ + ½ + ⅐
✓	2	4 + ⅓ + ¼ + 1/28

Hieroglyphs and Arithmetic of the Ancient Egyptian Scribes

✓	4	$9 + 1/6 + 1/14$
✓	8	$18 + 1/3 + 1/7$
Ignore	½	$1/2 + 1/3 + 1/4 + 1/14$
✓	¼	$1/4 + 1/6 + 1/8 + 1/28$
Totals =	14 + ¼	$32 + 1/2 + 1/4 + \; + 1/28$

As you can see using a value for X of 14 ¼ is only a tiny fraction short of 33, short by 5/56 to be exact. After extensive use of tables and inclusion of a factor or 42, derived from the product of all the denominators in the equation, the scribe eventually comes up with the correct answer for a value of X.

The scribe's final words on the problem are; *hence, after arranging the fractions in decreasing order, the total unknown quantity sought is 14 + ¼ + 1/56 + 1/97 + 1/194 + 1/388 + 1/679 + 1/776, which when multiplied by 1 + ⅔ + ½ + 1/7, makes the total 33, as given in the enunciation of the problem.*

X =	$14 + 1/4 + 1/56 + 1/97 + 1/194 + 1/388 + 1/679 + 1/776$

Part way through the solution to this problem, there is a mathematical blunder with totals. Later on in the workings the calculations then get back on track to produce the correct answer. This is an indication that the scribes worked from copies of the mathematical papyri and an error had been made in the transcription while copying. Errors such as this, crop up in many of the mathematical papyri. Scribes do make genuine errors in arithmetic that produce the wrong answer, but not on this occasion.

Also, because the scribes worked with unit fractions so much, many unit fractions created as the result of a calculation represented very tiny amounts. Sometimes a scribe would decide to ignore a fraction completely when its size was insignificant in relation to the whole sum.

This was a useful technique because it allowed the scribe to significantly simplify his calculations. I am sure this practise has caused many Egyptologists to think a blunder on the part of a scribe had been uncovered, when in reality the slight alteration or exclusion of something might have been deliberate.

Some people would surely hold up their arms in horror at the prospect of fiddling the figures. It must be remembered this technique is being applied nearly all the time whenever we encounter any sort of measuring or calculation.

For example, engineers and scientists work with tolerances; the best chefs never measure anything. When we perform calculations, we always work to a set number of decimal places; just look more closely at how a computer spreadsheet does your calculations; accountants and even the tax authority's round-up and round-down numbers. Some methodologies such as Calculus actually rely on certain terms being ignored completely during calculations.

§ 2.22.24 Notes of Interest

Although, only a small percentage of ancient Egyptians were literate not all writing was related to record keeping, crafts, business, religion, medicine, mathematics, or science. Literature was also important, it basically had two forms. One form of literature was called "Wisdom Literature" or simply called "Instructions"; the other was fiction and comprised of stories or poems, and was written for pure entertainment. Wisdom literature acted as a guide to younger generations. Aristocratic authors would thus instruct their sons how to attain high positions in office and prosper. The fictional literature dealt with magic, mystery, heroes, bravery, and love; and almost always had happy endings.

2.22.25 Rhind Mathematical Papyrus Problem 32

If a scribe says to you; 'A quantity, ⅓ of it, and ¼ of it added together become 2. What is the quantity?'

In algebraic terms, this would look like the following:

$$x + \frac{1}{3}x + \frac{1}{4}x = 2$$

The scribe goes on to say, *'Adding together the multipliers we find that the total of the required quantity is $1 + 1/6 + 1/12 + 1/114 + 1/228$'.*

	Multiplier	Times(1+⅓+¼)
✓	1	1 + ⅓ + ¼
Ignore	⅔	1 + 1/18
Ignore	⅓	½ + 1/36
✓	1/6	¼ + 1/72
✓	1/12	⅛ + 1/144
✓	1/114	1/72
✓	1/228	1/144
Totals=	1+1/6+1/12+1/114+1/228	2

The list of multipliers used in the table above was not chosen at random by the scribe. Prior to creating this table which delivers the solution for X, he had to perform numerous calculations which were also in table format. Similar to problem 31, the scribe included a factor in his calculations based on the product of all the denominators in the original equation. He probably thought of using 12 but this was not suitable, so 144 was used instead. The scribe also provided an extensive proof which accompanied the solution as well.

> § 2.22.25 Notes of Interest
>
> A scribe to Queen, Ahmose-Nefertari, instructs his son with some wisdom literature; he tells his son to stay out of pubs:
>
> Don't' indulge in drinking beer, lest you utter evil speech, and don't know what you are saying. If you fall and hurt your body, no one will hold out a hand to you; your drinking companions will stand up saying, 'Out with the drunk!'

2.22.26 Rhind Mathematical Papyrus Problem 33

This problem goes as follows; *a quantity, ⅔ of it, ½ of it, and ⅐ of it, added together become 37. What is the quantity?*

In algebraic terms, this problem would look like:

$$x + \frac{2}{3}x + \frac{1}{2}x + \frac{1}{7}x = 37$$

This algebraic expression is very simple to solve using modern techniques as follows.

$$x\left(\frac{97}{42}\right) = 37 \quad x = \frac{(37)(42)}{97} = 16 \frac{2}{97}$$

The scribe starts by creating a table to see how close he can get to a true value for X.

	Multiplier	Times $(1 + \frac{2}{3} + \frac{1}{2} + \frac{1}{7})$
Ignore	1	$1 + \frac{2}{3} + \frac{1}{2} + \frac{1}{7}$
Ignore	2	$4 + \frac{1}{3} + \frac{1}{4} + 1/28$
Ignore	4	$9 + \frac{1}{6} + 1/14$
Ignore	8	$18 + \frac{1}{3} + \frac{1}{7}$
✓	16	$36 + \frac{2}{3} + \frac{1}{4} + 1/28$
Totals	16	$36 + \frac{2}{3} + \frac{1}{4} + 1/28$

Unfortunately after using 16 as a value for X, the scribe finds that the whole equation is short of equalling 37 by a fractional amount. He does not know it yet but it is 1/21!

To help find this missing fraction, the scribe uses a numerical factor of 42 in his calculations. This is derived from the product of all the denominators in the original equation.

§ 2.22.26.1 Notes of Interest

Remember; solving problems by false position begins by selecting a convenient answer or making an educated guess, one that makes the calculations of the problem simpler. It does not have to be the correct answer. After calculating the result from the convenient answer, a ratio is found which is applied to the first guess to make it correct.

Multiplier	Times (42)
2/3	28
1/4	10 + ½
1/28	1 + ½
Total =	40

The scribe after taking into account the results of his table shown earlier, he multiplies the three fractions by the factor 42:

From the figures opposite, the scribe now says; the total is 40; with the remainder of 2 as part of 42. Since 1 ⅔ ½ 1/7 of 42 gives 97, this last number, 1/21, with the product already obtained gives a total of 37.

What the scribe means here is, when we used 16 as a value for X, we had to add 2/42 or rather 1/21 to the equation total to get 37. We also now know that 1 ⅔ ½ 1/7 of 42 gives 97, therefore the reciprocals; 1/42 and 1/97 are still proportional; proportionality is still maintained if we double these.

For example 2/42 is proportional to 2/97. As 2/42 or rather 1/21 is the missing fraction to make 36 + ⅔ + ¼ + 1/28 up to 37, then 2/97 is the amount 16 must be increased by to become the correct value of X.

The scribe then goes on to say; *37 is equal to the number specified in the enunciation of the problem.*

So the quantity sought for X *is 16 + 1/56 + 1/679 + 1/776.*

The answer is easier to understand if we see it as: $x = 16\frac{2}{97}$

You are welcome to check out: $16\frac{2}{97} = + 16 + \frac{1}{56} + \frac{1}{679} + \frac{1}{776}$

Best of luck!

§ 2.22.26.2 Notes of Interest

Wisdom literature: Instruction to Kagemni. The respectful man prospers. Praised is the modest one. The tent is open to the silent. Modesty, calmness, and restraint are all virtues to be cultivated and will lead to advancement.

Gluttony is base and is rebuked. A cup of water quenches the thirst; a mouthful of herbs strengthens the heart.

2.22.27 RHIND MATHEMATICAL PAPYRUS PROBLEM 34

The problem states; *a quantity, ½ of it, and ¼ of it, added together, become 10. What is the quantity?*

In algebraic terms, this would look like the following:

$$x + \frac{1}{2}x + \frac{1}{4}x = 10$$

The scribe pronounces, 'Multiply 1+ ½ + ¼ so as to get 10'.

§ 2.22.27 Notes of Interest

Converting a number into a reciprocal basically makes a unit fraction of it; the reciprocal of 4 becomes ¼. When we make a fraction into a reciprocal, we flip it upside down; the reciprocal of 4/5 is 5/4.

	Multiplier	Times (1+ ½ + ¼)
✓	1	1+ ½ + ¼
✗	2	3 + ½
✓	4	7
✓	1/7	¼
✗	¼ + 1/28	½
✓	½ + 1/14	½ + ¼ + ⅛ + 1/14 + 1/28 + 1/56
Totals	5 + ½ + 1/7 + 1/14	10

As they say, 'You can't get it wrong all the time'. This table has produced 10, the exact value for the equation. It is interesting to observe, you can almost sense the scribe's thinking as he completes the multiplier column. He probably realizes while entering 4, that he might be able to get his table to provide the complete answer.

After entering 1/7 in one row, he enters both ¼ and a 1/28 in the next row that follows. 1/28 could have had a row to itself but the scribe knew that the two together would allow a single fraction of ½ as the product. For economy of space and simplification, the ½ and the 1/14 in the multiplier column would have been better suited to their own rows; but by this time the scribe knew he had solved the equation.

The scribe then makes the statement, '*the total is the required quantity: 5 + ½ + ⅟₇ + 1/14*'. Then he follows this with a proof table.

1	5 + ½ + ⅟₇ + 1/14
½	2 + ½ + ¼ + 1/14 + 1/28
¼	1 + ¼ + ⅛ + 1/28 + 1/56

The scribe totals the product column to prove his calculations are correct.

2.22.28 COMPLEXITY IN A SOLUTION

With respect to problems 30-34 taken from the Rhind Mathematical Papyrus, it only takes a glance at the answers to convince us that these problems could have had no practical applications.

They were meant to illustrate one method for the solution of simple equations of this type, and although they did this, the simplicity of the method has been masked by the complexities of the unit fractions that arise in the process and by the unexpected operations to which the scribe was forced to resort.

§ 2.22.28 Notes of Interest

A love poem; as in all love poems, separated lovers pine for each other:

I will lie down in my house and pretend to be dying.

When the neighbours come to see me, perhaps my love will come with them.

She will make the doctors unnecessary, because she knows what's wrong with me!

In one part of the proof of problem 33, the scribe found that he had to add up 16 fractions, of which the last half-dozen were 1/1164, 1/1358, 1/1552, 1/4074, 1/4753, and 1/5432. This is a formidable task in anyone's language or notation, to do it with only unit fractions and without any knowledge of zero, is incredible. Incidentally all of the answers to these questions were quite correct!

2.23.0 Ship's Part Problems

2.23.1 Indecipherable Ship's Problems

Problem 2 and 3 in the Moscow Mathematical Papyrus relate to parts of a ship. The text in problem 2 is damaged and unreadable.

All that can be retrieved and translated for problem 2 goes as follows;

> *Example of the calculation of a ship's rudder from . . . If someone said to you, take a ship's rudder made from . . . Oh, let me know.*

2.23.2 Problem 3 from the Moscow Papyrus

> *Example of the calculation of a ship's mast from a cedar log. If someone says to you, 'Make a mast from a cedar log 30 cubits long such that the mast is $\frac{1}{3} + \frac{1}{5}$ of the length of the log'. Calculate $\frac{1}{3} + \frac{1}{5}$ of this 30.*

In algebraic terms, this problem quite simply looks like the following:

$$\left(\frac{1}{3} + \frac{1}{5}\right) 30 = \left(\frac{8}{15}\right) 30 = x = 16 \text{ cubits}$$

§ 2.23.2.1 Notes of Interest

To facilitate the grinding of grain into flour, sand, or ground stone such as quartz or granite was added to the grind stones. Powdered stone acted as an abrasive and helped grind the flour more quickly. Unfortunately, this grit caused excessive wear on the teeth of the ancient Egyptians.

§ 2.23.2.2 Notes of Interest

Most of us are familiar with the following rhyme; the wording varies slightly depending upon which version you are reading:

> As I was going to St Ives
> I met a man with seven wives
> Each wife had seven sacks
> Each sack had seven cats
> Each cat had seven kits
> Kits, cats, sacks, wives
> How many were going to St Ives?

The earliest version of it is dated circa 1730, but it differs, by referring to 9 rather than 7 wives. The modern form on the left dates to circa 1825. A similar problem appears in the Rhind Papyrus – problem 79.

All potential answers to this riddle are based on its ambiguity because the riddle only tells us the group has been met on the journey and gives no further information about destinations, only that of the narrator. As such, any one of a number of answers is plausible. The answer to the total number of people, sacks, and felines involved, is 2,802, calculated as follows:

Narrator: 1, The man he met: 1, His wives: 7, The sacks: 49, Adult cats: 343, Kittens: 2,401

2.24.0 Pefsu Problems

2.24.1 A Measure of Flour

The solutions to the problems provided for the Egyptian student can sometimes be more complex that the original problem itself. Take the following Pefsu problem as an example, remembering that a pefsu is a measure of the strength of bread and relative strength of beer.

The Pefsu number gave an accurate measure of the amount of flour or grain content of bread and beer in terms of Hekats. The Pefsu number was a good indicator of alcohol content in beer if the recipe contained only grain or flour. The Pefsu number could be misleading when used to indicate the alcoholic content of a beer if other ingredients had been added to the recipe. A typical alcoholic strength beer, that was mainly grain or flour based, would have a Pefsu of 2.

This system is unlike modern units of measure for the strength of alcohol by percentage volume or original specific gravity. Modern units do not measure any specific ingredient such as fruit or malt in the recipe.

Although it could be argued that a similar process is taking place when the original gravity is recorded in a brewing process before fermentation begins. This original gravity is measured by using a hygrometer, which measures the sugar content of the wort. There is a direct relationship between the amount of sugar consumed by the yeast and the amount of alcohol created. The source of the sugar is irrelevant as far as the tax officials are concerned.

Adding other ingredients to a beer recipe was very popular with the ancient Egyptians to enhance the flavour of the beer. This process would have considerably boosted the alcohol content. In fact, it could easily have doubled or tripled it.

For example 'besha' was a beer consisting of grain mixed with fruit; this was very popular. The fruit would probably have raised the alcohol content close to that of a modern wine.

A beer which included malt and dates was also popular. One particular type of beer called ½ ¼ malt-date beer was classed as a weak beer because it usually had a Pefsu of 4, although its alcohol content was high due to fermentation of the additional ingredients. The significance of these fractions may have been lost to antiquity; possibly they represent a ratio of ingredients in the recipe, or even a blend of beers and wines.

The fractions in the title may look a bit obscure, but remember without their use of unit fractions, they might even have prefered to call it ¾ malt-date beer. This sounds like something you would see advertized today. Obviously, the name of a beer was more important to the ancient Egyptians as an indicator of beer alcohol strength rather than Pefsu.

To assist with the fair sharing, bartering, and exchange of bread with beer, the ancient Egyptians used specific measuring jugs for different beers. They often used specific sizes of jug for different beers.

A 'Des' or 'ds' was a name given to a particular type of stoneware beer jug. A des-jug had a capacity of approximately ½ litre. Measuring jugs usually varied between about a ½ and 1 litre.

All the ancient Egyptian beers were probably very tasty as there are quite a few ancient Egyptian hieroglyphs and texts that relate to wine, beer brewing, and even inibriation. It is unlikely that any hard working pyramid builder would have happily settled for being short measured on the quality or strength of his ration of beer.

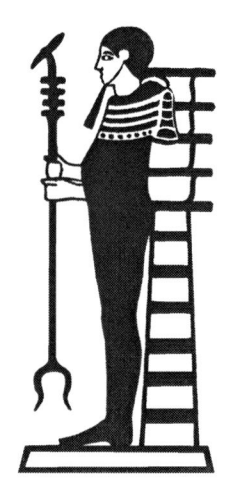

§ 2.24.1 Notes of Interest

Problem 79, 'The 7's', from the Rhind Papyrus, provides very little detail other than the outlines stated below and there are no workings to indicate as to where the number 2801 comes from, it can only be assumed the scribe obtained it from a set of tables. Therefore, we cannot delve into this problem too far.

A house-inventory shows how to find the multiplication by 7 to find each term as a product in a series.

1	2801
2	5602
4	11204
Total	19607

The same procedure is followed to multiply each term in the following series of five numbers by 7, which then may be summed

houses	7
cats	49
mice	343
spelt	2401
hekat	16807
Total	19607

A scribal error of using 2301 instead of 2401 in the table suggested that this papyrus was copied, because the totals are correct.

O! Beer
O! Wine
O! Joy

O! You are drunken

Determinative - Brewer

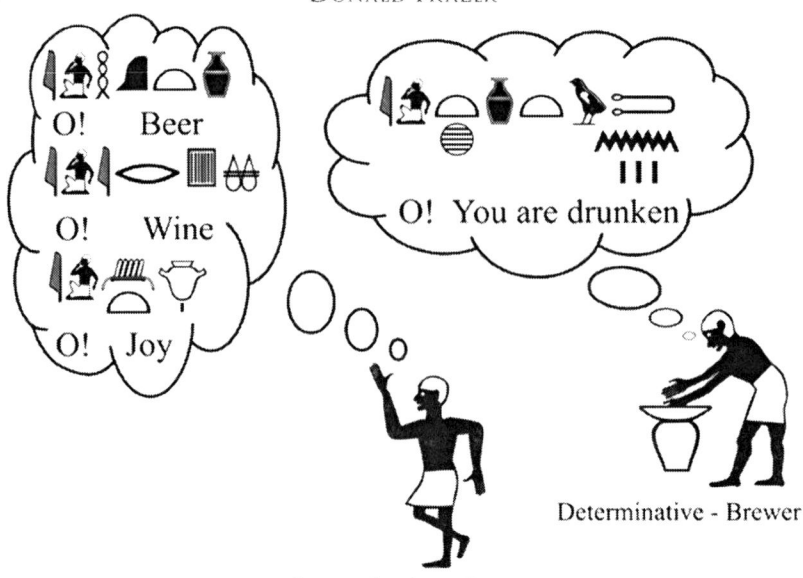

Determinative - Dance

2.24.2 Problem 8 from the Moscow Papyrus

Example of calculating 100 loaves of bread of pefsu 20. If someone says to you, 'You have 100 loaves of bread of pefsu, 20 to be exchanged for beer of pefsu 4, like ½ ¼ malt-date beer'. First calculate the grain required for the hundred loaves of bread of pefsu 20. The result is 5 hekat.

This statement translates into a simple algebraic equation as follows:

$$20 = \frac{100}{x} \qquad x = \frac{100}{20} = 5 \text{ Hekat of Grain}$$

Then reckon what you need for a 1 des-jug of beer like the beer called 1/2 1/4 malt-date beer. The result is 1/2 of the hekat measure needed for 1 des-jug of beer made from Upper-Egyptian grain.

Calculate 1/2 of 5 hekat, the result will be 2 ½, take this 2 ½ four times. The result is 10. Then you say to him, 'Behold! The beer quantity is found to be correct.'

> § 2.24.2 Notes of Interest
>
> In all the examples where a number of des-jugs of ½ ¼ malt-date beer have been produced as the result of a calculation, the number of jugs is halved. The alcoholic strength of normal beer is 2 pefsu; a beer of 4 pefsu is very weak, the higher the pefsu number, the weaker the beer! One logical reason for treating weak beer like strong beer is because the pefsu unit of strength is only based on grain or flour. Adding fruit to the brew during the fermentation process would increase the alcohol content of the beer considerably, without affecting the pefsu number.

As requested by the scribe, we half the quantity of grain and get 2 ½ Hekat. Using the formula:

$$\text{Pefsu} = \frac{\text{Number of Jugs of beer}}{\text{Number of Hekats of Grain}}$$

We get 4 Pefsu times 2 ½ Hekat = 10 Des-jugs of Beer.

Considering that the students were probably beaten with a stick if they got their sums wrong, you wouldn't blame them for drinking their homework.

2.24.3 PROBLEM 69 FROM THE RHIND MATHEMATICAL PAPYRUS

This problem like all the other problems relating to the strength of bread and beer can be solved with modern straight-forward arithmetic. These problems can also be expressed in very simple algebraic terms; simplicity as far as the scribe's were concerned was not in their interest; well let's say they were on to a good little earner by keeping things complex.

$$x = \frac{80}{3\frac{1}{2}} = \frac{80}{\frac{7}{2}} = \frac{80(2)}{7} = 22\frac{6}{7} \quad Pefsu$$

The problem is documented by the scribe as follows:

> 3 ½ Hekat of meal is made into 80 loaves of bread. Make known to me the amount of meal in each loaf and their pefsu; cooking potency. Multiply 3 ½ so as to get 80.

	Pefsu	(Times) 3+½
✗	1	3 + ½
✗	10	35
✓	20	70
✓	2	7
✓	⅔	2 + ⅓
✓	1/21	⅙
✓	1/7	½
Totals	22 ⅔ 1/7 1/21	80

The Pefsu is 22 + ⅔ + 1/7 + 1/21 and 1 Hekat makes 320 Ro, so:

Hekats	(Times) 320
1	320
2	640
1/2	160
Totals = 3 ½	1120 Ro

Hence multiply 80 so as to get 1120. The procedure is as follows:

	Ro	(Times) 80
✗	1	80
✓	10	800
✗	2	160
✓	4	320
Totals	14	1120

So the amount of meal in one loaf is 14 Ro or 1/32 Hekat + 4 Ro

2.24.4 PROBLEM 69 PROOF USING EYE-FRACTIONS

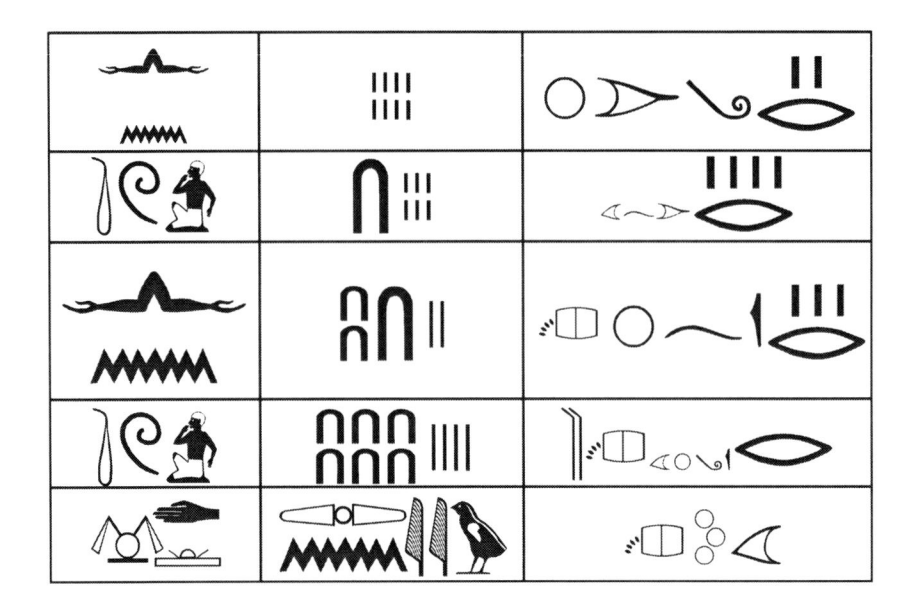

The result is 3 ½ Hekat of meal for 80 loaves, as was specified.
To prevent the reader suffering too much, the table above has been translated as follows:

	Loaves	Hekat
✗	1	1/32 Hekat 4 Ro
✗	2	1/16 1/64 Hekat 3 Ro
✗	4	⅛ 1/32 1/64 Hekat 1 Ro
✗	8	¼ 1/16 1/32 Hekat 2 Ro
✓	16	½ ⅛ 1/16 Hekat 4 Ro
✗	32	1 ¼ ⅛ 1/64 Hekat 3 Ro
✓	64	2 ½ ¼ 1/32 1/64 Hekat 1 Ro
Total	80	3 ½ Hekat

§ 2.24.4.1 Notes of Interest

Doctors were formally trained in an institution called 'The House of Life', where they gained scribal, medical, and priestly training. Most of these institutions were attached to temples. Ancient Egyptian doctors did not need to pass any exams to practice, although a strict hierarchy existed according to their ability and experience. The job titles were:

- Senenu (lay physician); a scribe that could read medical texts, they were a very low-ranking doctor.
- Kherep Senenu (overseer of Senenu); general controller of doctors.
- Sau (magic physicians); medically qualified priests who only treated people punished by a god.
- Shepherd of the Anus of Pharaoh; a physician who gave enemas to the king. The figs didn't work then?
- Specialists (particular ailment experts); each dealt.

§ 2.24.4.2 Notes of Interest

The gods were often considered the source of dreams. This is why the ancient Egyptians spent a lot of time having their dreams interpreted.

A 19th dynasty papyrus in the British Museum is possibly the oldest dream book in existence. It is even thought that this book might date back to the 12th dynasty. The following extracts are just few dream interpretations.

A crane; is a good sign, it means prosperity will come to him. Munching lotus leaves; is a good sign, it means something enjoyable will happen. Seeing the god above; is a good sign, it means there will be much food. Looking out of a window; is a good sign, it means that his god will hear his cry. Seeing himself on a roof; is a good sign, it means he will find what he is looking for. Seeing a large cat; is a good sign, it means there will be a large harvest.

Drinking warm beer; is a bad sign, it means he will experience suffering. Removing one of his legs; is a bad sign, it means judgment will come upon him by those yonder, the dead. Seeing his face in a mirror; is a bad sign, it means another wife. Eating figs and grapes; is a bad sign, it means he will become ill. Looking after monkeys; is a bad sign, an unwelcome change awaits him.

2.25.0 BAKU PROBLEMS

2.25.1 PROBLEM 11 FROM THE MOSCOW PAPYRUS

This problem involves calculating the productivity of a worker moving logs. There is some disagreement between Egyptologists as to the translation and exact wording of this problem. This is mainly due to the deterioration and damage to the original papyrus and the fact that the scribe who authored the material did not pay as much attention to detail as he could have. The problem is described as follows:

> *Example of reckoning the work of a man in logs. If someone says to you, 'The work of a man in logs; the amount of his work is 100 logs of 5 hand-breadths section; but he has brought them in logs of 4 hand-breadths section.' You are to square these 5 hand-breadths. The result is 25. You are to square the 4 hand-breadths. The result is 16. Reckon with the 16 to get 25.*

In today's English, this problem states that a man brought a number of logs with an end area of 16 which were equivalent to a 100 logs with an end area 25. What is the number of logs that he brought? This is quite a simple problem in algebraic terms:

$$25x = 100(16) \qquad x = 156\frac{1}{4}$$

The scribe gives the students a clue of how to start by telling them to use the area of the ends of the logs.

> § 2.25.1 Notes of Interest
>
> Ancient Egyptian physicians seemed prepared to have a go at treating most things although, if an ailment was internal with no obvious cause, it was believed to have a supernatural origin. For these situations, magic and the gods were employed in the cure.

Then the scribe gives the method of solving the problem:

Reckon with 16 to get 25.

✓	1	16
✓	½	8
✗	¼	4
✗	⅛	2
✓	1/16	1
Totals	1 + ½ + 1/16	25

The result is 1 + ½ + 1/16 times. You are to take this number 100 times. The result is:

156 + ½ + 1/16, (This result was an error in the papyrus! It should have read 156 + ¼).

Then you shall say to him, 'Behold, this is the number of logs which he brought of 4 hand-breadths section. You will find that it is correct'.

1	100
½	50
1/16	6 ¼
Total	156 ¼

2.25.2 Problem 23 from the Moscow Papyrus

This problem involves calculating the productivity of a shoemaker. As an equation the problem looks very basic; a job of 10 pairs of shoes cut, takes the same time as a job of 5 pairs decorated, that's 1 day for each job:

10 Pairs Cut + 5 Pairs Decorated = 2 Days
10 Pairs Complete = 3 Days
10/3 Pairs Complete = 1 Day

The problem is described as follows:

> *Example of reckoning the work of a shoemaker. If someone says to you, 'Regarding the work of a shoemaker, if he is cutting out only, he can do ten pairs of sandals per day; but if he is decorating, he can do five per day. As for the number, he can both cut and decorate in a day, what will that be?'*
>
> *You will calculate the sum of the day equivalences of the ten and the five. Add the one day for cutting out the ten pairs of sandals and the two days for decorating them. The result for them together is three days. Take this to find ten. The result is 3 + ⅓ times. Behold it is 3 + ⅓ pairs of sandals per day to be fully cut and decorated.*

The ancient Egyptians would have had no difficulty working this one out in their head's. Take a ⅓ of 3 to get 1, therefore ⅓ of 10 is 3 ⅓. If they couldn't solve the problem with mental arithmetic, they had access to plenty of tables listing multiplications of ½, ⅓, ¼, ⅔ and 1/10 etc. All of these tables could be used in reverse to give the answer to divisions by whole numbers and fractions.

§ 2.25.2 Notes of Interest

Not all ancient Egyptian medicine was quackery. For example, the physicians were quite capable of removing arrow heads, performing amputations, stitching wounds, and making potions and ointments. Some cures were a bit dubious such as the use of hot-broken glass for some eye treatments, but many would have worked. The following remedies were quite valid; figs were used to treat constipation, honey for coughs and cataracts, copper for cleaning wounds, poppies used as a sedative and yeast was used for digestive disorders. These medications are just a few of the many prescribed by Egyptian physicians.

3.0.0 Chapter Three

Reference Material

3.1.0 SELECTED BIBLIOGRAPHY

The works which was of particular relevance for topics covered in the writing of this book was most definitely 'Egyptian Grammar' written by Sir Alan Gardiner. There have been very few books or articles written since Sir Alan Gardiner had his book published that have not relied upon his work as source material. In many modern publications by other authors, Gardiner is quoted literally word for word from various sections of his book 'Egyptian Grammar'. This must be a compliment to him and a first class reference to the high standard of his work which has stood the test of time.

Adel Emil; Reading Hieroglyphs, *Published by Adel Emil,* New York: NY, 1997.

Angela McDonald; Write Your Own Egyptian Hieroglyphs, *British Museum Press*, London, 2007.

Amr Hussein; ABC Hieroglyphics, *Amr Hussein Abdel Aal Press*, UK, 2000.

Barbara Watterson; Introducing Egyptian Hieroglyphs, *Scottish Academic Press*, London, 1983.

Barbara Watterson; More about Egyptian Hieroglyphs, *Scottish Academic Press*, London, 1985.

Bob Brier and Hoyt Hobbs; Daily Life of the Ancient Egyptians, *Greenwood Press*, New York: NY, 1999.

Charlotte Booth; The Ancient Egyptians for Dummies, *John Wiley & Sons, Ltd.*, New York: NY, 2007.

Christian Jacq; Fascinating Hieroglyphics, *Sterling Publishing Co., Inc.*, New York: NY,1997.

David Sandison; The Art of Egyptian Hieroglyphics, *Hamlyn Publications*, London, 1997.

E. A. Wallis Budge; A Hieroglyphic Vocabulary to the Book of the Dead, *Dover Publications, Inc.,* New York: NY, 1991.

James P. Allen; Middle Egyptian, *Cambridge University Press*, New York: NY, 2009.

John H. Taylor; Ancient Egyptian Book of the Dead, *The British Museum Press*, 38 Russell Square, London, 2010.

Lorna Oakes and Philip Steele; Everyday Life in Ancient Egypt and Mesopotamia, *Southwater Press*, 88-89 Blackfriars Road, London, 2005.

Marshall Clagett; Ancient Egyptian Science: A Source Book—Knowledge and Order—Volume 1, Tome One, *American Philosophical Society*, Philadelphia: PA, 1989.

Marshall Clagett; Ancient Egyptian Science: A Source Book—Knowledge and Order—Volume 1, Tome Two, *American Philosophical Society*, Philadelphia: PA, 1989.

Marshall Clagett; Ancient Egyptian Science: A Source Book—Calendars, Clocks and Astronomy—Volume 2, *American Philosophical Society*, Philadelphia: PA, 1995.

Marshall Clagett; Ancient Egyptian Science: A Source Book—Ancient Egyptian Mathematics—Volume 3, *American Philosophical Society*, Philadelphia: PA, 1999.

Mark Collier and Bill Manley; How to Read Egyptian Hieroglyphs, *British Museum Press*, London, 2006.

Peter A. Clayton; Chronicle Of The Pharaohs, *Thames and Hudson*, London, 1994.

Philip Ardagh; The Hieroglyphs Handbook: Teach Yourself Ancient Egyptian, *Faber and Faber Press*, London, 1999.

Richard Parkinson; Pocket Guide to Ancient Egyptian Hieroglyphs, *British Museum Press*, London, 2003.

Richard J. Gillings; Mathematics in the Time of the Pharaohs, *Dover Publications*, New York: NY, 1982.

Robert Hamilton; Ancient Egypt: The Kingdom of the Pharaohs, *Atlantic Publishing*, Massachusetts, 2007.

Sir Alan Gardiner; Egyptian Grammar, *Griffith Institute, Ashmolean Museum*, Oxford, 2005.

Theoni Pappas; The Joy of Mathematics, *Wide World Publishing/Tetra Press*, New York: NY, 2009.

Theoni Pappas; More Joy of Mathematics, *Wide World Publishing/Tetra Press*, New York: NY, 2003.

Trevor Anderson, Hazel Norris, Gary Dexter, Michael Munro; Book of Facts, *Chambers Harrap Publishers Ltd.*, New York: NY, 2004. Egyptian Designs, *Dover Publications, Inc.*, New York: NY, 1998. Rhind Mathematical Papyrus, *The British Museum*, London.

§ 3.1.0 Notes of Interest

Considering how intrinsically important the decorative arts were to the ancient Egyptians for the adornment of their architecture, papyri, and everyday objects, it's remarkable to learn that there appears to have been no cult of the artist. Indeed, there does not even seem to be any hieroglyphs for the words painter or artist.

3.2.0 GLOSSARY

1-consonant—Alternative name for a hieroglyph that represents a uniliteral. Uniliterals are the most important hieroglyphs; each contributes a distinct sound to a spoken word.

2-consonant—Alternative name for one or more hieroglyphs that represent a biliteral. These sound-signs contribute two consonants to the reading of a word.

3-consonant—Alternative name for one or more hieroglyphs that represent a triliteral. These sound-signs contribute three consonants to the reading of a word.

Accent—Stress or pitch in speaking.

Adjacent Side—The base of a right-angled triangle.

Adze—Carpenter's tool, like an axe but with an arched blade, set at right angles to a long-shafted handle.

Aliquot Fraction—Aliquot means dividing exactly or without remainder. An unrepeated individual fraction which is a member of a sequence of unique-unitary fractions; the sum of which makes up a non-unitary proper fraction. For example, the aliquot fractions of ¾ are ½ and a ¼. The sequence ¼, ¼, ¼ would not be aliquot fractions of ¾.

Alluvial Plain—Land formed by washed-up earth and sand.

Alphabetic Writing—Words formed by letters that represent sounds rather than pictures that represent real items.

Ancient Egyptian Alphabet—An alphabet made up of hieroglyphs that make twenty-four distinctive sounds.

Ancient Moscow Mathematical Papyrus—The Moscow Mathematical Papyrus is an ancient Egyptian mathematical papyrus, which probably dates to the Eleventh dynasty of Egypt, roughly 1850 BC. The papyrus is also called the Golenischev Mathematical Papyrus after its first owner, Egyptologist Vladimir Goleniščev. It is now on display at the Pushkin State Museum of Fine Arts in Moscow. The format of the papyrus consists of twenty-five mathematical problems and their solutions.

Ancient Rhind Mathematical Papyrus—The Rhind Mathematical Papyrus was named after Alexander Henry Rhind, a Scottish antiquarian, who purchased the papyrus in 1858 in Luxor, Egypt; it was apparently found during illegal excavations in or near the Ramesseum. It dates to the Second Intermediate Period of Egypt, about 1,650 BC and is the best example of Egyptian mathematics ever discovered. The papyrus was acquired in 1864 by the British Museum who currently has it on display.

The papyrus consists of mathematical tables and eighty-seven mathematical problems and their solutions.

Anthropomorphic—Of human form or in human shape.

Coffin Texts—A collection of funerary spells to help the deceased in the afterlife, used mainly during the Middle Kingdom. They are derived from the Pyramid Texts.

Ascending Order—A sequence of numbers where each value is the same or greater than the previous one.

Bark—Large-sailing ship.

Base Ten—A positional numerical counting system based upon ten. The first column can represent values zero to nine and the remaining columns represent multiples of ten, hundreds, thousands, and so on respectively.
Beard—The beard was a symbol of kingship. It appeared in paintings, carvings, and the sarcophagi of the pharaohs. Ruling queens had fake beards for special ceremonies.

Biliterals—See 2-consonant.

Binary Numbers—A sequence of numbers increasing by multiples of two. For example; 1, 2, 4, 8, 16, 32, 64, 128 . . .

Cardinal Number—Cardinal numbers, also known as counting numbers, are those which represent quantity.

Cartouche—A carved or cast ornamental tablet or panel in the form of a either a ring or lozenge-shaped frame. Cartouches are sometimes known as royal rings and are used to contain the name of a pharaoh.

Cartouche Determinative—See cartouche. They are a special type of determinative because they inform the reader that the name within the cartouche belongs to a pharaoh.

Corn-measure—Different fractional parts of the Wadjet eye represent fractions of a Hekat (Heqat) for measuring corn.

Consonantal—Non-vowel, sound-making hieroglyph(s).

Cosmogony—Myths relating to creation.

Counting Boards—Boards marked in columns or containing pegs, used by ancient Egyptian scribes to assist them with counting and basic arithmetic.

Crescent Moon—The moon in her first quarter.

Cubic Cubit—A unit of volume, a royal cubit multiplied by itself three times—cubit[3]. Remember that three-cubic cubits is a 1/27 of the volume of three cubits cubed.

Cylinder-Seal—Cylinder seals are made from stone such as hematite, obsidian, steatite, amethyst, and carnelian, or made from glass, or ceramics such as Egyptian faience. Of the many varieties of material used to make cylinder seals, lapis lazuli was especially popular because of the beauty of the blue stone.

The seals were engraved with hieroglyphs. They left an impression when they were rolled over mud or the damp clay covers that closed jars of valuable commodities such as wine. The cylinder seals were worn by the owner on the chest like a pendent, and were used as administrative tools, jewellery, and as magical amulets. Basically, they ensured that goods and documents were not tampered with.

Denary—See base ten.

Denominator—The denominator is the number below the line in a fraction, indicating how many parts the number above is to be divided by.

Diacritical Tick—A special mark attached to a hieroglyph. It indicates a special phonetic value and distinguishes this hieroglyph from those of similar form.

Des-jug—A jug for the volumetric measure of beer, approximately ½ Litre.

Determinative—A hieroglyph with no sound value. It ends a word to supplement its meaning, thus giving the reader a better understanding and clarification about the word.

Dialect—The characteristic speech of a particular district.

Divine Proportion—A style of painting and sculpting popular during Medieval and Renaissance times. Elements in the art work were laid out according to mathematical rules to achieve balance and beauty.

Dynamic symmetry—See Divine Proportion.

Dynasty—A line of succession of kings who are usually related.

Early Dynastic Period—Dynasties 0-3 (circa. 3100-2600 BC).

Egyptologist—A person that studies the archaeology and the language of ancient Egypt.

Epagomenal Days—Egyptian astronomers understood that the 360 day calendar was short by five days. So five days holiday were added to the existing 360 day calendar called epagomenal days.

Eye of Horus—The left eye; is also known as the Wadjet Eye, Udjat, or Utchat eye, meaning the sound eye. The left eye of Horus was ripped apart by his murderous uncle, Seth. It is also known as the Eye of Thoth, named after the god who repaired the damaged left eye.

The Eye of Horus was one of the most common amulets of ancient Egypt. This highly stylized eye of the falcon is associated with regeneration, health, and prosperity. This left eye is black and represents the moon. As an amulet, the Eye of Horus has three versions; a left, a right eye, and both eyes. The separate parts of the Horus eye represent fractions of a Hekat.

Over the millennia, the ancient Egyptians became to recognize the right eye as the Wadjet Eye mainly because the daytime sun was recognized as being more powerful than the night-time sun, the moon.

Eyes of Horus—Both eyes together are known as the 'Two Eyes of Horus the Elder'.

Eye of Ra (Re)—This is the right eye of Horus, it represents the sun and is coloured white. Sometimes this eye represents the Wadjet Eye because the Eye of the Sun is seen as the more powerful eye and the moon is seen as the nightly sun.

Eye of Thoth—This is the left eye of Horus. See Eye of Horus. Many authors, especially those providing fact sheets on the internet, appear to have problems distinguishing the left from right when facing a pair of eyes. *When you are facing someone, their right eye is on your left, and vice versa*. See Wadjet Eye.

Faience—Bluish-green man-made material used for jewellery such as amulets and decorative items.

Festivals—Ancient Egyptian festivals centred on procession by land and river, and were celebrated on particular days or a series of days in the official year. The official year was 365 days long, which was just short of the solar year which is 365 1/4 days; as a result, the official year gradually moved back, with the official 'winter' months and their festivals falling into the summer. There seems to be no attempt to move the festivals, even those relating to agricultural events in the solar year such as flood, or the low-river sowing season. Such fixed reference to the official year demonstrates the remarkable power of the centralised kingship, in determining the timing of festivals that would have been celebrated by large numbers across the country. The role of festivals in daily life is indicated by the names of months; these derive from names of festivals, and were kept in use even after the conversion of Egypt to Christianity in the early centuries AD.

Fire-drill—Used to make fire. A block of wood on which another piece of wood, like a dowel, is rotated to create heat by friction resulting in a small fire.

First Intermediate Period—Dynasties 7-11; period of political instability (circa. 2150-1950 BC).

Font—A table of characters accessible through the keyboard of a computer.

Fraction—A numerical quantity which is not an integer.

Frustum—A cone or pyramid with a smaller section resembling the overall shape removed from the top. The intersection plane that separates the top and bottom parts of the structure runs parallel with the base of the overall shape.

Fuller—A fuller was a person who cleaned and thickened freshly-woven cloth, especially wool in order to remove impurities such as oils and dirt, and make the cloth ready to use. This was achieved by beating and twisting the cloth with a fuller's club and scouring the cloth, with water and sometimes urine. The process often included dying the materials as well. To 'full' the cloth meant to clean and thicken it.

Fuller's club—A fuller's club was a staff of wood strong enough to wring out for washing and dying cloth and garments.

Geb—Geb was the god of the earth; he was also called, Seb, Keb, Gebb, and Kebb. His symbols were the goose and the earth. Geb was the son of Shu and Tefnut and the brother and husband of Nut. Through Nut, he had four children, Osiris, Isis, Seth, and Nephthys. Even though, he was the god of the earth, Geb guided the dead to heaven and gave them meat and drink. It is interesting to note that while in most cultures the deity associated with the earth and its bounty is a woman, 'Mother Earth', the ancient Egyptians chose a male for this role. Geb earned the exclusive title, 'Heir of the Gods.' Geb was so admired as a ruler that the Egyptian throne was known by the epithet, 'Seat of Geb.'

He is usually shown as a man wearing either the crown of the north or of the south. Added is either the Atef crown or a goose. The goose was a sacred animal to Geb, as such he was sometimes called 'The Great Cackler' It was said that Geb's laughter was the source of earthquakes.

Other images show him lying underneath his wife, Nut, goddess of the sky and his father Shu, god of the air. He reclines on one elbow with a knee and arm in the air. In this way, he symbolized the valleys and hills of the land, which was called 'The House of Geb.' He is shown either as a dark or green-skinned man, the colours of life, the soil of the Nile and vegetation, respectively, with leaves on his skin.

Gender—The ancient Egyptian language similar to modern French had a grammatical classification of nouns as either masculine or feminine, there was no 'it'.

Glottal stop—A speech sound made by closing the vocal chords and then releasing them, as in a cough; a stop consonant articulated by releasing pressure at the glottis, as in the sudden onset of a vowel. Technically, it is a voiceless glottal plosive.

Glyphs—Abbreviation for hieroglyphs.

Gnomon—A stationary arm in the form of a spike, pole, or even an obelisk that projects a shadow of the sun. The declination of the sun by measuring the shadow position and length throughout the year is used to determine the time of day. A sundial uses a gnomon.

Golden Mean—Also refered to as the Golden Ratio, Golden Section, Divine Proportion, and Divine Section; it is an irrational mathematical constant (Phi) ϕ. Many artists and designers, including those from ancient Egypt have proportioned their works to approximate to the Golden Mean.

Golden Pyramid—Any pyramid can be classed as a Golden Pyramid if its geometry is based upon the Golden Mean. The great pyramid of Giza is an excellent example of a Golden Pyramid.

There are two ways in which a pyramid can be based on the Golden Mean and consequently be classified as a Golden Pyramid. The first is when an isosceles triangle is constructed within the pyramid from the opposite sloping sides of the pyramid. These opposite sloping sides form the equal sides of the triangle; the base of the pyramid forms the base of the triangle. Also this isosceles trangle must be constructed from two 3:4:5 right-angled triangles.

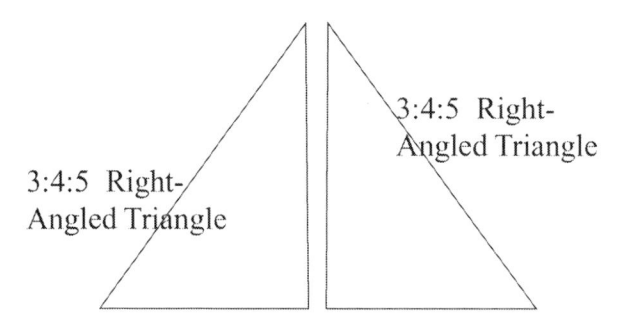

3:4:5 Right-Angled Triangle

3:4:5 Right-Angled Triangle

The second way in which a pyramid may be classed as a Golden Pyramid is when the perimeter of the base is equal to (2Pi) 2π times the height.

There is a mathematical relationship between (Pi) π and (Phi) ϕ the Golden Mean.

Golden Ratio—See Golden Mean

Golden Triangle—A Golden Triangle has sides in the ratio of 3:4:5. There are a number of proofs confirming this statement; some of the geometric proofs are based on the circle.

Graphic Transposition—Placing of one or more hieroglyphs out of the expected grammatical order for aesthetic reasons.

Greco-Roman Period—Final phase of Egyptian history under the Ptolemies and Roman Emperors (332 BC-AD 395).

Guttural Sound—The word guttural literally means 'of the throat' because they are produced in the back of the mouth. Guttural sounds have a harsh grating quality.

Hieroglyphs—the basic picture writing system as used in ancient Egypt. The pictures or symbols could represent an object, a sound or a concept or any combination of these, but not at the same time.

Hobble—A hobble is a device usually constructed from loops of rope. It is designed to prevent or limit the locomotion of an animal such as an ass. They work by tethering one or more of the animal's legs.

Honorific transposition—Placing of the signs in the name of a king or a god out of the expected grammatical order as a sign of respect.

Hypotenuse—The diagonal side of a right-angled triangle.

Ideogram—A picture hieroglyph showing actual objects or actions.

Inundation—Annual flooding of the River Nile

Infinity—A very large number; when you think you have it, add infinity to it, again and again, for ever!

Justified—The title given to those who had passed the final test of morality in the hall of judgement and so could enter the afterlife.

Kerning—The adjustment of space between pairs of letters or hieroglyphs to make them more visually appealing, by using their natural shape and slope to improve their appearance. Without kerning, several letter or hieroglyph combinations can look awkward. Kerning becomes more important as the size of the characters increases.

Keyboard Map—Also known as a keyboard layout. It is a table showing a font specific character set. It shows which character or hieroglyph is activated when a specific keyboard key is pressed.

Kiln—A furnace for firing, burning, or drying such things as bricks or porcelain.

Late Period—Dynasties 25-30 (circa. 700-331 BC).

Logogram—Hieroglyphic sign with both sound and meaning; showing actual objects or actions. Used to represent words directly with an image; also known as an ideogram.

Mathematical constant—Is a special number, usually a real number that arises naturally in mathematics. Unlike physical constants, mathematical constants are defined independently of physical measurement.

Middle Kingdom—Dynasties 12-14 (circa. 1950-1650 BC).

Moscow—See Ancient Moscow.

Multiplier—The number by which the multiplicand is multiplied.

Multiplicand—The number to be multiplied.

Netherworld—The underworld, in some religions a place called 'Hell'. The ancient Egyptians believed that after death they would go to the dark and terrifying place called the Underworld. The Underworld, called Duat, was a land of great dangers through which every Egyptian would need to pass through after death. There passage was determined according to the beliefs of the ancient Egyptian religion.

New Kingdom—Dynasties 18-20 (c. 1550-1050 BC).

Numerator—The top part of a fraction showing how many of the fractional units are taken.

Obelisk—Tall column with a pointed tip commonly setup in front of temple gateways.

Offering Formula—Conventional titles of status and authority were often laid out to the rules of standard formulae. They comprised of relatively fixed combinations of words and consequently can be read without a detailed understanding of their internal grammar.

The offering formula consists of a combination of two related functions; official and personal. In official terms, the status of the deceased was linked to the successful performance of official functions in royal service and ethical behaviour in life. The personal function relates more to the private family based aspects of the deceased. Private offerings to the dead could be physical or verbal and any offerings could be continued by living family members at the tomb or stela.

Old Kingdom—Dynasties 4-6 (circa. 2600-2150 BC)

Opposite Side—In a right-angled triangle, the vertical side which is perpendicular to the base. The opposite faces the angle at the base of the triangle which is not a right angle.

Ordinal Numbers—Ordinal numbers define the position of something in a series. For example; first, second, third, fourth.

Palace—The palace of the king was an itinerant community gathered around the king. As well as residing at a central residential and administrative complex, they also moved about the country in order to celebrate the festivals of Egypt's many gods. Today they would probably be called party animals!

Papyri—Plural of papyrus.

Papyrus—A species of reed, a sedge plant. Also a manuscript written on a kind of paper made from cutting this plant into strips and pressing it flat.

Paradox—A statement that appears to be self contradictory but actually has an element of truth.

Pharaoh Names—A new pharaoh was given five names. The two most important names are the prenomen (coronation name) and nomen (family name).

Pharaoh—The title of an ancient Egyptian king. Kings were not called pharaohs until the time of the Middle Kingdom. The word for 'pharaoh' actually means 'great house'.

Phi (ϕ)—An irrational mathematical constant approximately 1.6180339887 . . .

Phoneme—In a language dialect, a phoneme is the smallest segmental unit of sound employed to form a meaningful contrast between utterances.

Phonetics—Is concerned with the physical properties of speech sounds, auditory perception, and acoustic properties.

Phonogram—sound glyph that makes up words, used for its sound value only.

Pi (π)—A mathematical constant whose value is the ratio of any circles circumference to its diameter. It is approximately equal to 3.142. The ancient Egyptians used a value of approximately 3.160, which is very close to our modern day version of Pi (π).

Pictogram—Also called pictograph or ideogram. It conveys its meaning through its pictorial resemblance to a physical object. For example a picture of a cat would mean 'cat'.

Plosive—A plosive is a consonant sound produced by stopping the airflow in the vocal tract.

Polliwog—Another name for a tadpole.

Prime number—An integer that cannot be divided into other integers.

Pyramid—In the case of ancient Egypt, a solid object, where its base is a square and its sides are triangles, these triangle meet at a common apex.

Pyramid Texts—Collection of funerary spells to help the deceased in the afterlife. Used mainly in the Old Kingdom exclusively for royalty at first.

Quadratic—An equation involving a value squared of unknown quantity.

Ramesside Period—Term for Dynasties 19 and 20 of the New Kingdom, when a number of kings had the name Ramses.

Rebus Principle—Written symbols are borrowed to represent new words with the same sounds regardless of what these symbols originally mean. For example the picture of an eye could be used to represent the sound of a letter 'Y' in the word 'fry'.

Ready Reckoner—A set of tables used to facilitate computation.

Rhind—See Ancient Rhind

R-notation Fractions—One method the ancient Egyptians employed for expressing fractions was by writing a mouth above a denominator to express a fraction. The mouth represents 'r' in hieroglyphs, hence the term R-notation.

Ro-measure—The Ro was the smallest unit for grain by definition 320 Ro = 1 Hekat (Heqat). The symbol for the Ro is the mouth, basically it represented a mouthful.

Rosetta Stone—A large black slab of stone named after the location in 1799 in which it was found; Rosetta, Egypt. It has three deep bands of different types of writing on it; Greek, demotic and hieroglyphic all about Ptolemy V.

Sacred Ratio—The ancient Egyptians found some natural shapes and forms pleasing to the eye such as the swirls of shells and flowers. All these natural structures obey mathematical laws which can be expressed as ratios called the Golden or Sacred Ratio.

Sarcophagus—(Plural sarcophagi). A sarcophagus is a funerary receptacle for a corpse, most commonly carved or cut from stone.

The word 'sarcophagus' comes from the Greek meaning 'flesh eater', it came to refer to the limestone that was thought to decompose the flesh of corpses interred within it.

In ancient Egypt, a sarcophagus formed the external layer of protection for a royal mummy, with several layers of coffins nested within, and was often carved out of alabaster.

Scribe—The profession at first associated with the goddess Seshat is the source of the Egyptian word 'Sesh' meaning scribe. There appears during the Middle Kingdom the word 'seshet'; the feminine form of the male 'sesh'.

In the later dynasties, the profession became restricted to males.

All scribes were regarded with high status and were employed as state bureaucrats and administrators for the pharaohs. Scribes were also considered as part of the royal court and did not have to pay tax or join the military.

They were professional writers; administrative and economic activities were documented by them, they were also the accountants of their day and could perform complex mathematical calculations.

We also know that to be eligible for a scribal career, you had most likely to be well born. The sons of commoners did not reach the temple schools in general.

Second Intermediate Period—Dynasties 15-17; period of political instability and rule of the Hyksos kings (circa. 1650-1550 BC)

Sedge Plant—Also called the papyrus plant, (Latin; Cyperus Papyrus) was of great economic importance to the ancient Egyptians. Sedges are grass-like plants which generally grow in wet ground, have triangular stems and inconspicuous flowers. The sedge was the symbol for Lower Egypt, while the bee stood for Upper Egypt.

A type of writing paper called papyrus was made from this plant and also boats, baskets, and sandals were woven from it. It gained its major cultural impact when it was used in the manufacture of papyrus.

Seked—The Seked (Seqed, seqt or sqd) describes the slope of an inclined surface based on the linear unit, the Royal Cubit, which was equal to seven Palms or twenty-eight Digits.

The angle of a slope was therefore expressed as the number of Palms and Digits that had to be moved horizontally to give a vertical rise of one Royal Cubit.

Seqed—See Seked.

Sequential List—A list of numbers in either ascending or descending order of magnitude. Usually a sequential list of numbers is in ascending order.

Seqt—See Seked.

Sesh—See scribe.

Seshet—See scribe. The word seshet should denote a female scribe. But some scholars believe that this is a short version of a female title probably meaning 'painter of her mouth' or 'beautician' as it is found listed together with the word for hairdresser.

Despite the presence of the word seshet, there is not any sound evidence to suggest that women were able to read and write in ancient Egypt. The main reason for this may be that as they were not working within the bureaucracy, they were not given the opportunity to create any records that could have lasted to the present day. We may just lack the necessary proof that some documents were written by a woman.

In the Middle Kingdom there existed a woman called Seshet Idwy, who was the owner of a scarab seal. This seal indicated that she was of high status, a much higher status than that of a beautician.

Shen Ring—The shen ring is a stylised ring of rope with each end visible. It was almost always a symbol of eternity. However, the shen ring also held the idea of protection. It most often carried this connotation when seen in its elongated variation, the cartouche; which surrounded the birth names and throne names of the pharaohs.

Sickle—A sickle is a short handled agricultural tool with a semicircular curved blade. It is typically used for harvesting grain crops or cutting grasses such as papyrus.

Slope—A slope is either an upward or downward incline. The ancient Egyptians were only interested in upward inclines, typically those of the sides of a pyramid. The amount by which the incline of a slope can vary is determined by its gradient. See Seked.

Sound Complement(s)—One consonant phonogram used to echo the final consonant(s) of a two or three-consonant phonogram.

Sqd—See Seked.

Stela—Monument erected to commemorate a person or event, the plural is stelae.

Syllabic Writing—Uses a set of written unique symbols, which represent or approximate to each syllable that make up words of the language, or dialect. A symbol in syllabic writing typically represents an optional consonant sound followed by a vowel sound. The ancient Egyptian language is not syllabic. In a syllabic writing system, the overwhelming numbers of signs are used solely for their phonetic values. These phonetic signs are Syllabograms, meaning that they represent syllables rather than individual sounds.

Syllabogram(s)—A symbol that represents a syllable.

Tenet—A tenet is a core belief, dogma, doctrine, opinion or principle held by a group or individual. It is generally used to mean a position dearly held or valued and believed to be true, rather than a casual thought or opinion.

Third Intermediate Period—Dynasties 21-24; period of political instability (circa. 1050-700 BC).

Thomas Young—Thomas Young was an English genius in many fields of study, he was also a physician and physicist. By the age of fourteen, it is said that he was acquainted with Latin, Greek, French, Italian, Hebrew, Arabic, and Persian. So great was his knowledge that he was called Phenomena Young by his fellow students at Cambridge. He became very interested in Egyptology, and is famous for having partly deciphered the Egyptian hieroglyphs specifically on the Rosetta Stone which was discovered on one of Napoleon's expeditions in 1814. The key to his discovery was when he realized that the name 'Ptolemy' was repeated in each of the three languages on the Rosetta Stone. After working out the spelling for Ptolemy, he realized that demotic letters were a development from simplified hieroglyphs.

His studies of the Rosetta Stone, contributed greatly to the subsequent deciphering of all ancient Egyptian hieroglyphic writing. Contrary to popular myth, he achieved this partial translation before Jean Francois Champollion who eventually expanded on his work.

Translation—Is to copy a text from one language into another, such as from ancient Egyptian hieroglyphs to English. Translation also applies to the verbal conversion of one language into another and maintaining the meaning of what is spoken.

Transliteration—The recording of a series of hieroglyphs, using a standard set of simple symbols or letters to represent each hieroglyph. This saves a lot of time and effort laboriously drawing out each symbol in full.

Trilingual—Inscription in three languages, usually hieroglyphic Egyptian, demotic (cursive) Egyptian, and Greek.

Triliterals—See 3-consonant.

Uniliterals—See 1-consonant.

Units of Measure—Are standard quantities used to gauge the size of something by comparison. The ancient Egyptians had their own standard units for measuring most things such as length, gradient, area, volume, and time.

Uraeus—Sacred cobra depicted rearing up in attack position.

Vinculum—A line drawn above a group of mathematical terms such as the line separating the numerator from the denominator in a fraction.

Vowel—An alphabetic character that represents in speech a sound pronounced without stoppage or friction of breath.

Wadjet Eye—The evil God Seth tore the left eye of Horus into pieces then it was repaired by the God Thoth; hence the left eye gained its title; 'sound eye or Wadjet'. The separate parts of this eye represent fractions of a Hekat, in a system called the Corn Measure.

Wepwawet—Funerary stelae often show the god Wepwawet and Anubis alongside Osiris. Wepwawet was an ancient Egyptian god of Abydos that represented a jackal or a dog. The name 'Wepwawet' means 'lord of the sacred land', where 'sacred land' means the cemetery. Consequently this god was associated with cemeteries and funerals.

§ 3.2.0.1 Notes of Interest

The festival of drunkenness was celebrated every year in honour of the goddess Hathor. Hathor, the goddess of drunkenness and generally having a good time, was originally depicted as a cow. Later she was represented as a woman with a cows head, then as a woman with horns; some statues give her cow's ears.

The purpose of the celebration was to drink as much beer and wine as possible over a five-day period. This celebrating seemed to go on late into the nights as well as most of the day time.

Of course, the ancient Egyptians believed that the drunkenness associated with the festival was a means of achieving an altered state of mind, no doubt it did! This altered state enabled worshippers to see the divine or receive messages from the goddess. I wonder if the Sphinx ever got a red traffic road cone as a hat. Any excuse for a party!

HATHOR

§ 3.2.0.2 Notes of Interest

It was the duty of every pharaoh to ensure that order, or rather Maat was maintained in the same way that the god Ra had done so. The attitude that the ancient Egyptians took with respect to order was viewed strictly along class lines and should come as no surprise to us. If good fortune came to a poor person, it was not considered a blessing or something to celebrate, but rather a sign that something was wrong with the universe. This attitude is confirmed in the following lament.

> *He who possessed no property now is a man of wealth. The poor man is full of joy. Every town says; let us suppress the powerful among us. He who had no yoke of oxen is now possessor of a herd. The possessors of robes are now in rags. Gold and lapis lazuli, silver and turquoise are fastened on the necks of female slaves are free with their tongues. When their mistress speaks it is irksome to the servant. The children of princes are dashed against the walls.*

This lament follows a common theme found throughout ancient Egyptian literature. As long as the rich and powerful prospered while the poor remained in their places, order was maintained.

3.3.0 KEYBOARD MAPS

3.3.1 PHYSICAL KEYBOARD VIEWS

The following catalogue of keyboards show what each character key represents depending upon which Egyptian font is active at the time. The keyboard views also show any variations encountered when pressing keys if they are twinned with either, the shift key, capital key, or both simultaneously.

The location of any hieroglyphs or transliterative characters that were not tabularised earlier, will certainly be found in the following keyboard views.

You will find that some hieroglyphs that are phonograms are repeated on one or more keyboard maps. This is because these hieroglyphs represent the same or similar sounds of more than one alphabetical letter in the English language. For example the English sounds for the letters 'c' and 'k' often sound the same depending upon the context of their usage.

And you think pigeons are a problem!

My fangs are starting to itch.

3.3.1.1 Font Filename Egypt1.ttf

3.3.1.1 Font Filename Egypt1.ttf

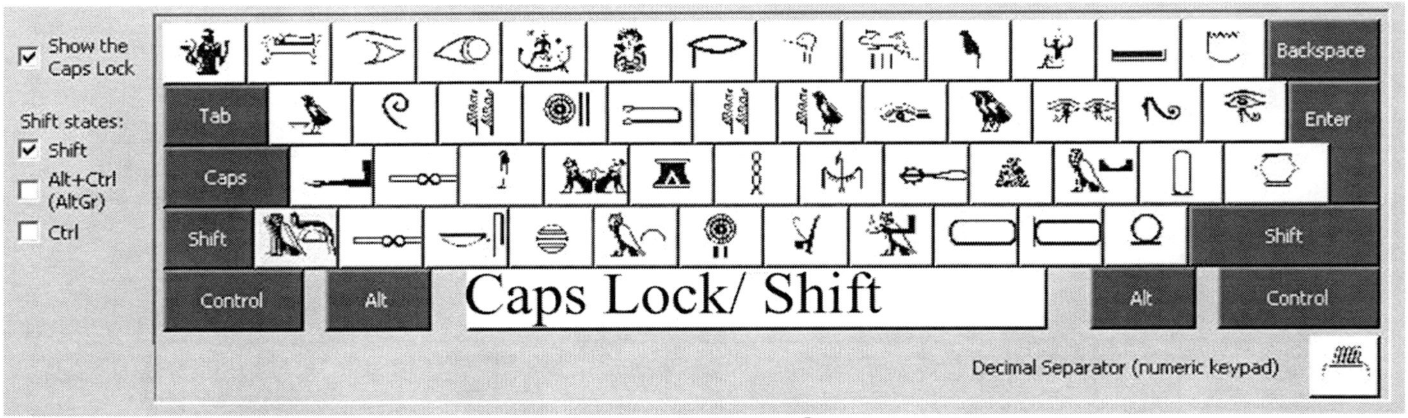

3.3.1.1 Font Filename Egypt1.ttf

3.3.1.1 Font Filename Egypt1.ttf

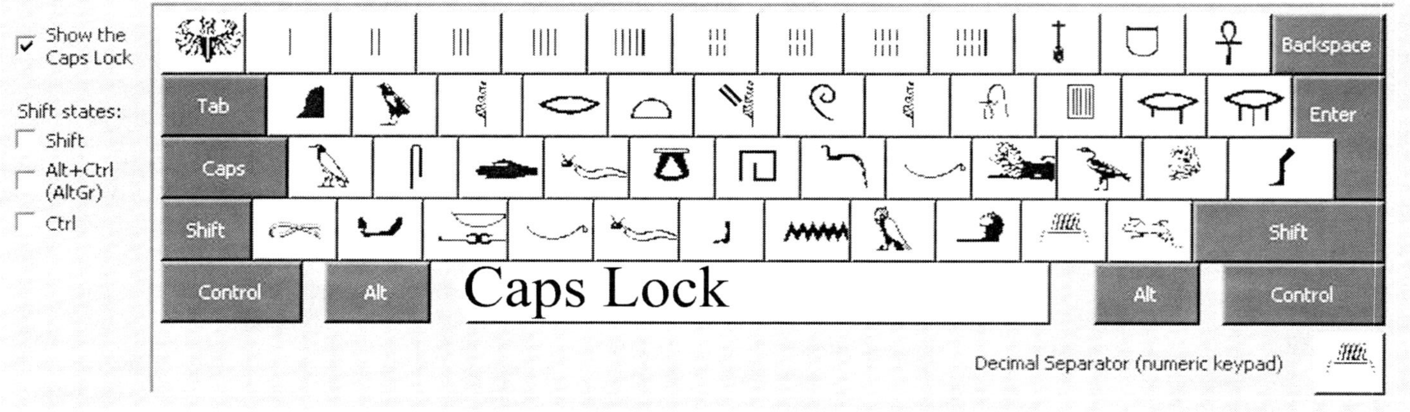

3.3.1.1 Font Filename Egypt1.ttf

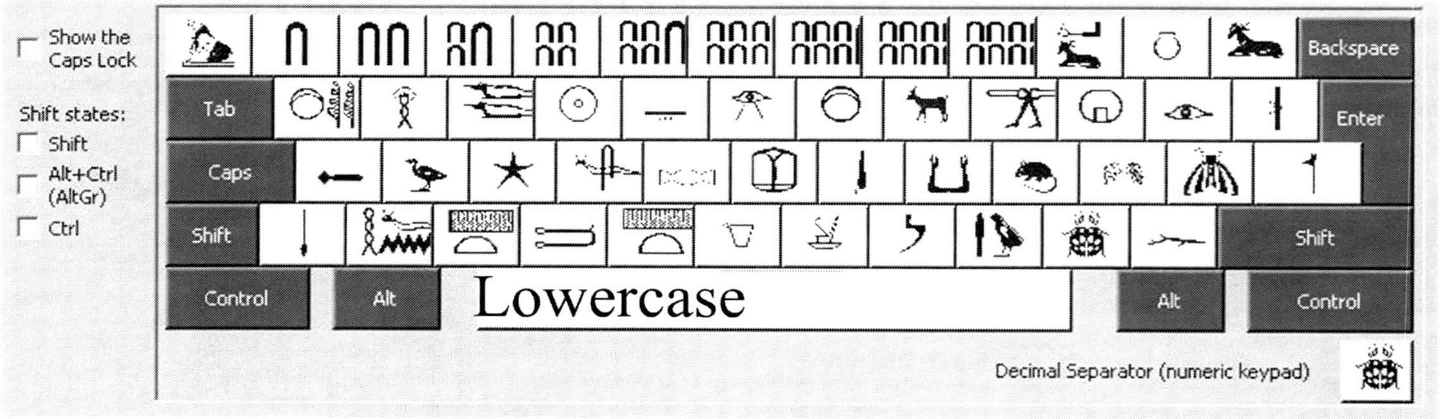

3.3.1.2 Font Filename Egypt2.ttf

3.3.1.2 Font Filename Egypt2.ttf

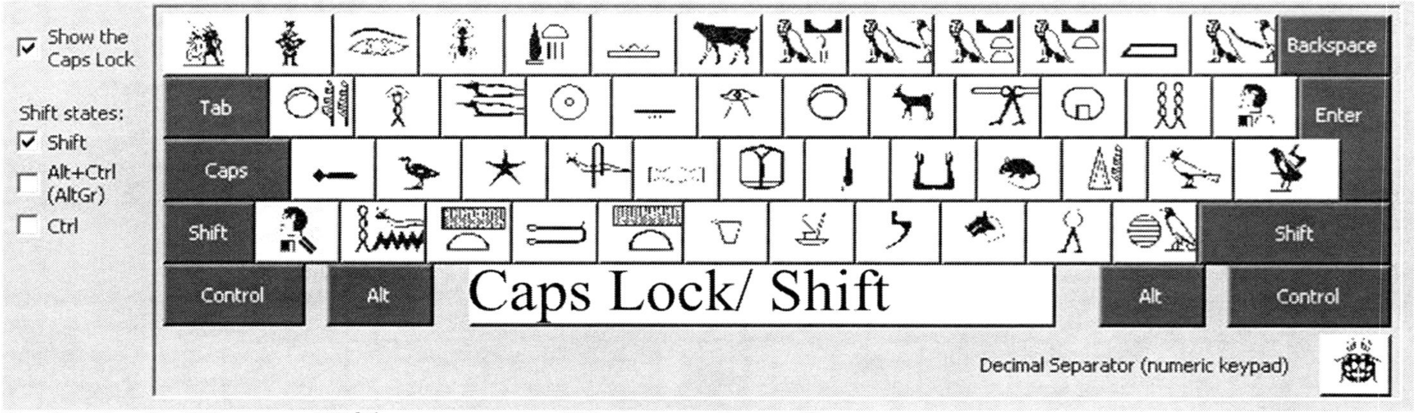

3.3.1.2 Font Filename Egypt2.ttf

3.3.1.2 Font Filename Egypt2.ttf

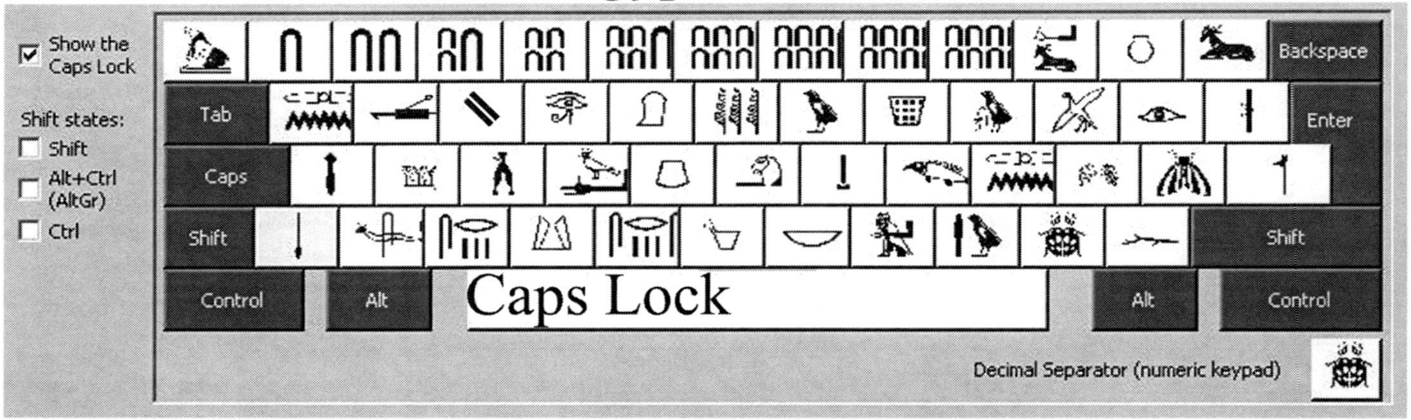

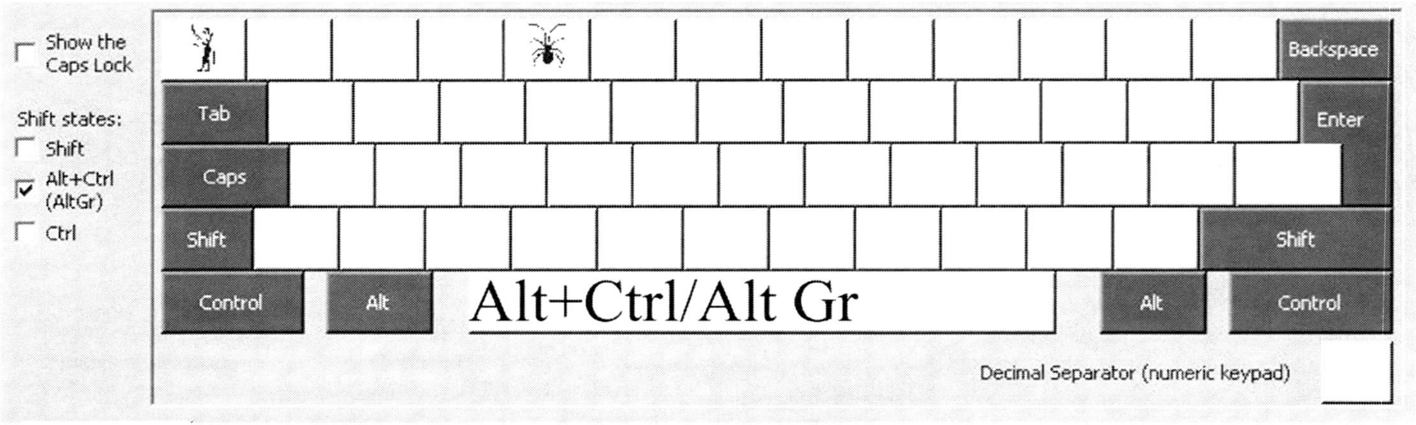

3.3.1.2 Font Filename Egypt2.ttf

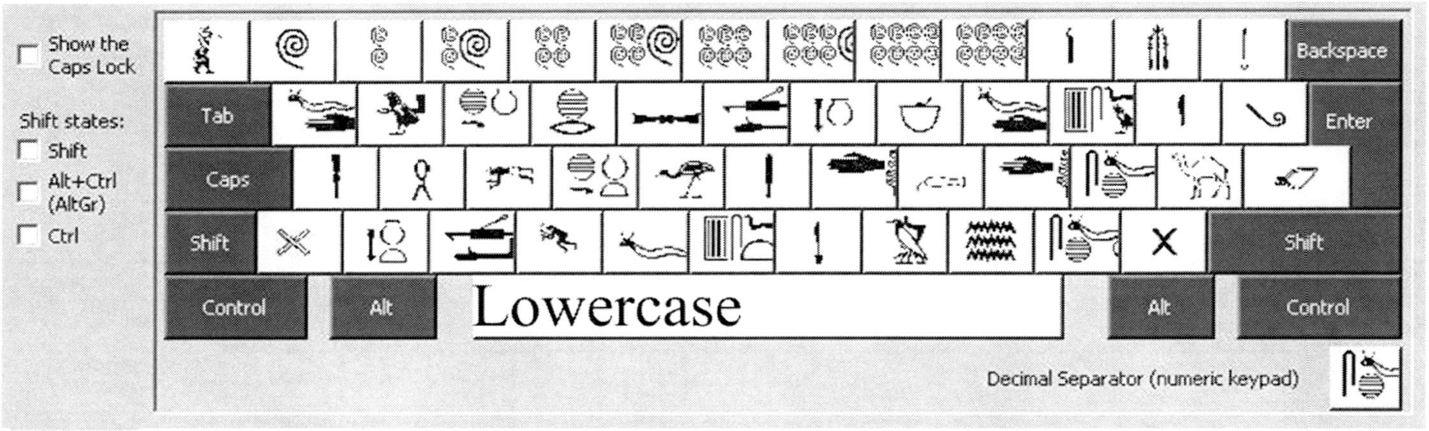

3.3.1.3 Font Filename Egypt3.ttf

3.3.1.3 Font Filename Egypt3.ttf

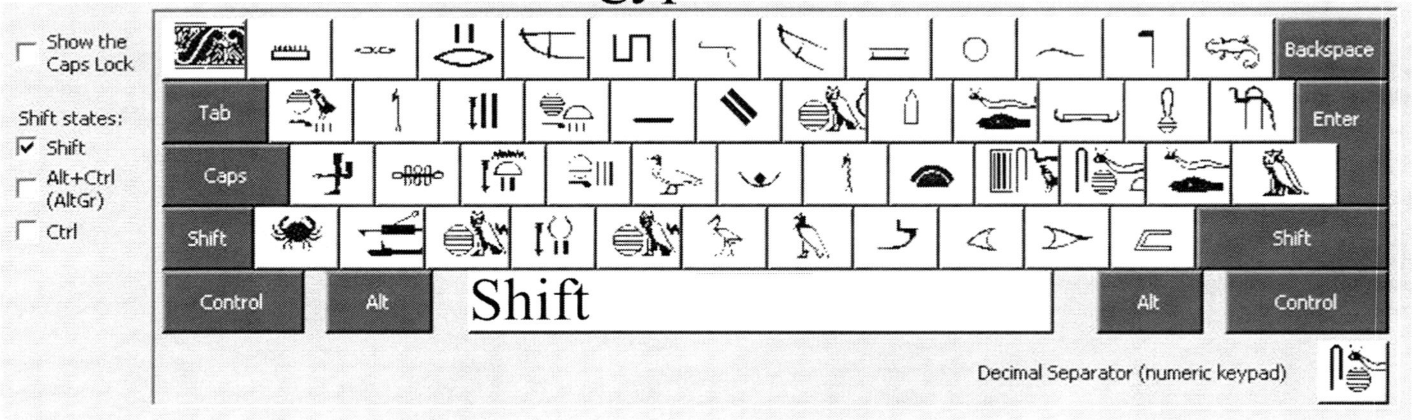

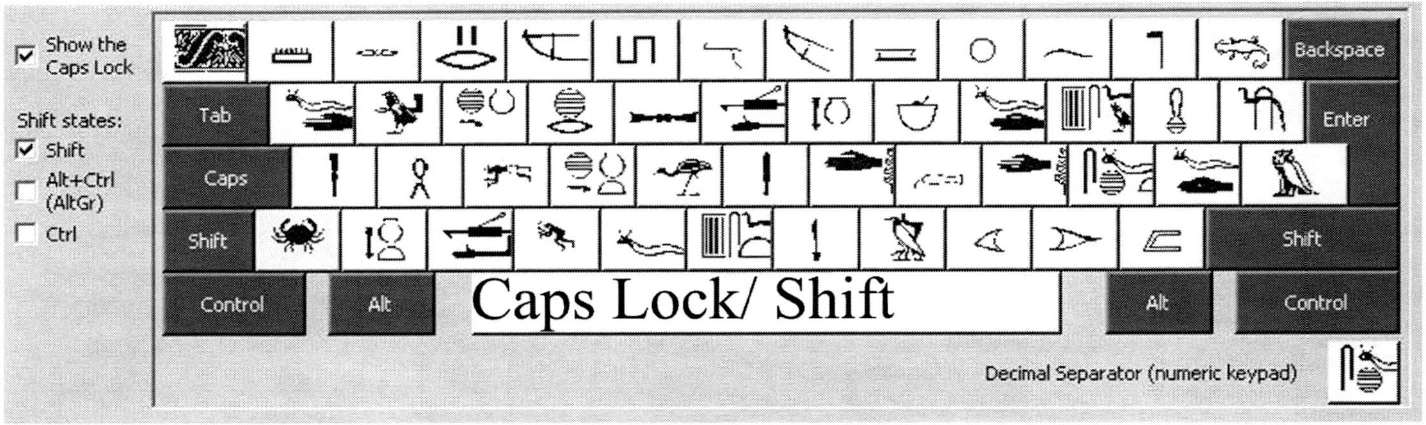

3.3.1.3 Font Filename Egypt3.ttf

3.3.1.3 Font Filename Egypt3.ttf

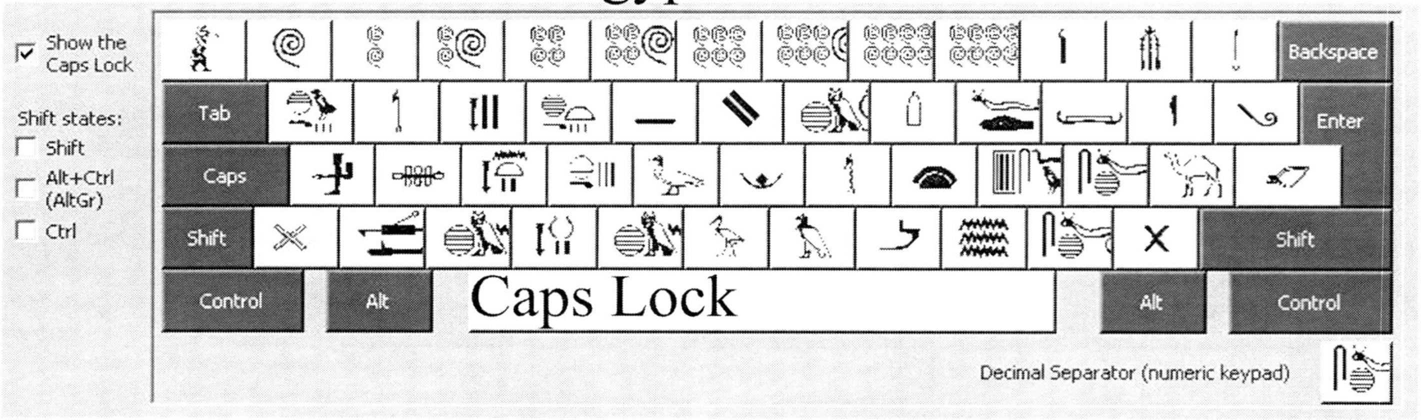

3.3.1.3 Font Filename Egypt3.ttf

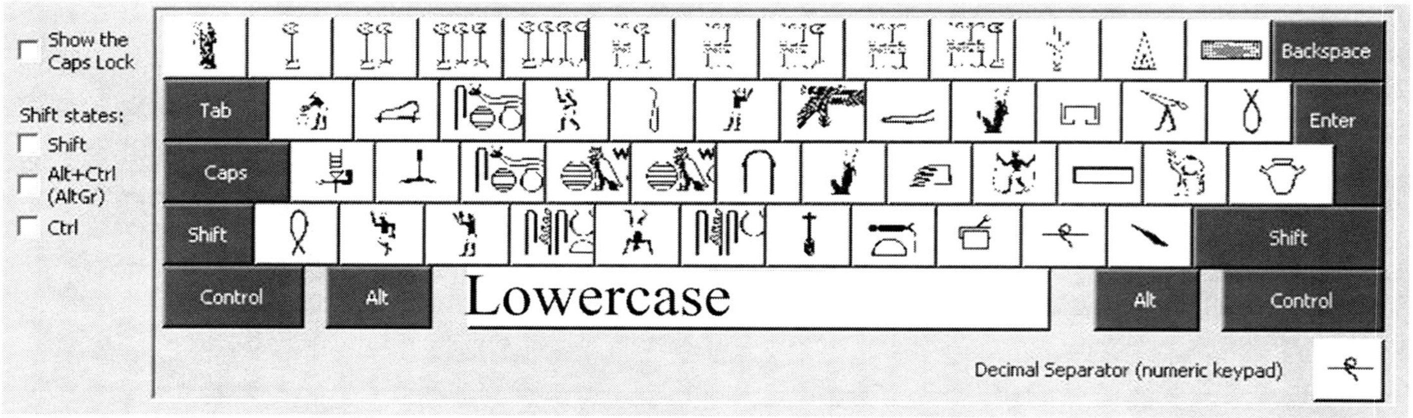

3.3.1.4 Font Filename Egypt4.ttf

3.3.1.4 Font Filename Egypt4.ttf

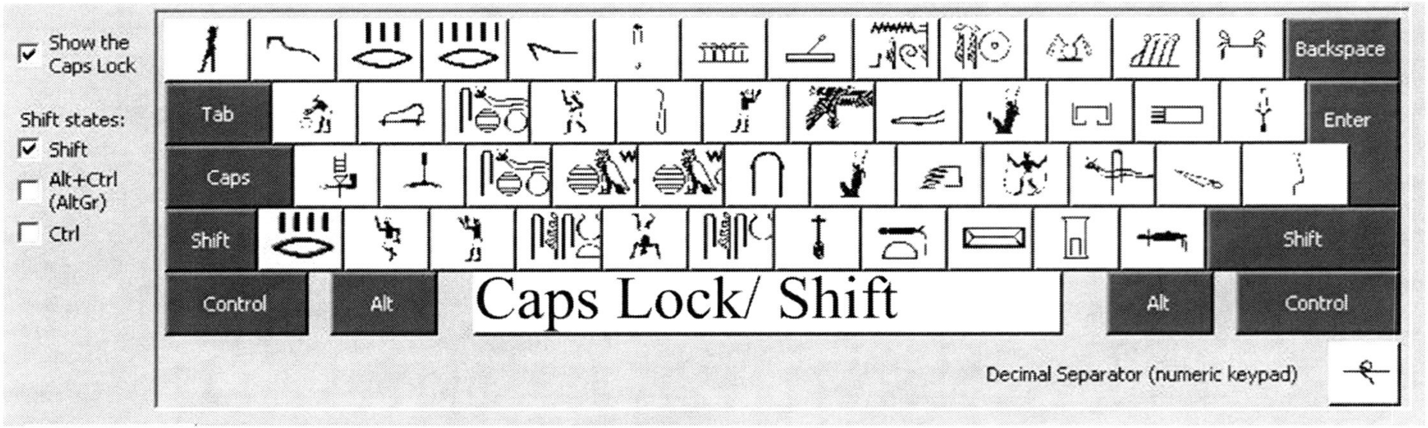

3.3.1.4 Font Filename Egypt4.ttf

3.3.1.4 Font Filename Egypt4.ttf

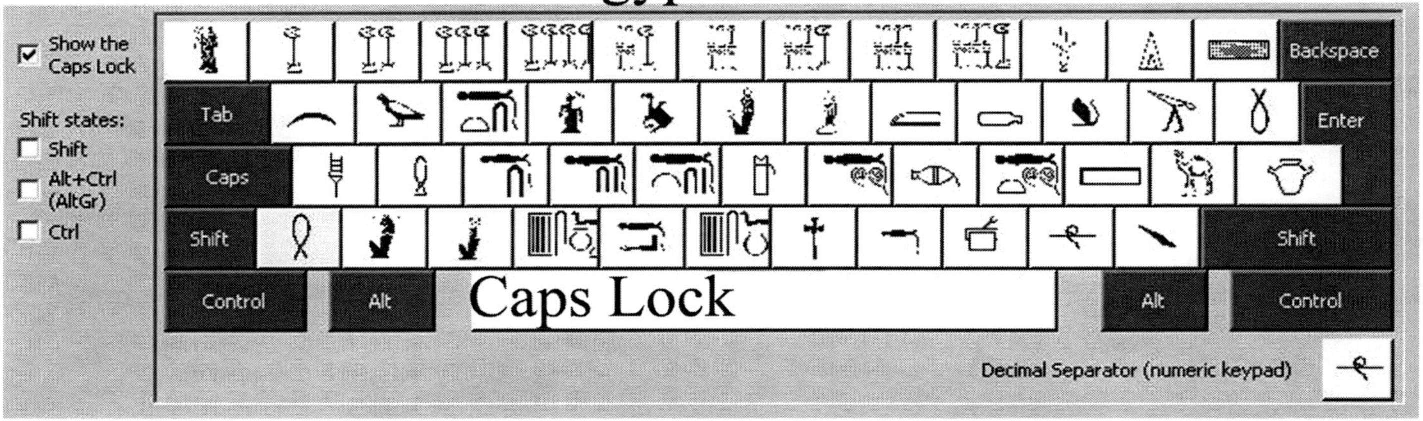

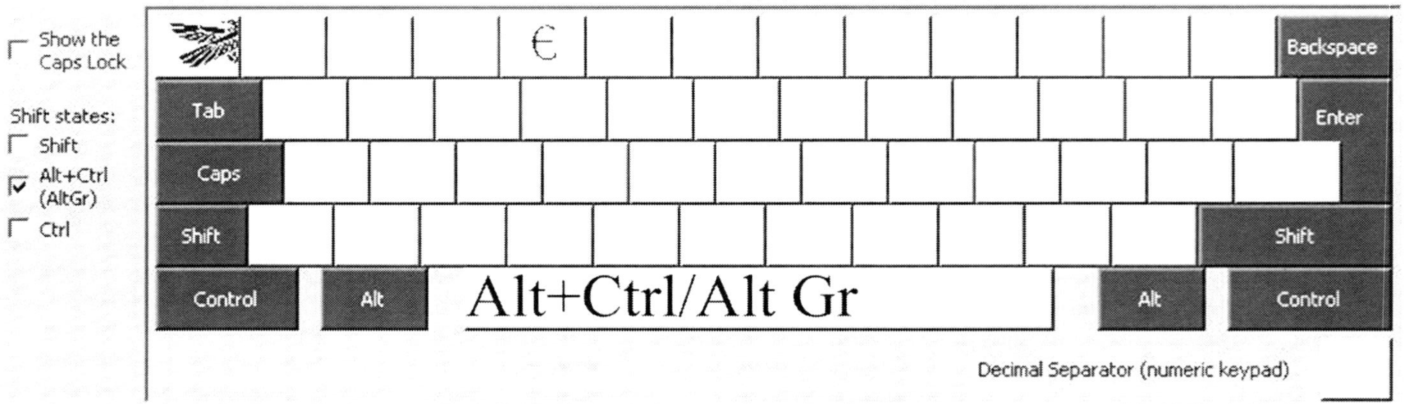

3.3.1.4 Font Filename Egypt4.ttf

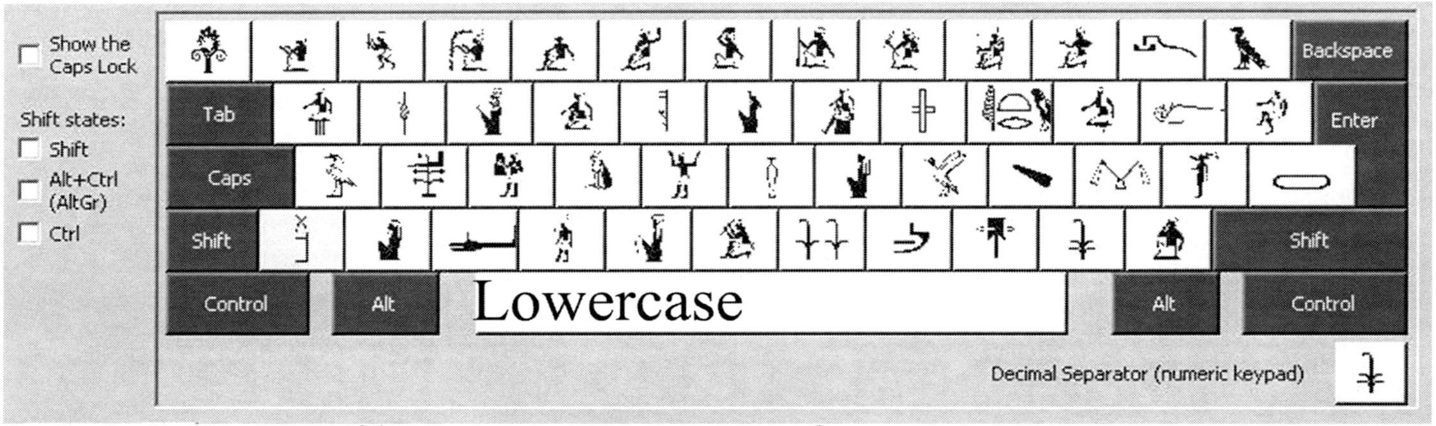

3.3.1.5 Font Filename Egypt5.ttf

3.3.1.5 Font Filename Egypt5.ttf

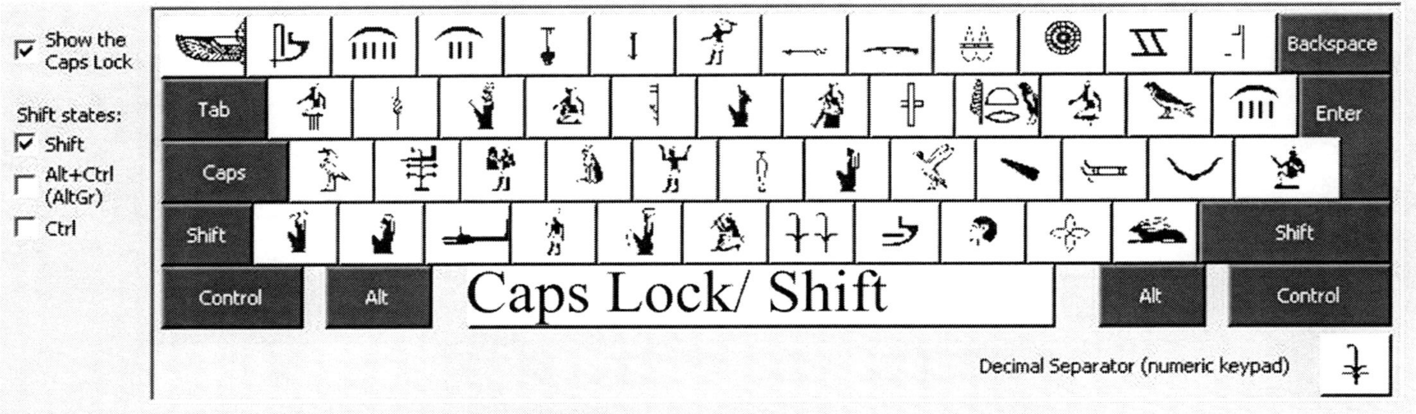

3.3.1.5 Font Filename Egypt5.ttf

3.3.1.5 Font Filename Egypt5.ttf

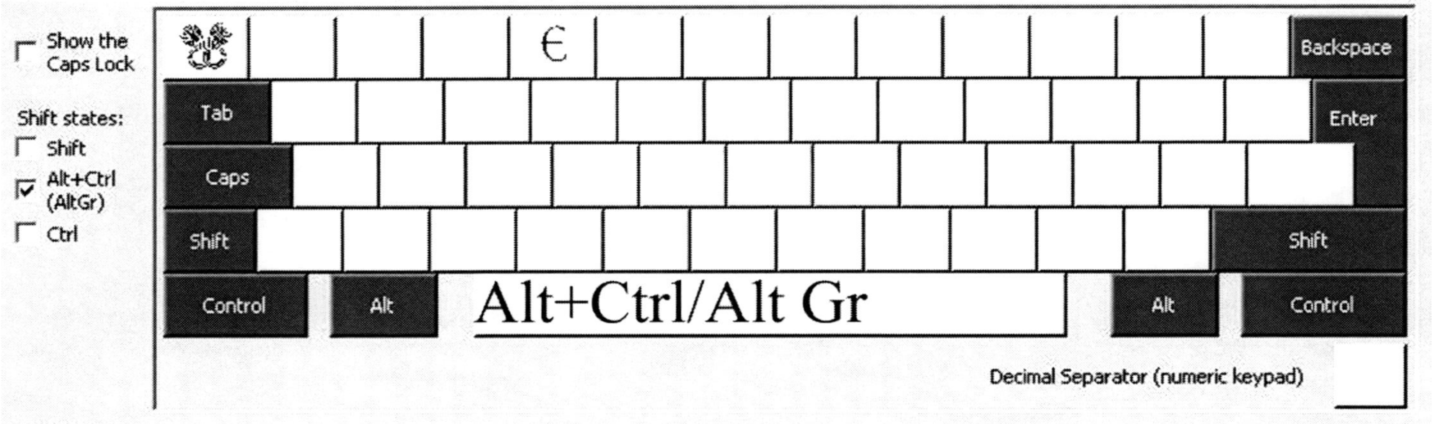

3.3.1.5 Font Filename Egypt5.ttf

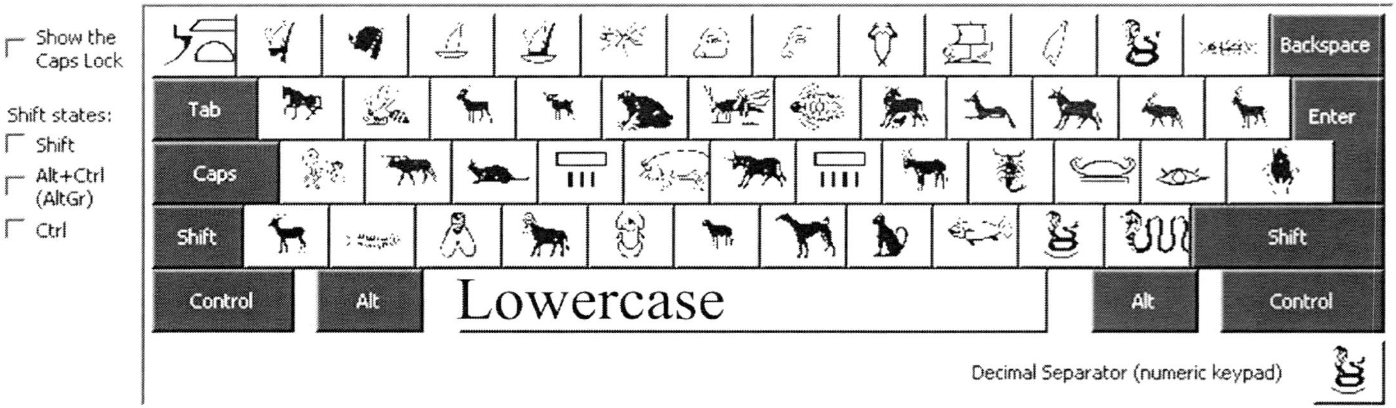

3.3.1.6 Font Filename Egypt6.ttf

3.3.1.6 Font Filename Egypt6.ttf

3.3.1.6 Font Filename Egypt6.ttf

3.3.1.6 Font Filename Egypt6.ttf

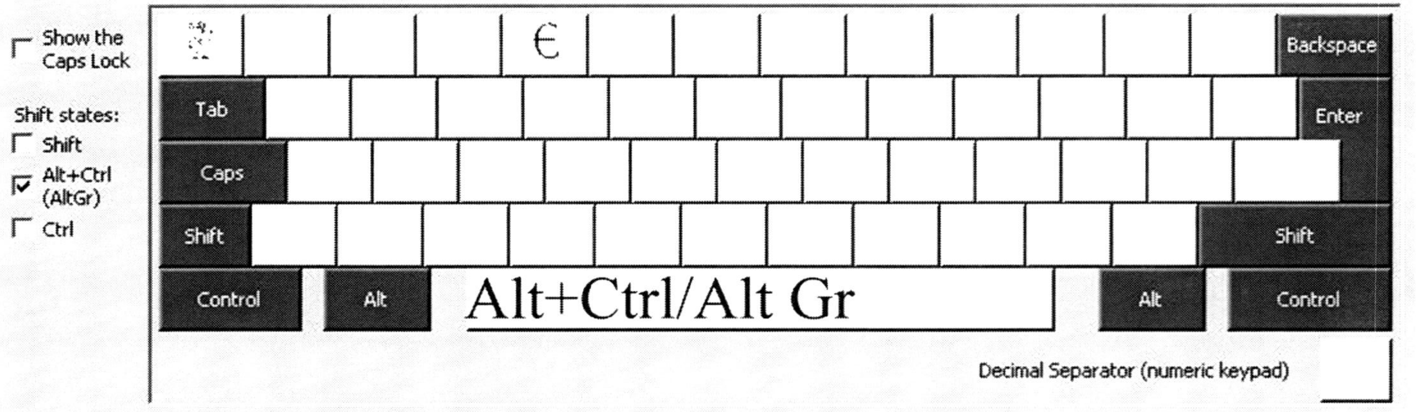
Show the Caps Lock
Shift states:
Shift
Alt+Ctrl (AltGr)
Ctrl
Backspace
Tab
Enter
Caps
Shift
Shift
Control
Alt
Alt+Ctrl/Alt Gr
Alt
Control
Decimal Separator (numeric keypad)

3.3.1.6 Font Filename Egypt6.ttf

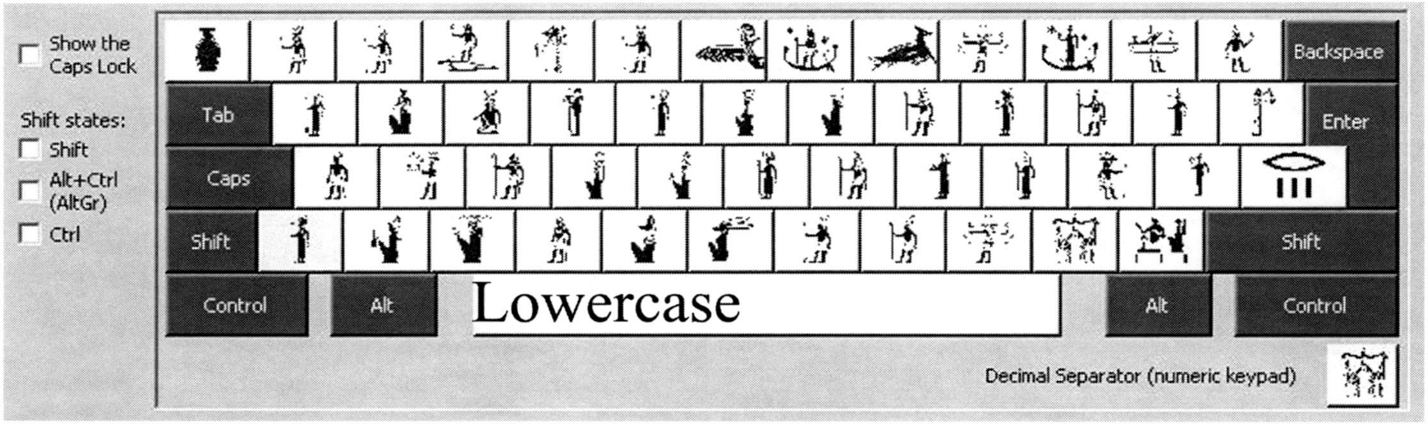

3.3.1.7 Font Filename Egypt7.ttf

3.3.1.7 Font Filename Egypt7.ttf

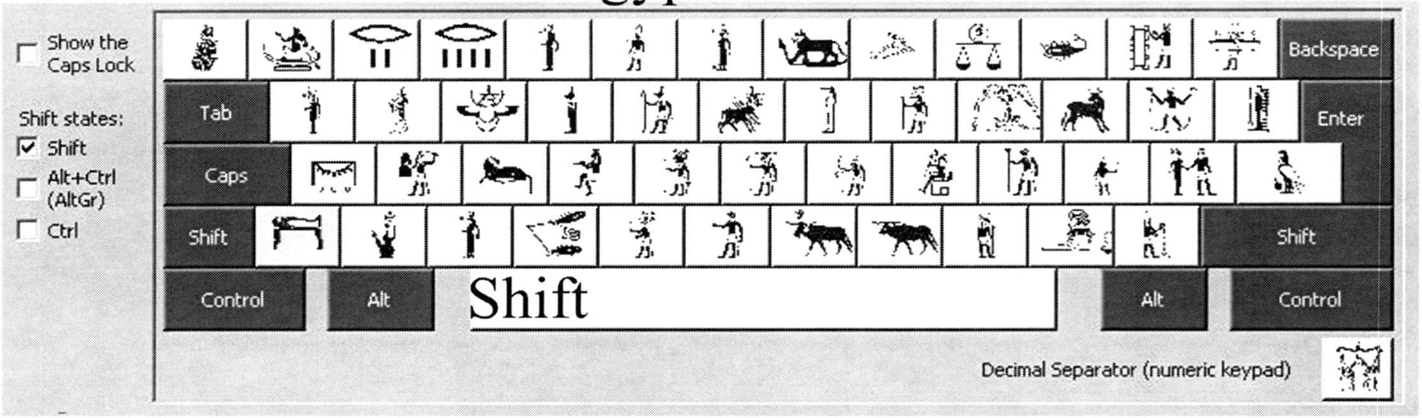

3.3.1.7 Font Filename Egypt7.ttf

3.3.1.7 Font Filename Egypt7.ttf

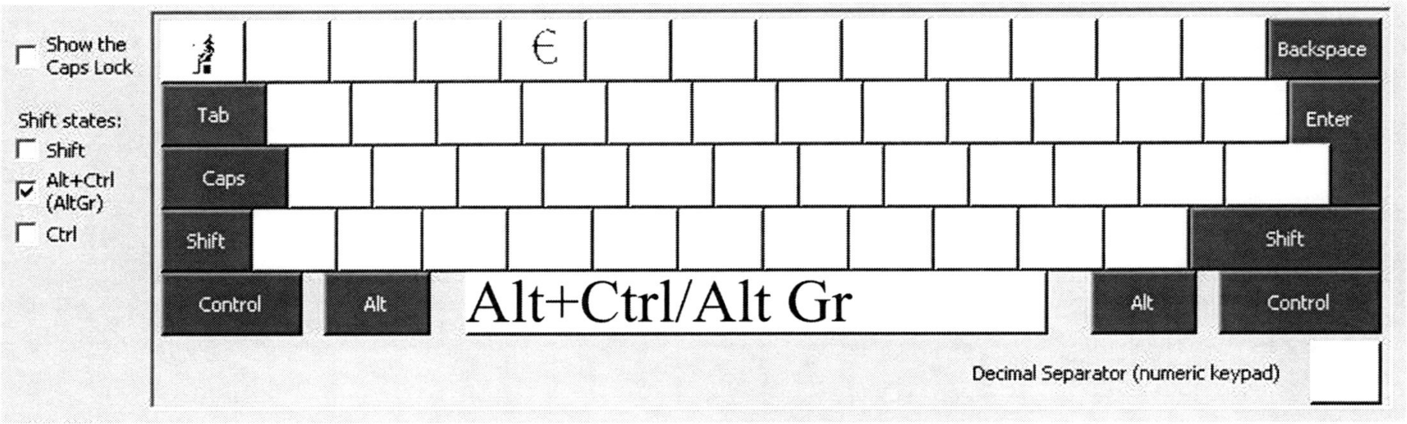

3.3.1.7 Font Filename Egypt7.ttf

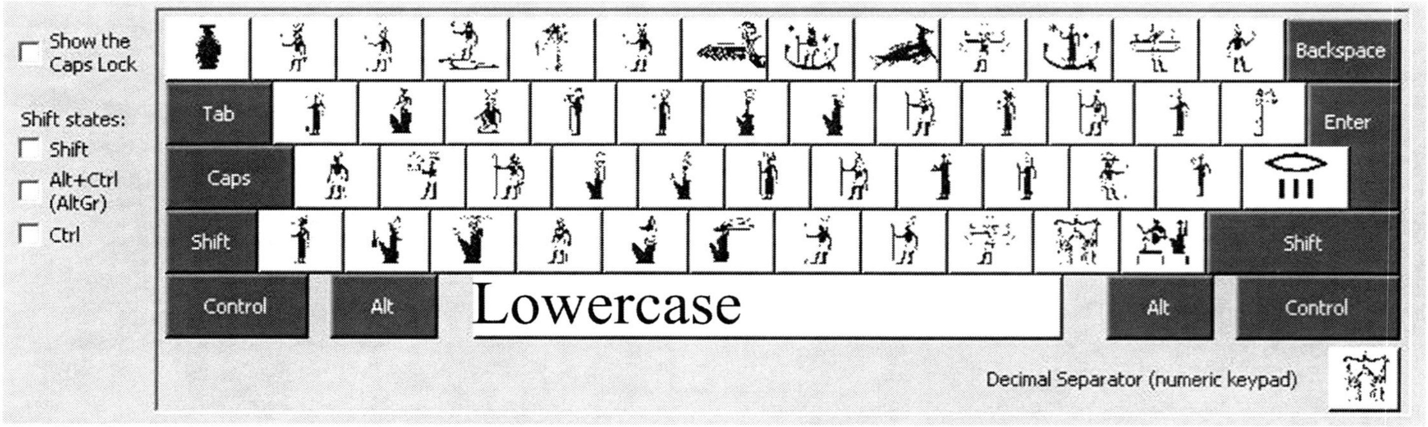

3.3.1.7 Font Filename Egypt7.ttf

3.3.1.7 Font Filename Egypt7.ttf

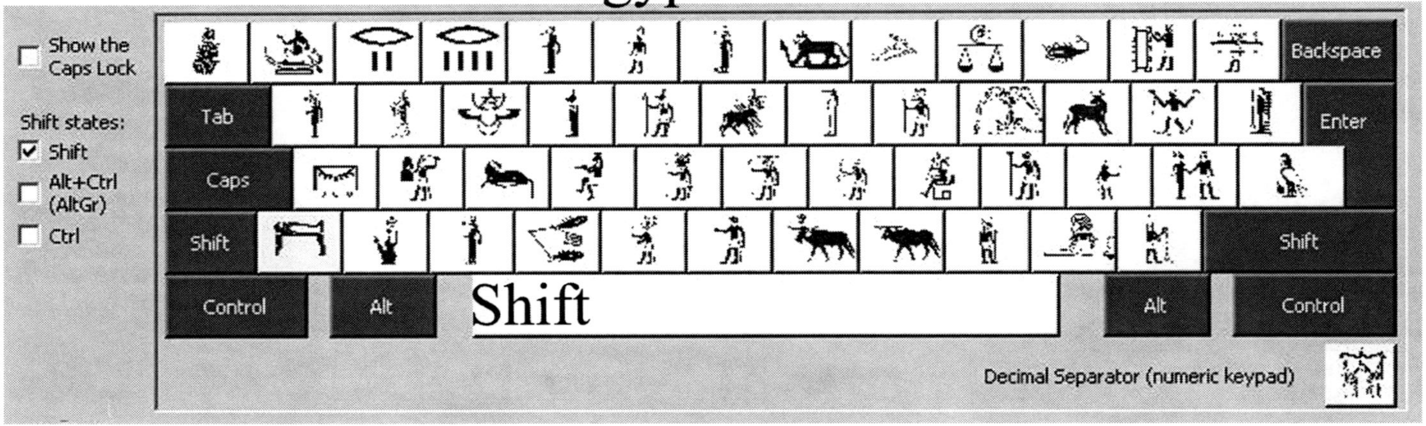

3.3.1.7 Font Filename Egypt7.ttf

3.3.1.7 Font Filename Egypt7.ttf

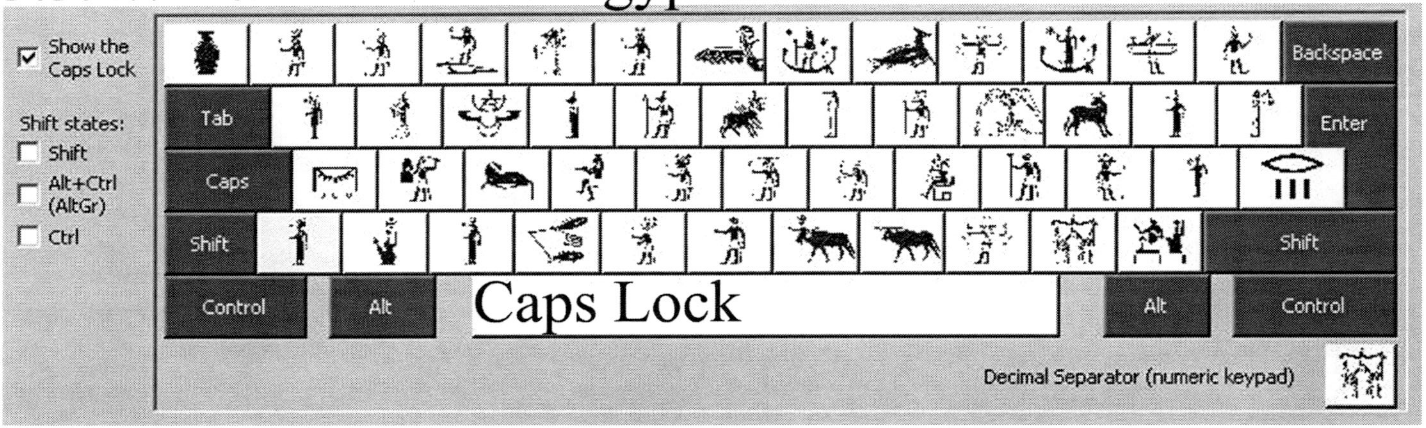

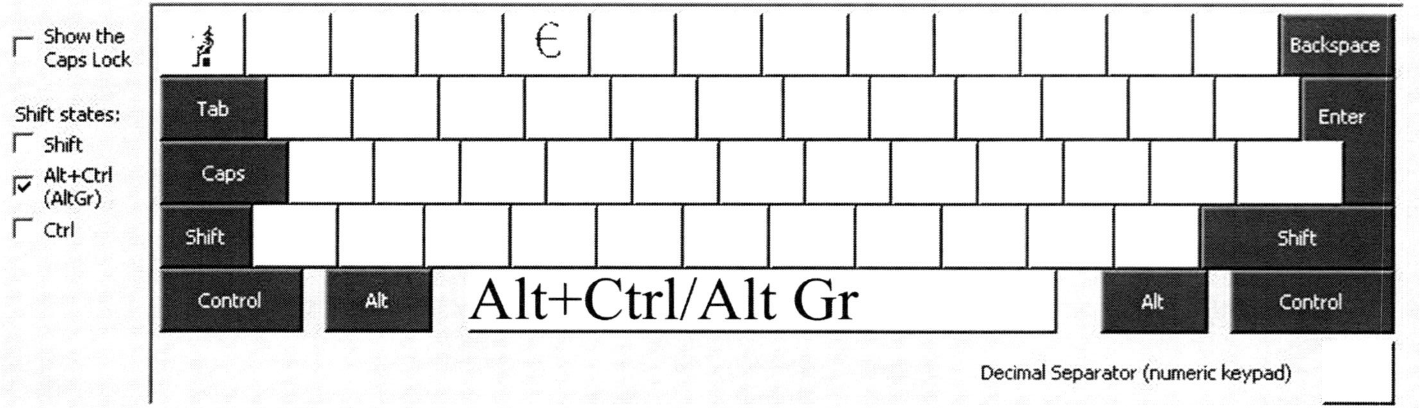

3.3.1.7 Font Filename Egypt7.ttf

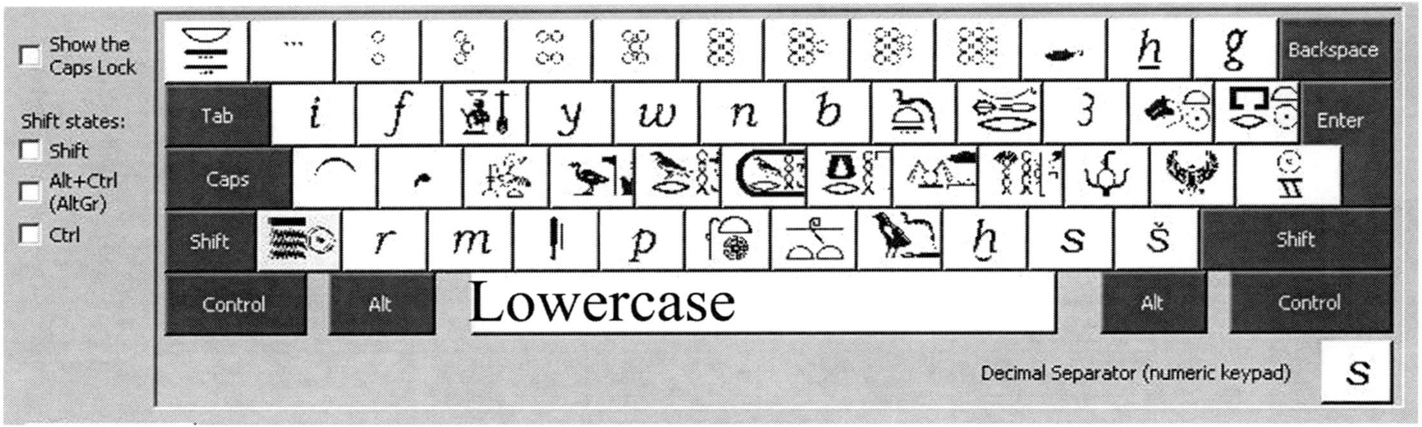

3.3.1.8 Font Filename Egypt8.ttf

3.3.1.8 Font Filename Egypt8.ttf

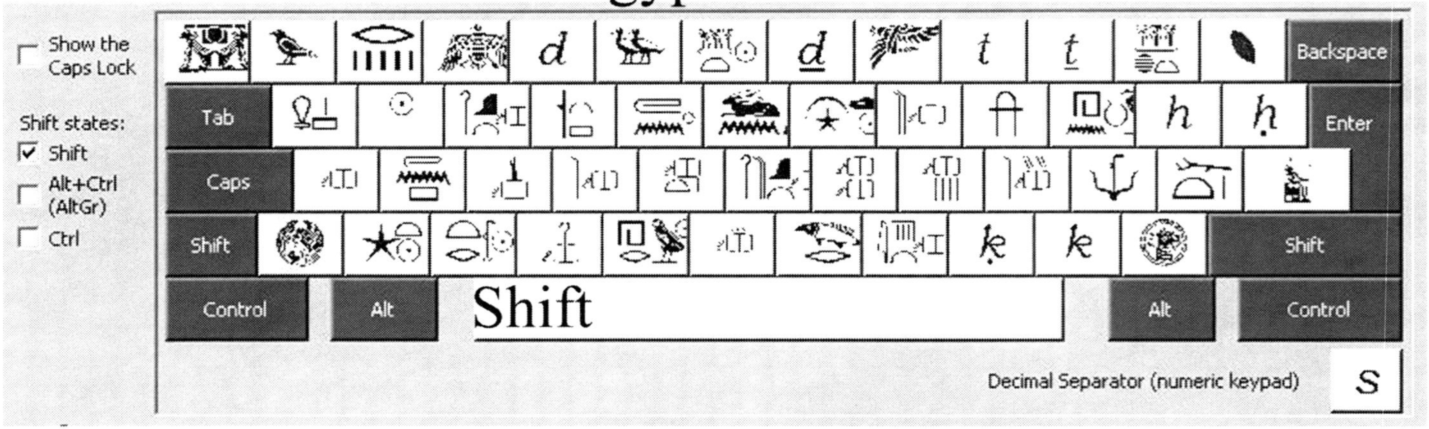

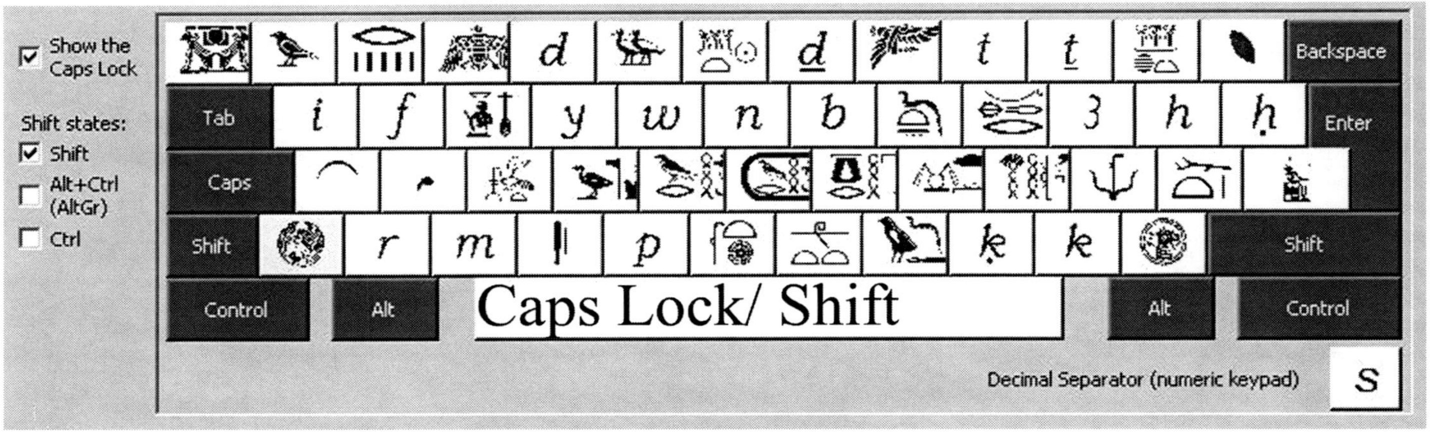

3.3.1.8 Font Filename Egypt8.ttf

3.3.1.8 Font Filename Egypt8.ttf

☑ Show the Caps Lock

Shift states:
☐ Shift
☐ Alt+Ctrl (AltGr)
☐ Ctrl

3.3.1.8 Font Filename Egypt8.ttf

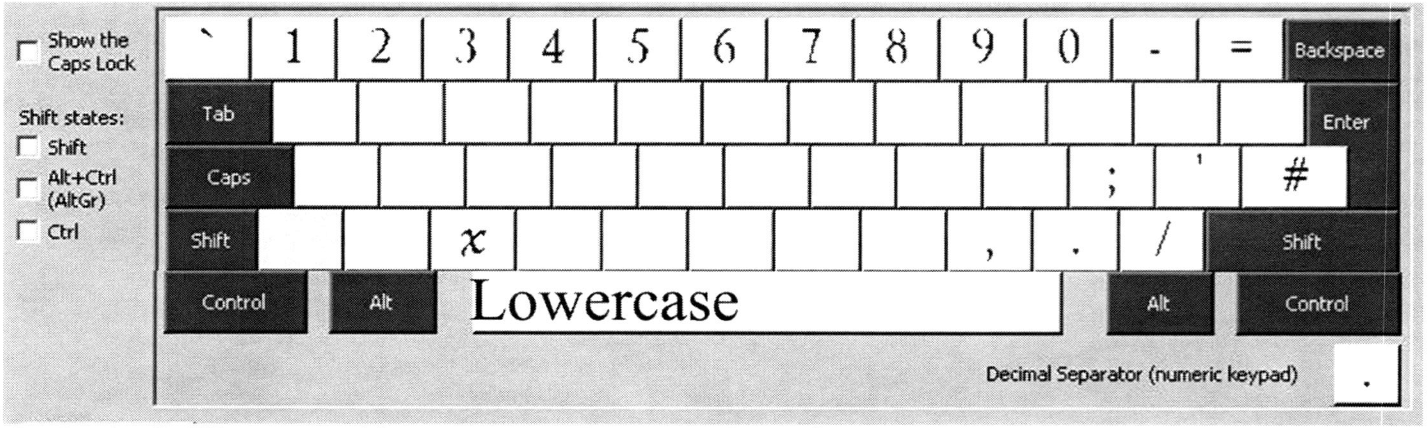

3.3.1.9 Font Filename Egypt9.ttf

3.3.1.9 Font Filename Egypt9.ttf

3.3.1.9 Font Filename Egypt9.ttf

3.3.1.9 Font Filename Egypt9.ttf

3.3.2 Character to Hieroglyph Index Mappings

3.3.2.1 Font Filename Egypt1.ttf

1	2	3	4	5	6	7	8	9
I	II	III	IIII	IIIII	:::	III	IIII	IIII
0	-	=	`	a	b	c	d	e
▯	▯	▯	▯	▯	▯	▯	▯	▯
f	g	h	i	j	k	l	m	n
▯	▯	▯	▯	▯	▯	▯	▯	▯
o	p	q	r	s	t	u	v	w
▯	▯	▯	▯	▯	▯	▯	▯	▯
x	y	z	[	]	;	'	#	\
▯	▯	▯	▯	▯	▯	▯	▯	▯
,	.	/	!	"	£	$	%	^
▯	▯	▯	▯	▯	▯	▯	▯	▯
&	*	(	)	_	+	¬	A	B
▯	▯	▯	▯	▯	▯	▯	▯	▯
C	D	E	F	G	H	I	J	K
▯	▯	▯	▯	▯	▯	▯	▯	▯
L	M	N	O	P	Q	R	S	T
▯	▯	▯	▯	▯	▯	▯	▯	▯
U	V	W	X	Y	Z	{	}	:
▯	▯	▯	▯	▯	▯	▯	▯	:
@	~			<	>	?	¦		
▯	▯	▯	▯	▯	▯	▯		

Hieroglyphs and Arithmetic of the Ancient Egyptian Scribes   335

3.3.2.2 Font Filename Egypt2.ttf

1	2	3	4	5	6	7	8	9
∩	∩∩	∩∩	∩∩	∩∩∩	∩∩∩	∩∩∩∩	∩∩∩∩	∩∩∩∩
0	-	=	`	a	b	c	d	e
f	g	h	i	j	k	l	m	n
o	p	q	r	s	t	u	v	w
x	y	z	[	]	;	'	#	\
,	.	/	!	"	£	$	%	^
&	*	(	)	_	+	¬	A	B
C	D	E	F	G	H	I	J	K
L	M	N	O	P	Q	R	S	T
U	V	W	X	Y	Z	{	}	:
@	~			<	>	?				

3.3.2.3 Font Filename Egypt3.ttf

1	2	3	4	5	6	7	8	9
0	-	=	`	a	b	c	d	e
f	g	h	i	j	k	l	m	n
o	p	q	r	s	t	u	v	w
x	y	z	[	]	;	'	#	\
,	.	/	!	"	£	$	%	^
&	*	(	)	_	+	¬	A	B
C	D	E	F	G	H	I	J	K
L	M	N	O	P	Q	R	S	T
U	V	W	X	Y	Z	{	}	:
@	~	|	<	>	?	¦		

3.3.2.4 Font Filename Egypt4.ttf

1	2	3	4	5	6	7	8	9
0	-	=	`	a	b	c	d	e
f	g	h	i	j	k	l	m	n
o	p	q	r	s	t	u	v	w
x	y	z	[	]	;	'	#	\
,	.	/	!	"	£	$	%	^
&	*	(	)	_	+	¬	A	B
C	D	E	F	G	H	I	J	K
L	M	N	O	P	Q	R	S	T
U	V	W	X	Y	Z	{	}	:
@	~			<	>	?				

3.3.2.5 Font Filename Egypt5.ttf

1	2	3	4	5	6	7	8	9
0	-	=	`	a	b	c	d	e
f	g	h	i	j	k	l	m	n
o	p	q	r	s	t	u	v	w
x	y	z	[	]	;	'	#	\
,	.	/	!	"	£	$	%	^
&	*	(	)	_	+	¬	A	B
C	D	E	F	G	H	I	J	K
L	M	N	O	P	Q	R	S	T
U	V	W	X	Y	Z	{	}	:
@	~	|	<	>	?	¦		

3.3.2.6 Font Filename Egypt6.ttf

1	2	3	4	5	6	7	8	9
0	-	=	`	a	b	c	d	e
f	g	h	i	j	k	l	m	n
o	p	q	r	s	t	u	v	w
x	y	z	[	]	;	'	#	\
,	.	/	!	"	£	$	%	^
&	*	(	)	_	+	¬	A	B
C	D	E	F	G	H	I	J	K
L	M	N	O	P	Q	R	S	T
U	V	W	X	Y	Z	{	}	:
@	~			<	>	?	¦		

3.3.2.7 Font Filename Egypt7.ttf

1	2	3	4	5	6	7	8	9
0	-	=	`	a	b	c	d	e
f	g	h	i	j	k	l	m	n
o	p	q	r	s	t	u	v	w
x	y	z	[	]	;	'	#	\
,	.	/	!	"	£	$	%	^
&	*	(	)	_	+	—	A	B
C	D	E	F	G	H	I	J	K
L	M	N	O	P	Q	R	S	T
U	V	W	X	Y	Z	{	}	:
@	~	|	<	>	?	|		

3.3.2.8 Font Filename Egypt8.ttf

1	2	3	4	5	6	7	8	9
...	∴	∴	∷	⁙	⁙	⁙	⁙	⁙
0	-	=	`	a	b	c	d	e
🐟	ḥ	g	〰	⌒	🏺	|	🐝	𓀁
f	g	h	i	j	k	l	m	n
🦅	🦅	𓍹𓅓𓇋𓇋𓆱𓍺	🔔	⚱	🦅	🦅	🦅	🐊
o	p	q	r	s	t	u	v	w
🐟	3	i	y	⸱	w	b	p	f
x	y	z	[	]	;	'	#	\
m	n	r	🦅	🏺	🦅	🦅	☉	〰
,	.	/	!	"	£	$	%	^
ḫ	s	š	🐦	🏛	🦅	d	🦅	🦅
&	*	(	)	_	+	¬	A	B
ḏ	🌿	t	ṯ	🏛	⬤	𓋹	🏺	🏺
C	D	E	F	G	H	I	J	K
🏺	🏺	🏺	🏺	🏺	🏺	🏺	🏺	🏺
L	M	N	O	P	Q	R	S	T
🏺	🏺	🐟	𓉐	🏺	🏺	🏺	🏺	🏺
U	V	W	X	Y	Z	{	}	:
🌟	🦅	☉	🏺	🐟	⭐	ḥ	ḥ	𓋹
@	~	|	<	>	?	¦	h	h
𓂀	🏺	🕊	ḳ	k	🏺	🏺	𓍹𓅓𓇋𓇋𓆱𓍺

3.3.2.9 Font Filename Egypt9.ttf

1	2	3	4	5	6	7	8	9
1	2	3	4	5	6	7	8	9
0	-	=	`	a	b	c	d	e
0	-	=	`					
f	g	h	i	j	k	l	m	n
o	p	q	r	s	t	u	v	w
x	y	z	[	]	;	'	#	\
x					;	'	#	
,	.	/	!	"	£	$	%	^
,	.	/	!	"	£		%	
&	*	(	)	_	+	¬	A	B
&	*	(	)	_	+	¬		
C	D	E	F	G	H	I	J	K
L	M	N	O	P	Q	R	S	T
U	V	W	X	Y	Z	{	}	:
			X			{	}	:
@	~	|	<	>	?			
@	~	|	<	>	?			

3.4.0 Fonts Copyright and Licence Information

3.4.1 Electronic License Agreement

This is a legal agreement between you, the end user, (Licensee) and EGYPTIAN PABULUM Systems hereinafter called PABULUM.

By opening and using any of the Egypt1, Egypt2, Egypt3, Egypt4, Egypt5, Egypt6, Egypt7, Egypt8, or Egypt9 fonts hereinafter called 'The Fonts' you agree to be bound by the terms of this Agreement, whether the source of the fonts were via an online download or any analog or digital storage medium such as CD-Rom.

The Fonts are owned by PABULUM and are protected by International copyright laws and trade provisions.

3.4.1.1 License Grant

Number of Users

In consideration of the license fee paid, PABULUM grants to you, personally or on behalf of your employer, the Licensee, a non-exclusive, non-transferable right to use and display The Fonts purchased as a companion to the book, 'The Hieroglyphs and Arithmetic of The ancient Egyptian Scribes' on a single computer at one time. You may make backup copies for archival purposes. All copies must remain in your possession and bear appropriate copyright notices as described herein. Multi-user license agreements may be granted in writing by PABULUM.

Electronic Documents

You may embed 'The Fonts' within PDF files or Postscript Language files for distribution, viewing, and imaging by other parties.
Alteration Restrictions

You may not alter, adapt, reverse engineer, disassemble, or create derivative works from The Fonts software without the prior written consent of PABULUM.

Third Parties

You may send a copy of The Fonts to a commercial printer or service bureau to enable editing or printing of your documents provided that such party owns a valid license to use that particular font software.

You may not sell, lease, loan, rent, transfer, distribute, copy, or electronically transfer any copy of the font software, in whole or in part.

3.4.1.2 COPYRIGHT

The font software and accompanying documentation are copyrighted. You may not distribute copies of The Fonts software or documentation in any form without prior written permission from PABULUM. Unauthorized copying of The Fonts software or written materials is strictly forbidden.

3.4.1.3 DISCLAIMER AND LIMITED WARRANTY

PABULUM warrants that The Fonts software is supplied free from defects in materials and workmanship under normal use for a period of thirty days from the date of delivery, as evidenced by a copy of your invoice.

With respect to The Fonts software, PABULUM's entire liability under this limited warranty and otherwise, is limited to the return of the software to PABULUM for a replacement or refund, at the discretion of PABULUM.

PABULUM shall not be responsible for replacing or refunding the purchase price if the product is lost or damaged due to theft, fire or negligence or if failure results from accident, abuse or misuse.

PABULUM does not warrant that the functions contained in this font software will meet your requirements or that the operation of the software will be error-free. Except as stated above, The Font software is provided 'as is' without warranty or condition of any kind, either expressed or implied, including, but not limited to, any implied warranties or conditions of fitness for a particular purpose. The entire risk as to the quality and performance of the software is with you.

3.5.0 FONT INSTALLATION INSTRUCTIONS

3.5.1 INSTALLATION GUIDE

Email the place you purchased your book from and its invoice or bill reference number to: EgyptianPabulum@sky.com. You will then receive your download instructions.

The following guidelines assume that you will be installing The Fonts from the *Egyptian Fonts* folder that you have placed on your computer desktop. The password for this zipped file is the first word in the heading to this page; this password is case sensitive. If you intend to install the fonts from an alternative source such as a CD-Rom, then the same password will suffice if you are asked for one.

3.5.2 FONT INSTALLATION FOR GENERIC WINDOWS® USERS

- Open the *Egyptian Fonts* Folder and click on *File, Extract All, Next, Password, enter password, Next, Finish*.
- Click *Start, Control Panel*.
- Double-click the *Fonts Icon* to open the font folder in the *Control Panel*. You will be able to view all the fonts currently installed.
- To install a font, click on the *File* menu and select *Install New Font*.
- Locate the directory where the fonts you wish to install are located; for the desktop this will probably be (C:\Documents and Settings*your user name*\Desktop\Egyptian Fonts). Double-click the folder *Egyptian Fonts*.
- Select all the fonts you wish to install and click *OK*.
- NOTE: you can also copy/paste fonts directly into the *Fonts* folder. This is usually easier.

3.5.3 FONT DELETION FOR GENERIC WINDOWS® USERS

- Click *Start*, and then click *Run*.
- Type the command *%windir%\fonts* then click *OK*.

- Click the font that you want to remove. To select more than one font at a time, press and hold the *Ctrl* key while you select each font.
- On the *File* menu, click *Delete*
- When you receive the prompt *Are you sure you want to delete these fonts?* Click *Yes*.

Note You can prevent a font from loading without removing it from the hard disk. To do this, move the font from the *Windows\Fonts* folder to another folder.

3.5.4 WINDOWS® XP USERS

- Open the *Egyptian Fonts* Folder and click on *File, Extract All, Next, Password, enter password, Next, Finish*.
- Click *Start, Control Panel*.
- Click *Appearance and Themes* category.
- Click *Fonts* from the *See Also* panel at the left of this screen.
- On the *File* menu, click *Install New Font* . . .
- Click the drive and folder *Egyptian Fonts* that contain the fonts you want to install.
- To select more than one font you wish to add, press and hold down the *Ctrl* key, click the fonts you want, and then click on *OK*.

3.5.5 WINDOWS® 95/98/2000/ NT4® USERS

- Click *Start, Control Panel*.
- Double-click the *Fonts Icon* to open the font folder in the *Control Panel*. You will be able to view all the fonts currently installed.
- To install a font, click on the *File* menu and select *Install New Fonts*. A new window *Add Fonts* should pop up.
- Locate the directory where the fonts you wish to install are located. This will be the folder *Egyptian Fonts*.
- Double-click on the font file you wish to install and click OK

3.5.6 Windows® 7 Users

There are two ways in which this can be accomplished for Windows® 7. The first is a simple; copy the fonts from the folder *Egyptian Fonts* to the Font Directory located at C:\Windows\Fonts. The second method is to click on the font file at its current location. It will then give you a screen that shows the font preview where click on the install font button.

3.5.7 Re-installation of Standard Fonts

Typically, Microsoft® Windows® XP (Home and Professional) and more recent versions of operating system, installs the following TrueType fonts into the Windows/Fonts folder. As Windows XP and other applications may need these fonts installed it is suggested that you do not remove any of these from your computer.

If you have doubts about removing a font, copy it to a folder before deleting it from the system font folder. Then if you have problems, you can always copy it back. It is probably wise to copy fonts to another folder anyway if you intend to delete them from the system; you never know when you or a software program may need them.

Default Fonts	
Font	File name
Arial	Arial.ttf
Arial Black	Ariblk.ttf
Arial Bold	Arialbd.ttf
Arial Bold Italic	Arialbi.ttf
Arial Italic	Ariali.ttf
Comic Sans MS	Comic.ttf
Comic Sans MS Bold	Comicbd.ttf
Courier 10,12,15	Coure.fon

Courier New	Cour.ttf
Courier New Bold	Courbd.ttf
Courier New Bold Italic	Courbi.ttf
Courier New Italic	Couri.ttf
Estrangelo Edessa	Estre.ttf
Franklin Gothic Medium	Framd.ttf
Franklin Gothic Medium Italic	Framdit.ttf
Gautami	Gautami.ttf
Georgia	Georgia.ttf
Georgia Bold	Georgiab.ttf
Georgia Bold Italic	Georgiaz.ttf
Georgia Italic	Georgiai.ttf
Impact	Impact.ttf
Latha	Latha.ttf
Lucida Console	Lucon.ttf
Lucida Sans Unicode	L_10646.ttf
Microsoft Sans Serif	Micross.ttf
Modern	Modern.fon
MS Sans Serif 8,10,12,14,18,24	Sserife.fon
MS Serif 8,10,12,14,18,24	Serife.fon
Mv Boli	Mvboli.ttf
Palatino Linotype	Pala.ttf
Palatino Linotype Bold	Palab.ttf
Palatino Linotype Bold Italic	Palabi.ttf

Palatino Linotype Italic	Palai.ttf
Roman	Roman.fon
Script	Script.fon
Small Fonts	Smalle.fon
Symbol	Symbol.ttf
Symbol 8,10,12,14,18,24	Symbole.fon
Tahoma	Tahoma.ttf
Tahoma Bold	Tahomabd.ttf
Times New Roman	Times.ttf
Times New Roman Bold	Timesbd.ttf
Times New Roman Bold Italic	Timesbi.ttf
Times New Roman Italic	Timesi.ttf
Trebuchet MS	Trebuc.ttf
Trebuchet MS Bold	Trebucbd.ttf
Trebuchet MS Bold Italic	Trebucbi.ttf
Trebuchet MS Italic	Trebucit.ttf
Tunga	Tunga.ttf
Verdana	Verdana.ttf
Verdana Bold	Verdanab.ttf
Verdana Bold Italic	Verdanaz.ttf
Verdana Italic	Verdanai.ttf
Webdings	Webdings.ttf
WingDings	Wingding.ttf
WST_Czech	WST_Czech.fon
WST_Engl	WST_Engl.fon

WST_Fren	WST_Fren.fon
WST_Germ	WST_Germ.fon
WST_Ital	WST_Ital.fon
WST_Span	WST_Span.fon
WST_Swed	WST_Swed.fon

The following are Fonts are Microsoft® Windows® XP protected system files. These fonts cannot be removed or overwritten.

- Micross.ttf
- Tahoma.ttf
- Tahomabd.ttf
- Dosapp.fon
- Fixedsys.fon
- Modern.fon
- Script.fon
- Vgaoem.fon

If any of the standard fonts that are included with Windows® XP are missing, you can run Windows® XP Setup again. Setup replaces missing or changed files. If these standard fonts are missing, other Windows XP files may also be missing, and Setup corrects these problems.

Warning If you run Windows® Setup, you may lose programs and hardware drivers that you have installed since the last time Windows was set up on your computer. If you need more information about the files you could lose, you might want to contact Support. For information about how to contact Support, please visit the following Microsoft® Web site: http://support.microsoft.com/contactus

HIEROGLYPHS AND ARITHMETIC OF THE ANCIENT EGYPTIAN SCRIBES   351

§ 3.5.7 Notes of Interest

Ancient Egyptians believed in the use of amulets to protect, strengthen, and bring health and happiness to them. An amulet is a symbol made of any kind of material that can be worn like jewellery such as part of a necklace. They were even placed on the dead for the same reasons they were used by the living. Depending upon the symbols used, the amulets provided different benefits.

3.5.8 FONT INSTALLATION FOR GENERIC MACINTOSH® USERS

- Open the *System Fonts* folder
- Copy and Paste the fonts into the *Fonts* folder. Alternately, while holding down the Options key, drag and drop the fonts into the *Fonts* folder.

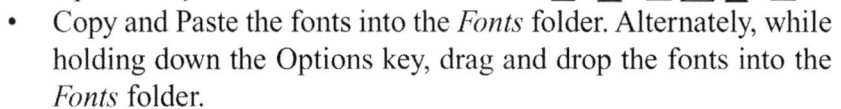

3.6.0 COMMON PROBLEMS ENCOUNTERED WITH FONT USAGE

3.6.1 KERNING PROBLEMS

Kerning is the name given to the process of either increasing or decreasing the size of the space allocated between a pair of characters to make them fit more comfortably. Sometimes you want their bearings to be different in special situations.

Usually the typical user is unaware that there exists a table of special individual characters and pairs of characters that exist alongside the font that they are currently working with. When you want to change the distance between two characters, you could use kerning pairs.

Many sophisticated word processors, desk-top publishing applications, and general applications that support a little word processing have a kerning facility.

For example individual alphabetic letters such as 'A, T, V, W, and Y' and pairs 'AT, AV, AW, and AY' are offered in kerning tables with most fonts.

Of the operating systems and applications that do not support kerning, they will simply ignore the tables of kerning letters and pairs. For applications like Microsoft® Word the feature of kerning is automatic by default, but it can be turned off if required.

When we are using fonts of a graphical nature such as hieroglyphic fonts, it is unlikely that we would be interested in any kerning features the application we are working with might offer.

The Egyptian fonts that are provided on the CD-Rom do not have any kerning tables associated with them. Therefore, if an application you are working with possesses any kerning facilities, they will be ignored while working with hieroglyphs. This applies whether the kerning feature is switched on or off in the application.

Where you may encounter a minor problem, is when you enter characters from an alternative font to Egyptian Hieroglyphs, then select these characters to convert them to hieroglyphs by changing your working font. If the spaces between the characters in the original font had been kerned, converting the text to a hieroglyphic font will return any spacing to normal.

The effects may be miniscule and not worth bothering about, but if the positioning of the hieroglyphs is critical, you may wonder what strange curse has affected your keyboard.

To turn the kerning feature off in Microsoft® Word, select *Font* from the *Format* menu and select the *Character Spacing* tab. There you can turn off kerning by clicking on *kerning for fonts*

According to the official TrueType font specifications, the maximum number of kerning pairs is 10920, I doubt whether this fact will ever be required in a pub quiz!

3.6.2 AutoCorrect Problems

Most modern word processing and desk-top publishing packages offer some sort of automatic correction facility as you type a line of text. This is also true of many image manipulation and engineering drawing packages that offer some sort of text manipulation.

This feature can be a great benefit to those dealing with ordinary fonts and lines text, but it is a nightmare for the user entering hieroglyphs who is unaware of what is going on.

Typically automatic correction detects and corrects; spelling mistakes, incorrect capitalization and, date format, text such as 'th' in ordinal numbers to superscript, for example a 5th, and will hyphenate words in the correct place, when the entered text reaches the end of a line.

Unfortunately, when you type three keys on the keyboard expecting to see three hieroglyphic characters, and you only get one character, you may wonder what is wrong. If you typed 1/2 with AutoCorrect switched on, it would replace these three characters by a single character the ½. You must remember that the computer is a stupid machine, it does not realize that the hieroglyphs (𓄿𓃀𓏏) do not represent a half.

The process of switching on or off any specific AutoCorrect features is usually quite simple. This applies to most packages and certainly to all the versions of Microsoft® Word and Microsoft® Works.

It is strongly recommended that all the auto-correction features are temporarily disabled while you are working with hieroglyphs. Don't forget to enable any required auto-correction when you are finished!

It would take volumes of text to explain how to change auto-correction features in all applications and their different releases. Therefore it is suggested that you look at the user manual or help system for whichever package you are currently working with.

To give you some idea of how to turn off AutoCorrect features, we will take a generic view at Microsoft® Word. It is strongly recommended that you check with your user manual or the help system before beginning this procedure of changing AutoCorrect settings.

- Start up Microsoft® Word.
- Click On the *Tools* menu and click *AutoCorrect Options* . . .
- Then click on each of the following tags and remove the ticks from as many of the feature boxes as necessary; *AutoText, AutoFormat, SmartTags, AutoCorrect, AutoFormat As You Type.*

When enabled, probably the most troublesome AutoCorrect features are quotes and ellipsis. Smart quotes, also known as curly quotes, are slanted characters which make text look better compared to the straight apostrophe (') and straight quote or inches character ("). Microsoft® Word also automatically changes three periods to an ellipsis. If you are not aware of what is going on, these automatic changes can be quite startling.

3.7.0 Hieroglyphic Character Manipulation

3.7.1 Formatting Fonts

All word processing and desk-top publishing packages offer some features for basic-font manipulation. If they didn't, they would be bordering on useless.

Whatever you can with normal text in your software can be done with a hieroglyphic font. Typically this includes switching between the different formats for: normal, bold, italic, bold italic, and setting the size of the font from a very tiny point size to enormous sizes.

Hieroglyphs can be underlined and the colour of the font can be changed quite easily in packages.

The best thing to do is to experiment with the features; but always take a backup of your work and read the user manual before doing anything.

3.7.2 Desk-Top Publishing

Desk-top publishing packages are an integration of word processing, artistic, graphic, and image processing packages, the options for text manipulation are endless.

With the multitude of packages available, it is well beyond the scope of this book to cover these features in any useful detail.

3.7.3 Word Processing

3.7.3.1 Generic Overview of Microsoft® Works

This package offers many of the usual features such as: Strikethrough, Superscript, Subscript, Shadow, Outline, Emboss, Engrave, Small Caps, and All Caps. The point size can be adjusted and the colour of the font changed.

The only way you are able to get hieroglyphs to face the opposite way as shown in section 1.6.1, or distort them in some way, is through the paint feature.

By selecting *Insert, Picture,* and *New Painting,* a frame appears on the word-processing page.

Hieroglyphs can then be entered into this paint window as text. By selecting this text or rather string of hieroglyphs, it can be flipped vertical or horizontally, stretched, shrunk, skewed, and generally distorted.

3.7.3.2 Generic Overview of Microsoft® Word

This package is much more powerful than Microsoft® Works. Microsoft® Word offers many more features. The features that this package offers for text formatting include: Strikethrough, Double Strikethrough, Superscript, Subscript, Shadow, Outline, Emboss, Engrave, Small Caps, All Caps and Hidden. The point size can be adjusted and the colour of the font changed.

There are other features such as blinking background, sparkle text, and shimmer that can be applied to hieroglyphic fonts in the same way as the standard fonts.

There are a number of useful options for placing hieroglyphs on a page in any position and these include WordArt, Text Boxes, and AutoShapes. The reversed hieroglyphs in section 1.6.1 could quite easily be produced by using the WordArt feature.

Here, we have another example of the powers of wordart on the right.

You generally find that there are more options available for manipulating and distorting Text Boxes and Auto shapes, if they are placed within a New Drawing frame first. To get a New Drawing frame to appear on the page select *Insert, Picture,* and *New Drawing.*

The WordArt feature allows hieroglyphs to be rotated, flipped vertically, horizontally, stretched, and generally distorted into most shapes you can think of.

3.7.4 Spreadsheets and Tables

It is worth investigating the character manipulation features of these packages. You can very often rotate lines of text to be read vertically or on the diagonal within a cell. The cell borders can usually be made transparent as well.

3.8.0 Trademark and Registration Notices

Microsoft® and Windows® are either registered trademarks or trademarks of Microsoft Corporation in the United States and/or other countries.

Mac®, Macintosh®, and TrueType® are trademarks of Apple computer®, Inc. registered in the United States and other countries.

Microsoft® Word is a copyright© of the Microsoft Corporation.

§ 3.8.0 Notes of Interest

Communities of people since time immemorial have had some means of entertaining, even if it was just watching someone being burnt to the stake or eaten alive by lions. You have to do something during the adverts on TV!

The ancient Egyptians also enjoyed various entertainments ranging from eating and drinking, to physical exercise, hunting, reading, music, dancing, storytelling, poetry, board games, and puzzles. Activities with a military founding such as chariot racing, target practice with spears and the bow and arrow were common. The modern game of darts has its origins in spear throwing!

One example of an ancient Egyptian crossword has been discovered. Unfortunately the clues to the crossword were not found with the solution. It was discovered with the grid filled in and with all the words interlocking as they do in a modern crossword. Although there is no evidence that the ancient Egyptians entertained themselves with Sudoku, papyri with a number of mathematical and geometric riddles have been found.

Have a go at the following puzzle it is based on a very, very, late period of Egyptian entertainment. The meanings of the hieroglyphs are irrelevant for this teaser.

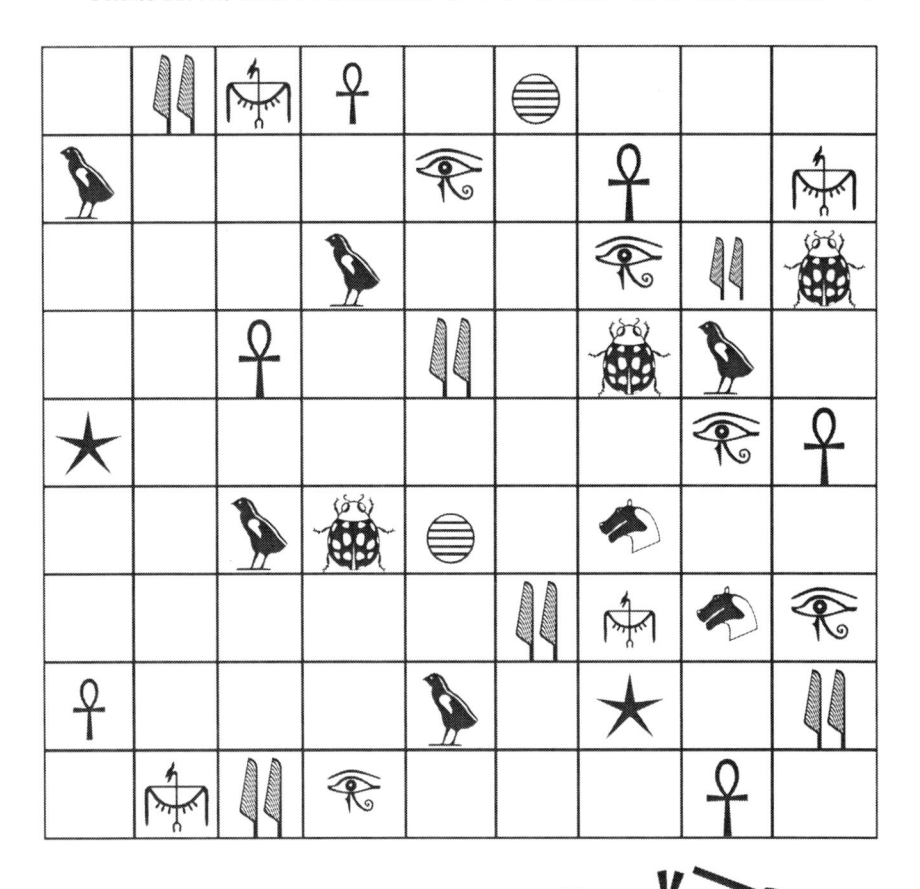

I'm Seth; here is another puzzle for you. Find out what a Seth animal is, this is a far bigger puzzle than the polliwogs ever were.

3.9.0 INDEX

A

accent 264
addition 167
adjacent side 264
adze 264
Ahmose-Nefertari (queen) 236
akh 118
Akhenaten (king) 199
algebra 200-1, 203
  modern day 208
Alluvial Plain 264
alphabet 35
  ancient Egyptian 56, 264
  English 36
alphabetic writing 264
amulets 351
anthropomorphic 265
area(s):
  adding 138
  of a circle 185, 190
  of a hemisphere 187
  measuring 135
  of a rectangle 183
  of a square *see* area, of a rectangle
  of a triangle 184
arithmetic: symbols of 119-21
aroura 135
ascending order 265
AutoCorrect 13, 353-4

B

ba 118
balance 120, 200
base ten 54, 265
BCE (before the Common Era) 17
beard 265
beer 158, 245-6
  drinking 236
  malt-date 246, 249
  measuring strength of 157
besha *see* beer
biliteral 38, 40, 264
Book of the Dead 27
bread 158
  measuring strength of 157
  work and 182

C

calendars 144, 148
cartouche 45
CE (Common Era) 17
centaroura 131, 137
Champollion, Jean 24
circumference 164
coffin texts 31, 265
consonantal 266
corn-measure 125
cosmogony 266

counting boards 266
crescent moon 266
cubic cubit 188, 266
cubit 131, 136, 138, 163
cubit strip 136
cylinder-seal 266
Cyperus papyrus 26, 277

D

day, twenty-four-hour 147
daytime 32
deben 143
deben rings 144
decade 147
decans 147
decaroura 137
Degree Rule 10, 202
denary *see* base ten
denominator 116, 267
des-jug 267
desktop publishing 355
determinative 42, 267
　double 52
　or plurality 48
　repeating 48
diacritical tick 267
dialect 267
digits 101
divine proportion 128-9, 267
division 177-80
　by fractional expressions 227-9
　solving equations by 227
doctors 253
Dog Star *see* Sirius
double-remen 131
dreams 254
duals 47
dynamic symmetry *see* divine proportion
dynastic period 5, 19
　early 267

E

Egypt: Lower 26, 277
Egypt: Upper 26, 277
Egyptologist 36, 267
epagomenal days 145, 267
epithet 149
equal sign 203, 213
equations:
　algebraic 200
　division method to solve 227
　first-degree 201
　second-degree 201
　third-degree 202
eye fractions *see* fraction(s): Horus eye
Eye of Horus 122-4, 267-8
Eye of Ra *see* Eye of Horus
Eye of Re *see* Eye of Horus
Eye of Thoth *see* Eye of Horus

F

faience 268
falcon god *see* Horus
false position 209-10, 212
festivals 145, 268
find 120
fingers 96
fire-drill 269
fist 133
font 269
foot 133
fraction(s) 269
　aliquot 115, 180, 182, 264
　breaking down 182
　bulky 116
　hekat 126-7
　Horus eye 127
　paradox of ordinal 117
　R-notation 114, 116, 276
frustum 269

Moscow papyrus problem of 196
  volume of 194
frustum formula 196
  modern derivation of 197
fuller 269
funerary text 27, 31

G

Geb (god) 269
gender 7, 50, 112, 270
glottal stop 270
glue 226
gluphe 23
glyphs *see* hieroglyphs
gnomon 270
gold 143
Golden Mean 128-30, 270-1
golden pyramids 8, 130, 163, 271
golden ratio *see* golden mean
Golden Rectangle 129
Golden Triangle 135, 162, 271
gradient 159
graphic transposition 271
Greco-Roman Period 20, 271
guttural sound 272

H

hand 133
Hathor (goddess) 34, 282
hekat 125-6, 139
  double 140
  quadruple 140
heqat *see* hekat
hieroglyphs 23, 32, 35, 37-8
  direction of reading 46
  English phonetic for Egyptian 59
  for numbers 0 to 9 *102*
  for numbers greater than 1000 *104*
  for numbers in multiples of 10 7, *102*
  for numbers in multiples of 100 *103*
  for numbers in multiples of 1000 *103*
  for whole numbers 96
hieros 23
hin *see* hinu
hinu 140
Hittites 160
hobble 272
honorific transposition 272
Horus 8, 46, 59, 122-4, 126, 139, 145, 267-8, 281
hour 146
  Egyptian 155
hypotenuse 272

I

Ibis (god) *see* Thoth (god)
ideograms 33
infinity 272
Intef (king) 29
interjections 41
intermediate period:
  first 19
  second 265
  third 19
inundation 144-5, 272
Ity 154

J

justified 272

K

ka 118
Kadesh 160
kerning 272, 352
keyboard map 272
khar 190
Kheperkara (king) 154

khet   188
kiln   272
kingdoms   5, 19
kite   143-4

L

length:
  Egyptian units of   132
  measuring   131
Leonardo da Vinci   128

M

Maat (goddess)   189, 283
mathematical constant   273
mathematical symbols *see* arithmetic, symbols of
medicine   258
Middle Kingdom   19, 273
month   146, 151
Moscow papyrus   205
  frustum problem of   196-7
  problem 3 of   243
  problem 8 of   248-9
  problem 11 of   255-7
  problem 23 of   257
multiplicand   273
multiplication   7, 107, 173
  in reverse *see* division
multiplier   273

N

netherworld   273
New Kingdom   19, 31, 273, 275
New Year's Day   144, 150
Nile   24, 149, 155
no   79
nouns   50
Nubia   26, 124

number(s):
  ad hoc   7, 105
  binary   174, 265
  cardinal   7, 109-10, 266
  development of a system of   7, 101
  Egyptian hieroglyphs for whole   96, 104
  examples of big   7, 106
  feminine   110
  keyboard locations of hieroglyphic   104
  masculine   7, 109
  ordinal   112-13, 274
  prime   275
numerator   116, 273

O

obelisk   148, 273
offering formula   273
oipe   140
Old Kingdom   12, 19, 82, 274-5
1-consonant *see* uniliteral
opposite side   274
Osiris (god)   124

P

paint   206
palace   274
palm   121, 166
papyri *see* papyrus
papyrus   26, 28, 31
paradox   274
pefsu   157, 204
  formula of   158
  problems   245
period, late   273
pesu *see* pefsu
pharaoh   189, 274, 283
  names of   274
phi(φ)   129
phonemes   35, 275

phonetics 275
phonogram 35, 275
pi(π) 275
pictogram 16, 275
plosive 275
plurals 47
plywood 226
pole 76, 134
polliwog 275
prepositions 52
priesthood 59, 106
Ptolemy 20, 24-5
pyramid 275
  building 167
  first Egyptian 196
  shape of 130
  volume of 194
Pyramid of Giza 130
pyramid texts 275

Q

quadratic 275

R

Ramesside Period 275
ready reckoner 276
rebus principle 36-7, 276
reciprocals 240
reference tables 164
regnal year 150
remainder 120
remen 131, 135
Rhind Mathematical Papyrus 207
  problem 24 of 216-18
  problem 25 of 218
  problem 26 of 212, 220-1
  problem 27 of 221
  problem 28 of 223-4
  problem 29 of 224-6

problem 30 of 229-32
problem 31 of 232-4
problem 32 of 235
problem 33 of 236
problem 34 of 240-1
problem 40 of 207-9
problem 50 of 185-6
problem 56 of 164
problem 69 of 250-2
river 134
ro 127, 276
  fractions and 126
Ro-measure 8, 115, 127, 276
rod 184
Rosetta stone 5, 24, 276
royal cubit 131
rulers 19

S

sack 140, 142
sacred ratio 128-9, 276
sand 143
Saqqara 196
sarcophagus 276
scarab seal 278
scribe 209, 277
seal 143
season 145-6
sedge 26, 277
seked 158, 166, 277
seqed *see* seked
seqt *see* seked
sequential list 278
sesh 26, 277 *see also* scribe
seshet 278 *see also* scribe
setat 136
Seth (god) 281
shen ring 278
short cubit 131
sickle 76-7, 88, 278

Sirius (star)   144
slope   278
  angle of   161
  measuring   158
sound complement   279
sound-writing   35
spreadsheets   356
sqd *see* seked
square cubit   136
stela   154, 279
subtraction   167
summer   147, 152
syllabic writing   279
syllabogram   279

T

tables   356
tadpoles   7
tenet   279
therefore   58, 68, 119
Thoth (god)   28, 123-4
3-consonant *see* triliteral
time:
  Egyptian units of   146
  to measure distance   157
  measuring   144
  ordinal units of   152
  vocabulary of   150
total   120-1
translation   55, 280
transliteration   55, 280
trilingual   280
triliteral   38, 41, 264
2-consonant *see* biliteral

U

Udjat *see* Eye of Horus
Ujat eye *see* Eye of Horus
uniliteral   5, 38-40, 264, 280

units of measure   280
uraeus   280
Utchat eye *see* Eye of Horus

V

vertical stroke   32
vinculum   280
Vladimir, Golenišev   265
volume:
  of a block   188
  of a cylinder   189
  Egyptian units of   139
  of a frustum   194
  jars used for   188
  of a pyramid   194
vowels   37, 280

W

Wadjet Eye   123, 281 *see also* Eye of Horus
week   146
weight, measuring   8, 143-4
Wepwawet (god)   281
wheels   12
winter   147, 268

Y

year   145, 147
Young, Thomas   24, 279

4.0.0 Chapter Four— Special Edition CD-Rom

Only the special edition version of this book provides the purchaser with a CD-Rom containing nine sets of Egyptian Hieroglyphic fonts. Do not despair, please read on . . .

Purchase of this book entitles you to download your nine sets of complimentary Egyptian Hieroglyphic fonts, yes, absolutely free!

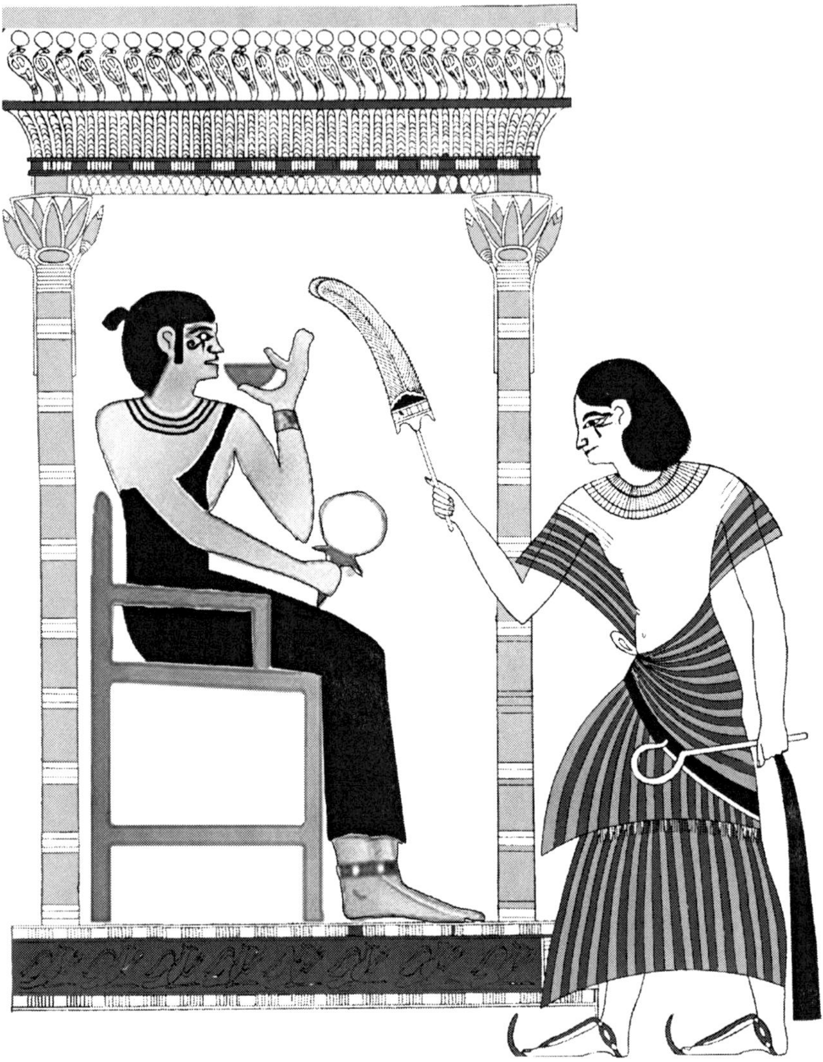